Jorella Andrews//Michael A
Roy Ascott//Elma Askham//
Bailey//Lars Bang Larsen//C
Benn//Claire Bishop//Black
Pierre Bourdieu//Julie Brook//Luis Camnitzer//Paul Clements//Pen Dalton//Alain Darbel//Paul Dash// Thierry de Duve//John Dewey//Dinah Dossor//Jimmie Durham//Elliot W. Eisner//David Elliott//Alex Farquharson//Bruce Ferguson//Joanna Fiduccia// Harrell Fletcher//Andrea Fraser//Paulo Freire//Johnny Gailey//Claire Gibb//Henry A. Giroux//Dr Annette Gomperts//Janna Graham//Michael Hardt//Paula Harper//George E. Hein//Pablo Helguera//Patrick Heron//Tom Holert//Allan Kaprow//Vincent Katz// Mary Kelly//Grant H. Kester//Eve Kosofsky Sedgwick// Tamara Krikorian//Suzanne Lacy//Darcy Lange//Dieter Lesage//Les Levine//Lawrence McDonald//Carmen Mörsch//Antonio Negri//Emily Pethick//Andrea Phillips//Griselda Pollock//Ernesto Pujol//Radical Philosophy Collective//Jacques Rancière//Herbert Read//Adrienne Rich//Bridget Riley//Irit Rogoff// Suely Rolnik//Monica Ross//Ziauddin Sardar//Miriam Schapiro//Allan Sekula//Rebecca Sinker//Frances Stark//Harry Thubron//Lisa Tickner//Caroline Tisdall// Jan Verwoert//Henry Ward//WEB//Virginia Woolf

Education

Whitechapel Gallery
London
The MIT Press
Cambridge, Massachusetts

Edited by Felicity Allen

EDU CAT ION

Documents of Contemporary Art

Co-published by Whitechapel Gallery
and The MIT Press

First published 2011

Whitechapel Gallery is the imprint of Whitechapel Gallery Ventures Limited

ISBN 978-0-85488-192-5 (Whitechapel Gallery)
ISBN 978-0-262-51636-5 (The MIT Press)

A catalogue record for this book is available from the British Library

Library of Congress Cataloging-in-Publication Data

Education / edited by Felicity Allen.
p. cm. – (Whitechapel : Documents of contemporary art)
Includes bibliographical references and index.
ISBN 978-0-262-51636-5 (pbk. : alk. paper)
1. Art—Study and teaching—History—20th century. 2. Art—Study and teaching—History—21st century. 3. Art and society—History—20th century. 4. Art and society—History—21st century. I. Allen, Felicity.
N90.E33 2011
707.1—dc22

2011011786

10 9 8 7 6 5 4 3 2 1

Series Editor: Iwona Blazwick
Commissioning Editor: Ian Farr
Project Editor: Hannah Holloway
Publications Assistant: Sarah Auld
Design by SMITH
Printed and bound in China

Cover, Thomas Hirschhorn, *Cavemanman* (2002), installation: wood, cardboard, tape, aluminium foil, books, posters, videos of Lascaux 2, dolls, cans, shelves and fluorescent light fixtures. Installation view, 'Life on Mars', 55th Carnegie International, Carnegie Museum of Art, Pittsburgh. © Thomas Hirschhorn. Photograph: Tom Little. Courtesy of the artist and Gladstone Gallery, New York.

Whitechapel Gallery Ventures Limited
77-82 Whitechapel High Street
London E1 7QX
www.whitechapelgallery.org
To order (UK and Europe) call +44 (0)207 522 7888
or email MailOrder@whitechapelgallery.org
Distributed to the book trade (UK and Europe only) by Central Books
www.centralbooks.com

The MIT Press
55 Hayward Street
Cambridge, MA 02142
MIT Press books may be purchased at special quantity discounts for business or sales promotional use. For information, please email special_sales@mitpress.mit.edu or write to Special Sales Department, The MIT Press, 55 Hayward Street, Cambridge, MA 02142

Whitechapel Gallery

Documents of Contemporary Art

In recent decades artists have progressively expanded the boundaries of art as they have sought to engage with an increasingly pluralistic environment. Teaching, curating and understanding of art and visual culture are likewise no longer grounded in traditional aesthetics but centred on significant ideas, topics and themes ranging from the everyday to the uncanny, the psychoanalytical to the political.

The Documents of Contemporary Art series emerges from this context. Each volume focuses on a specific subject or body of writing that has been of key influence in contemporary art internationally. Edited and introduced by a scholar, artist, critic or curator, each of these source books provides access to a plurality of voices and perspectives defining a significant theme or tendency.

For over a century the Whitechapel Gallery has offered a public platform for art and ideas. In the same spirit, each guest editor represents a distinct yet diverse approach – rather than one institutional position or school of thought – and has conceived each volume to address not only a professional audience but all interested readers.

I DO NOT WANT

ART

FOR A FEW ANY MORE THAN I WANT

EDUCATION

FOR A FEW OR

FREEDOM

FOR A FEW

William Morris quoted by Jeremy Deller on placard for student protest, London 2010

PRIMER

INDISCIPLINE

Felicity Allen
Introduction//Art: Education

The subject of art's relation to education could hardly be more contested: since the turn of the century numerous significant projects and publications concerned with art and education have emerged from museums, galleries, educational institutions, international biennials and conferences. Each of these sources contributes to the production of education about art which, within modernizing cultures, implicitly contributes to revisions in the production and reception of art. Art education is therefore generated, to a greater or lesser extent, in all Western educational institutions, from playgroup through school and youth club to art school and university. And in the name of reform or punishment it is withheld or instrumentalized, most overtly in prisons. It is keenly identified, therefore, with developing an individual's sense of personal and social identity: it is cultural. So it is taught and learned not just in institutions but in the home, out on the street, or online. Educational strategies are employed equally by ad hoc artist collectives and by established cultural institutions whose central purpose is to buy, sell, collect and disseminate art. Since an ideal of universal education was endorsed within the democratic movement that built nation states, education has been promoted and experienced as both emancipatory and regulatory. Art education has hovered at its edges, poised as dormant, rumbling or actively counter-cultural. It is not surprising that as democracies are internally tested by the shift against the state towards the market, art education comes into focus.

This anthology divides into four interrelated sections which aim to provide an overview of the multiple ways that art and art education produce each other: *Primer* aims to set out some key ideas, while playing with the concept of a unifying primacy by including the incidental as well some essentials. *Indiscipline* mostly centres on school and on teaching students who are considered to be school age. The texts here frequently explore the tensions between school and life outside, the personal and the social, the boundaries to be regulated and crossed. Together they suggest the challenges to 'schooling' that art commonly presents, reflecting art's critical and potentially destabilizing social roles. *Art School* speaks for itself: re-reading the historical material aims to help map how we arrived here and what those involved in teaching artists imagine for a future. *Pedagogy as Medium* explores the type of practice artists make across art and education with exhibitionary intention, its values and its critical reception.

Although the writers are international, most texts tend to focus on education situated in North America and Europe, and mostly in anglophone culture. Why?

Because they share a common language through which to discuss similarities in educational systems, which are, above all, cultural. While the social position of mainstream art may be similar enough across Western countries, attitudes underpinning formal education reflect national cultures and political boundaries, as a comparison between France and neighbouring Britain demonstrates. An attempt to translate the different educational codes which are commonly understood by schoolchildren and their teachers in these respective countries denoting age, progression and examination readily demonstrates the disparities.

In *Hornsey 1968: The Art School Revolution*, Lisa Tickner assesses the impact of developments in the late 1960s and early 1970s that were pivotal for much of what is traced and discussed here: the embrace of new technologies; the emergence of conceptualism; the rise of theory; shifts in managerial and political structures; demands for participation to replace the failures of representation.[1] And although second-wave feminism registered mostly in later narratives, ideas central to the women's movement have frequently been intrinsic to the subject of art and education. The feminist texts selected here offer potential theoretical models for critique of the meetings of art and education but also reflect the highly significant roles women have played in art teaching and as artist educators.[2]

Among the most significant insights handed down from that period is that authority is always contingent – and this is reflected in the structure of this book. Its impulse, at times, is to tell, but at others to try something out, to pursue a thought, to compose, to lay bare, or to suggest. Sometimes a sequence of texts might form a kind of run, creating a collective pace. It could be visualized as an arabesque of texts whose lines and runs spiral with and against each other, across the different sections – reflecting the way one learns, usually in more or less anything other than straight lines. It incorporates texts that implicitly interpret others or address issues around learning in ways that weave in and out of experience and knowledge. It aims thus to demonstrate the mutable nature of teaching and learning, the different types of relationship a learner has to a teacher; a teacher to a student; an artist to a potential viewer or audience. This might include applying theory to practice (as Tickner demonstrates in applying Thierry de Duve's triad of 'attitude, practice and deconstruction' to her historical analysis); building practice into theory (Jacques Rancière on the schoolmaster Jacotôt); exploring not only intentional but unintended reflexive learning (Stuart Bailey); teaching and learning through argument (Griselda Pollock challenging Phillip King); homage (Henry Giroux on Stuart Hall); or practice-sharing (Harrell Fletcher). One can always know more: one text leads to another, as the process of producing this book has demonstrated. We publish for the first time in English the conclusion of Thierry de Duve's paper whose first section has already had significant influence. Many additional but invisible texts inform this book: some well known figures are omitted in favour of the less known, to indicate the breadth and range of writing on the subject.

A text, like a teacher, can act as an important interpolation of another. While Rancière's *The Ignorant Schoolmaster* (1987) seems in principle to contest interpolation as an educational value, his translator Kristin Ross' introduction needs to be cited briefly here for the deeper political and historical contextualization of his text that it provides. Rancière was responding to Pierre Bourdieu (and the new sociology) whose 'structuralist rigour', developed in the 1960s, permitted 'an analysis that could carry on an existence entirely divorced from the practical hypotheses of Marxism or the naïvetés of hope for social transformation'. Rancière proposed that Bourdieu and the new sociology derived 'its authority from the presumed naïveté or ignorance of its objects of study'. It followed that there was an almost academic investment in perpetuating that ignorance: 'not only did the sociologist see what teacher (and student) did not, he saw it because the teacher and student could not.' Ross goes on to contextualize these ideas in educational policy divisions within the Mitterand government. These tensions continue to play out, in analysis if not always practice, in the present. She describes how, on one hand, the first Minister of Education, Alain Savary, 'argued that a new educational community must be established; one based on undoing the rigid stratification of scholars and their knowledge – a kind of levelling at the top – and creating a convivial, open, egalitarian atmosphere in schools, which would be attentive to the "whole personality" of the child.' This position 'favoured a compensatory attitude to unequal opportunity'. On the other hand, the subsequent Minister, Jean-Pierre Chevènement, reinforced Enlightenment values and, as Ross puts it, 'a kind of curricular "back to basics" and a return to the rhetoric of selection that so long characterized French schooling'. This, it was argued, would promote France's prosperity in the face of technological change and competition. Ross situates this in relation to Louis Althusser's proposition that communist students 'must first develop their knowledge of Marxism-Leninism and then conduct scientific analyses that would yield objective knowledge of the University'. In Althusser's words, it is the 'quality of knowledge itself' that matters, less so the 'pedagogical relation in which knowledge was disseminated', and 'it is by the very nature of the knowledge that it imparts to students that the bourgeoisie exerts ... the profoundest influence over them'. Rancière, Ross observes, saw the function of the 'science/ideology distinction' as a means by which power or 'eminent dignity' is attributed to those who possess that knowledge.

Despite the different contexts of *The Ignorant Schoolmaster* and the American Ivan Illich's *Deschooling Society* (1971), both examine the notion of a 'hidden curriculum' underpinning educational structures. Illich writes that 'many students, especially those who are poor, intuitively know what the schools do for them. They school them to confuse process and substance.' His de-regularized proposals for 'skill exchanges', 'peer-matching' and 'reference services to educators-at-large' anticipate many of the networked and informal artists' pedagogical programmes and events that now populate virtual, international and local art-educational co-operatives. These often connect artists across geographical and cultural boundaries; some go in and out of activity but even if dormant they are usually retrievable online, from the US-originated Center for Urban Pedagogy, the Public School or the Mountain School of Arts, to the European-originated Independent Art School and the Parallel School of Art. The New International School's Map 2 expresses the potential that the Internet has generated in realizing some of Illich's utopian proposals, through its 'collective intelligence', 'networked decision-making' and 'distributed collaboration'. The idea, though, of a hidden curriculum seems to have been subsumed in the managerial mapping conventions that new technologies have made ubiquitous. Turning away from the virtual, the artist Annette Krauss has developed pedagogic art projects such as *Hidden Curriculum* to work with school students investigating the underlying material aspects of their corporeal and social experience of school. It focuses on 'unidentified, unintended and unrecognized forms of knowledge, values and beliefs'. Accessibly documented via the Internet, art magazines and books, the project was developed with and exhibited at Utrecht's Casco – Office for Art, Design and Theory, registering the current role of art venues as agents for experimental pedagogy as much as for exhibitions.

Recent criticism of shifts in education policy for the arts and humanities has focused on what has been called 'cultural apartheid': purchasing higher education individually at source rather than socially through tax reinforces the social 'distinction' (and exclusions) of those studying - and, by extension, producing - art, exponentially segregating class through cultural divisions.[3] However, at least as significant is the fact that technology and the sciences are privileged not to be cut, that is, unhinged from educational integration. While Michael Hardt and Antonio Negri maintain that we are in a state of perpetual war, it is worth recalling that one of the First World War's causes was the escalation of technological 'advances' such as armaments, in the preceding years. John Dewey's *Democracy and Education* (1916) implicitly repudiates these values, and Virginia Woolf made an explicit connection in *Three Guineas* (1938), arguing that the education system of the time ineluctably produced a warrior culture, and proposing a system founded on the arts that would build a culture of peace. In *Education through Art* (1943) Herbert Read wrote in the same spirit of a remodelling of society and its values through an education system with art at its centre, collapsing the disciplinary divides.

Progressive educational models such as these often focus on the understanding of individual socializing experiences. The transcripts from Mary Kelly's artwork

Post-Partum Document (1973–79) which open this collection – diary texts about the moment a mother prepares to relinquish her child to the first experience of nursery school – reveal the primal anxieties typically expressed by parents, wishing 'the best' for their children. Kelly's work also marks a highly influential moment in art, where education and the culture of everyday life came together in the programmed event of discussing an artwork with the artist in the gallery.[4] Two significant areas related to this lie beyond the scope of this book: developments in neuroscience which have important implications for our understanding of early learning processes, and advances in digital technologies, often associated in themselves with interactivity but here discussed only in so far as they support projects that include interaction or dialogue – participatory practices having been intrinsic to this area long before the digital revolution.

Over the post-1960s decades that are the focus here, we have seen political authorities ensure that state schools relinquish any attempt at a 'progressive' educational model (i.e. a modernist pedagogy built on ideas of discovery and volition – sometimes elided with what is now termed child-centredness – in which good teachers could encourage students to root out their own learning in their own time) in favour of reinforcing, through corporate accounting values, an 'industrial model'.[5] Meanwhile art schools have built on the challenges of the late 1960s to develop not just new curricula and teaching models, but new identities as institutions, as discussed by de Duve, Ernesto Pujol and Irit Rogoff.

It is hoped that these texts might further this endeavour of challenging divisions and hierarchies. Art education seems to provide an alternative career path for many artists who either cannot or choose not to enter the art world's more prestigious but precarious route of exhibition career-building. Class (e.g. the need for a stable salaried income) might be one factor in this; others touch on aesthetic, cultural, professional and political allegiances, as well as temperament. Political challenges, from both left and right, to the idea of a single professional identity, together with theoretical challenges to notions of artists' social purpose (see Suzanne Lacy and Allan Kaprow) – and, indeed, to concepts of what constitutes art and where it is situated – raise concomitant questions about identification in teaching. If we use Bourdieu's term 'cultural production' to include the performance-based practices documented by artists such as Kaprow, Lacy or Fletcher, the self-identifying 'attitude' described by de Duve (it's art because I say so; I'm an artist because I say so) and the practical pedagogy of the schoolteacher Henry Ward, it is difficult to maintain any consistent distinction between teaching activities and art practice. It is understandable, though, that those with nominally distinct professional identities can often fail to understand each other's terms and standards. Thus there are artists and artist educators who think teachers sell art short; teachers and artists who think artist educators are weak artists or poor pedagogues; teachers and artist educators who think artists' 'pedagogical' practices are naïve or exploitative; or art critics who tend only to acknowledge art as pedagogy if it is mediated through an exhibition-based model.

Real questions remain about definition and criteria for judgement across rather than within these different categories: artists producing work or exhibitions that incorporate pedagogy as a 'medium';[6] self-identified artist educators who undertake project work that may or may not be exhibited; and art teachers. Describing a 1960s project with teenagers decades later, Kaprow wonders if from this vantage point it is no longer blurred with everyday life but has become 'merely' art; Jorella Andrews considers the artists Liam Gillick and Edgar Schmitz's *Kiosk* (ICA, London, 2005) in terms of its efficacy in engaging visitor (learner) responses to its didactic discourses; artist educator Rebecca Sinker introduces the sociologist Roger Hart's 'Ladder of Young People's Participation' as a set of values through which to examine a gallery project with young people; Ward, teaching in a school, subverts the regulatory values of the inspectors, using exhibitionary models in his educational practice; Claire Bishop and Grant Kester, as critics and teachers, challenge each other's terms of reference in relation to collaborative practices and the critical discourses underpinning them.

As well as regulatory, education is understood to be emancipatory, but how and for whom? As Western societies shift from Enlightenment agendas, notions of 'potentiality', 'individuation', 'collaborative learning' and 'dialogic education' are common on the left, while in the mainstream education is pragmatically associated with skills, jobs, social mobility and economic success. In contrast, Caroline Benn's impassioned call for common education and an enabling State articulates both regret and determination. Significantly her text speaks of 'the kind of society that education and work are both supposed to serve', rather than the professionals education is supposed to produce; her model is the common good, rather than the prevailing notion of a market of consumers (applied to art schools by Bruce Ferguson). A continuing commitment to commonality can be heard, with different emphases, in more recent texts by Luis Camnitzer and Michael Archer.

Tickner's *Hornsey 1968* vividly demonstrates the tensions that arose in the late 1960s between the model of art taught in art schools and increasingly conceptual art models in the world outside. Gradually what kind of art was taught in art school, and how, shifted to more closely approximate contemporary practice. By contrast, art lessons for younger groups in schools still remain for the most part based on a modernist curriculum and the interests of individual art teachers. Art teaching will typically allude neither to contemporary art practices nor to the art world's infrastructures through which employment might be gained. But for decades the arts sector has been engaging groups of school students with artists and art contexts, often in unexpectedly productive ways.

Increasingly this has been in partnership with schools, although many artists devise projects that create alternative models of artistic practice as education.

Intermittently, in isolated instances, school-age students have had access to the kind of autonomy represented by the Room 13 Art Studio, in which they can run their own art business, as described by Claire Gibb. Is this where the modern concept of childhood bites the dust? By the mid twentieth century many progressive Western educationalists had aimed to extend the Enlightenment project beyond the professional classes to include the masses by protecting children from the stress and exploitation of earning a living: learning was to be for the sake of learning. Governments, however, as Benn shows, regularly shifted the emphasis away from concepts of universal knowledge towards employment-oriented learning – as George Hein describes it: 'learning to learn'. Based on a sensitive critique of the power structures underlying the prevailing educational and assessment model, Dennis Atkinson proposes the development of a pedagogy against itself: 'not focused on what we are and should be' (transcendence), 'but upon the potentiality and "unknown" of becoming'.[7] In this he reinforces the arguments of theorists who have explored similar questions in the context of the art school. Rogoff, for example, citing Giorgio Agamben, suggests abandoning the focus on results, instead favouring potential and the notion of a 'pedagogy not preoccupied with succeeding but with trying'. The desire to avoid exclusions and assessments has a long history. Joseph Beuys was sacked by the Kunstakademie Düsseldorf for it; Black Mountain College awarded graded degrees without disclosing them to the students, only passing on the information to expedite entry into postgraduate courses or work.

Atkinson's approach is situated within the political discourses of critical theory and is therefore distinct from educationalists whose research is focused on creative and cultural learning. The latter frequently use sociological models (often connected to developmental psychology, critiqued here by Pen Dalton) which involve assessing students' educational progress. Problematic issues around psychology, assessment and regulation are highlighted in Paul Clements' discussion of prison education.[8] He shows the shifts in 'art education' that evidence-based policy, a key tenet of both neoliberalism and social democratic pragmatism, has forced on British prisoners and their teachers. Distinct from modernist ideas of self-expression, or current ideas of potentiality, prison art education has been subsumed within the instrumentalist and economic imperatives which have accrued to practices such as cognitive behavioural therapy. CBT is also used in schools to address behavioural 'problems' that can be seen as the result of trying to fit too many 'square pegs' into a single round hole; those who demonstrate 'square peg' behaviour might otherwise be identified as 'creative'; their 'learning style' may not be met by school orthodoxies. Closely related is the model of medication following diagnosis of Attention Deficit Hyperactivity Disorder (ADHD). The arts education specialist Ken Robinson has challenged ADHD's 'epidemic' status, using the subversively absurd technique of mapping its incidence in the USA to unravel its rationale: 'Attention deficit disorder increases as you travel east across the country. People start losing interest in Oklahoma; they can hardly think straight by the time they get to Arkansas and by the time they get to Washington they've lost it completely.' He diagnoses medical fashion as the cause, and continues: 'Our children are living in the most intensely stimulating period of the history of the earth. They are being besieged with information and calls for their attention from every platform ... and we're penalizing them for getting distracted [at school] ... It seems to me not entirely a coincidence that the incidence of ADHD has risen in parallel with the incidence of standardized testing ...' He goes on to relate the aesthetic experience with being fully alive, in contrast to this model of anaesthetization.[9]

The reader, the learner and the viewer, as producers of meaning through doing and making, dialogue and reflection, run between the lines of this book. Hein cites John Dewey, Jean Piaget, Lev Vygotsky; Adrienne Rich cites Walter Ong. The ideas of these and others are intrinsic to a system of developing knowledge and sharing it for a public good. The privatization of scholarly knowledge (for instance, patenting scientific research) is a clear challenge to this notion, and movements such as Creative Commons are counterweights that reinforce the concept and practice of knowledge as public and collectively developed. Dissonance can occur between the broader art education arena – predominantly publicly oriented – and academic pedagogy because the latter has developed a commercial sector of its own. Since the 1980s former teachers have left public teaching to set up private employment agencies that sell temporary teaching staff back to schools, and academic educationalists have sold knowledge back to the public sectors through professional and management development programmes. Their services include 'managing change', which may aim to support the shift of schools and universities into models artists and art theorists call for, but the underlying management methodology almost always results in education's increased 'corporatization'. As well as privatizing free universal education, it also undermines professional specialism by introducing tiers of non-specialist management. Alex Farquharson's text on the artist Carey Young shows how her mimetic performance work embodies this kind of transition, in this case from artist as guru (Joseph Beuys), to management trainer as guru. In the context of this series and its readership, examples such as Young's have been selected rather than academic work which is influential in both art education and professional development; to cite just a few names: Donald Schön on the processes and development of reflective practitioners;

David Kolb on experiential learning; Howard Gardner on learning styles; or many, including Gardner, Guy Claxton and Anna Craft, who have contributed to debates on creativity.[10]

The pressure for governments to argue for the arts from an 'evidence-base' has created an industry for evaluators and assessors. Elliot Eisner's text articulates issues for assessing development in students' art. It is not surprising that the students of the late 1960s were demanding that art schools eliminate entry requirements and grading; their leaders were challenging the fundamentals of what was being taught. Never mind the content of conceptualism, how could assessment keep up with this revolution in practice? Attempts to overthrow regulation contribute to a site-specific, reality-based fantasy based on Leeds Polytechnic that the artist Paul Rooney describes, via the fictional persona of Dr Annette Gomperts, in his work *Thin Air* (2009). Gomperts notes that the [real] art historian Griselda Pollock was a member of the Leeds Fine Art Review Body which compiled an internal report in 1985 in response both to the impact of the new market economics and the hangover from 'a lack of teaching ... disrepair ... falling apart.'[11] In the 1980s the women's movement was beginning to achieve legislation to clear up discriminatory employment and teaching regimes, especially in the form of personal behaviours at work and education. But although the pejorative expression 'nanny state' arose at the same time, rather than emergent neoliberalism countering such ideas it effectively co-opted many of them. As Nancy Fraser puts it: 'Interestingly, second-wave feminism thrived in these new conditions. What had begun as a radical countercultural movement was now en route to becoming a broad-based mass social phenomenon.' But now, she says, is 'a moment in which feminists should think big. Having watched the neoliberal onslaught instrumentalize our best ideas, we have an opening now in which to reclaim them.'[12]

Art education's regulatory systems often run counter to one's motivation to learn about and practise art; to the fact that an intellectual subject can be explored through personal, emotional and tactile behaviours and that, intrinsically, it involves the frustrations and pleasures of fumbling in the dark. The ambiguities of judgement in teacher-student relationships are revealed in Eve Kosofsky Sedgwick's text. Judith Scott's teachers have supported her while believing her potential to be constrained, Sedgwick suggests, because of their own limiting vision of what art can be, what intentional thinking it must involve, what outcome it must have implied by its process. This sense of endless potential, but equally the exhausted nature of existing pedagogies, is represented in many of the texts of the 1970s, whether exploring newly-developed feminist pedagogies or transforming the art school as it emerged out of its skills-based ancestry into an interdisciplinary, intellectual and technological unknown. As, in turn, these possibilities have closed down institutionally, Pollock and others reflect on what is lost, the more clearly to focus on what is most valuable for the future.

These texts include the personal and affective no less than the specific and intelligent; they explore the relationships between art and education in the broadest, most inclusive terms. Central is a concern for people, beginning with Mary Kelly's maternal reflections on her infant's emergence into a 'pre-school' child of the 1970s – not divided from but interwoven with her rigorous psychoanalytic analysis – and ending with Harrell Fletcher's participatory art projects of the twenty-first century that reveal 'uninteresting' people as interesting teachers and older women as valued collaborators and audience. From this selection of texts – and its leads into many potential others – you are invited to begin making your own collection.

1 Lisa Tickner, *Hornsey 1968: The Art School Revolution* (London: Frances Lincoln, 2008).

2 The term 'artist educator' here indicates artists involved in delivering any form of education.

3 See Richard Eyre: 'Arts Cuts will Result in Cultural Apartheid' at http://www.guardian.co.uk/culture/culture-cuts-blog/2011/feb/15/arts-funding-arts-policy

4 For example, Mary Kelly's seminar on *Post-Partum Document* at the 'Feminist Interventions' Symposium, Hayward Gallery, London, in 1978. The work was included in the concurrent 'Hayward Annual II'. Its first exhibition was in 1976 at the Institute of Contemporary Arts, London.

5 Ken Robinson, 'Changing Education Paradigms' (RSA Animate series, 14 October 2010) at http://sirkenrobinson.com/skr/rsa-animate-changing-education-paradigms

6 Most work in this category might be identified as post-conceptual, in Peter Osborne's definition, and therefore involve a 'principled destruction of an ontological conception of "medium" ... [demonstrating] the radically *distributive* character of the unity of the work' (Peter Osborne, 'Art Beyond Aesthetics', *Art History*, vol. 27, no. 4 [September 2004] 665). However, some approaches clearly identify with pre-conceptual practices while others are developed in other terms, or in terms that are in transition, or between positions. It seemed therefore useful to raise the question of medium in relation to art practices that dialogue with a pedagogical momentum.

7 See Dennis Atkinson, 'Pedagogy of the Event' (2009) in this volume, 101–3.

8 The manifestation of the control society through significantly increasing the imprisoned population is important to reference, since education symbolically plays as regulatory, democratizing, emancipatory and liberational.

9 Ken Robinson, 'Changing Education Paradigms', op. cit.

10 e.g. Anna Craft, Guy Claxton, Howard Gardner, *Creativity, Wisdom and Trusteeship: Exploring the Role of Education* (Thousand Oaks, California: Corwin Press, 2007).

11 Paul Rooney, *Thin Air: The Psycho-Vocalic Discoveries of Alan Smithson* (http://www.thinair.org.uk/resources/Thin-Air.pdf) 25.

12 Nancy Fraser, 'Feminism, Capitalism and the Cunning of History', *New Left Review* (March/April 2009) 107; 117.

I'M NOT SO INTERESTED IN
ART AS EDUCATION
AS IN
EDUCATION
AS
ART

I'M INTERESTED IN
EXPLORING THE WAYS IN
WHICH THINGS BECOME
ART

I'M INTERESTED IN
SEEING WHAT MAKES
A MOMENT
ART,
A MOMENT
THAT COMES FROM
THE REALM OF
THE POLITICAL

Tania Bruguera, Transpedagogy: Conversation with Pablo Helguera, 2009

PRIMER

Mary Kelly
Post-Partum Document//1973–79

[...] (age 3.6) e IS FOR ELEPHANT. He calls it the 'curvy one' and pronounces it 'eeh'. He often forgets it and sometimes writes it upside down – 'a'. When he sees an e, a present or a breast, he says, 'what's that?' Something at once lost, forgotten, remembered and hoped for. 'a' as in 'me'. E IS FOR ALLIGATORS ENTERTAINING ELEPHANTS. E IS FOR AN EAGLE ON AN ELEPHANT IN AN EGG AND SPOON RACE. GOOD NIGHT EDWARD ELMER ELEPHANT. GOOD NIGHT LITTLE E.

February 22, 1977: I noticed the general conditions more than the children this time, like the rubbish outside the building and the dust inside. When I washed the cups the rag looked so grey I couldn't bring myself to use it. But I suppose they do the best they can, it isn't their own space, it's only rented during the day from a boys' club. There's no playground and the children have to stay indoors. All but about 20 mins of the 2 hrs. is 'unstructured' and seems to get out of hand. I'm afraid they'll get hurt. I can't stand the bad grammar after about an hour of it – I can't believe I could be so uptight and pretentious. I feel inadequate myself because I can't offer Kelly more. I wish he could go to a good school, but it's hopeless in this area. I went to the Social Services Dept. and self-righteously demanded the names and addresses of proper nursery schools. They just smiled and refused, saying it would be of no use since all of them had at least a 2 yr waiting list.

[...] (age 4.5) B IS FOR BALLOON. This is the first letter he has constructed with the express purpose of writing a special word – his surname. He draws P and carefully adds Ↄ. Learning to write 'Barrie' has also sorted out his backwards 'b' and the upside-down 'a'. B IS FOR ALLIGATORS BURSTING BALLOONS. B IS FOR BEARS PLAYING BAGPIPES IN A BAND. GOOD NIGHT LITTLE B. BERTRAM BULLFINCH BASSET HOUND

April 19, 1978. Now Kelly is at school all day Ray insisted that he was ready to stay for school dinners. He said Kelly was quite happy and I had to admit it did seem to be true so far. When he comes home I try to ask him what he does at school, what he has for lunch, but he's usually not very informative he's in such a hurry to change his clothes and go out to play with Ronnie. They've become very good friends. Once he said he didn't think he needed a mummy and daddy because he and Ronnie could live together and look after themselves. He brought home some flash cards which seem to take the place of our 'a.b.c.' sessions and he keeps a little notebook at school which I can go and look at from time to time. Things have definitely changed, and so quickly. When I told Rosalind that he'd started infant's school she said 'well, you're a real mother now.'

Transcribed extracts from the slate incised relief panels by Mary Kelly: *Documentation VI: Prewriting Alphabet, Exergue and Diary* and *Experimentum Mentis VI: On the Insistence of the Letter*, from *Post-Partum Document* (1973–79). Above the first of each of the texts transcribed here are early examples of writing by the artist's infant son. The first of each text by the artist is in handwriting, the second in typescript.

Bridget Riley
In Conversation with Nikki Henriques//1988

Nikki Henriques Who has inspired you?

Bridget Riley My mother certainly. [...]

Henriques What did you learn from her?

Riley During the War my father was a Japanese prisoner of war on the Siamese railway. In three years we had only three postcards from him. We had very little money; we lived in a cottage in Cornwall that was a paradise for children but must have been a nightmare for my mother. There were few amenities: no bath; we got water from a brook; the roof leaked; we had tarpaulins over our beds. [...]

My mother took us for walks on the cliffs. She was always pointing out colours: in the sea; the sparkle of dew; changes of colour when the dew was brushed away. If she arranged anything on the table like a bowl of fruit (we only saw two bananas in the village the whole time we were there!) she would point out the colours: 'Look, it's almost got a blue on it.' She wasn't a painter, she was a 'looker'. The pleasure that one could get from looking was part of her personality.

She was very well read. She read to us in the evening. When I was ten or eleven we would have a hip bath in the winter, in front of the fire, once a week. At other times we'd have a lick and a promise. My mother would read something from the classics, we would say our prayers together and go to bed. That gave me a taste for reading. As soon as I could I bought a torch and continued to read under the bedclothes. [...]

My father thought my education had gone to pot. It was probably true; the War had completely disrupted it. He realized that I was fairly illiterate and should go to a better school.

I went with my younger sister to a splendid academic school – Cheltenham Ladies' College. The headmistress was a great support to children of prisoners of war but was disconcerted and unhappy when she saw that she would have to put me in the lowest class. In terms of my age I should have been halfway up the school. I told her not to worry, I would work out my own timetable. She was very relieved and let me go ahead. I came up with art every day: art on Monday morning, art on Tuesday afternoon, art on Wednesday morning and art on Thursday afternoon ...

Cheltenham had a wonderful art wing. I had never seen such a palace. I was allowed to study there most of the time, but there was also a particularly good course called Citizenship. This involved reading newspapers, visiting prisons (though not in the lady bountiful manner), factories, law courts, and included a great many other things. Citizenship was supposed to be a one-year course but because it was the only thing I could do I repeated it for three! [...]

The Royal College [of Art] philosophy was stated to me by one member of staff as 'It's going to very tough outside, so you might as well have it tough in here.' So we were left to work it out for ourselves. We were abandoned, when what we needed (and hoped for) was help towards independence rather than having independence thrust down our throats. We could ask questions, but the trouble is that you don't necessarily know when you have a problem and students can be either too proud or too diffident to ask for help. Advanced teaching ought to help a student to discover his or her problems. We were anxious to find out as much as we could but this was ignored – a certain fundamental bargain was not kept. There was an overpowering sense of a vacuum in the College. There were exceptions, of course. Among the tutors, Colin Hayes was a good friend, and the warmth and heart of the school was John Minton, whose compassion, sophistication and wit were immensely reassuring. You realized at once that he was aware the problems he faced were in essence common ones. He was much loved by the students.

We were an immensely varied group. There were some fifty of us, with a wide range of backgrounds, interests and aspirations. That, I am sure, was very significant; and some had served in the War, so there was a wide range of experience and maturity. We were not ambitious in the way students are today. We did not expect attention from the commercial galleries, or to command the interest of a wide public. We didn't think far ahead, and that was excellent. [...]

Bridget Riley, extracts from conversation with Nikki Henriques (1988), *The Eye's Mind: Collected Writings 1965–1999*, ed. Robert Kudielka (London: Thames & Hudson, 1999) 21–3; 35–6.

Ziauddin Sardar
British, Muslim, Writer//1997

[...] My mother was distraught when she learned that my father was leaving for England. He '*had* to go', he said. But there was nothing to worry about as we would be joining him within a year or so – 'as soon as I find a job and a place to stay'. Within a week of his announcement my father was gone. [...]

I struggled with the books that my father kept sending me. Sometimes I was helped in this endeavour by my aunts and other regular visitors to our house. I started with *Black Beauty*. One of my aunts read *Treasure Island* and *Kidnapped* aloud to me. Ploughing through *Oliver Twist* and *David Copperfield* was a real chore. *Wuthering Heights* marked the outer limit. [...]

This eclectic introduction to the English language came with a whole set of associations. I came to think of England through the aura created by what I read. It seemed that England was indeed the centre, possibly the original home of what it claimed were all 'the great books of mankind'. In the pages that I stumbled over were all the polite civilities and the high-flown notions of justice, fairness, democracy, order. [...]

The day after I returned from [a convalescent home for children in] Broadstairs I walked into Brooke House Secondary School at Clapton Pond and asked to be enrolled. The school secretary to whom I presented my request was astonished, but eventually allowed me to see the headmaster, Mr Harris. He was a very gentle and considerate man, who, I would later learn, loathed punishing his pupils, but the lack of discipline at the school often left him no choice. Mr Harris asked me to come back a couple of days later and take an 'intelligence test'. I failed the test – miserably – and consequently joined the bottom stream: 1.6. I had problems at the school right from the start. By far the worst of my problems was Mr Brilliant, our history teacher. He looked like Einstein, without the moustache, and thought himself pretty clever, too. First, I found it difficult to understand how Mr Brilliant could talk about Victorian England without talking about what Victorian England did to India and Africa. Then I found his account of the 'Indian Mutiny' too difficult to swallow. But most of all I resented the fact that he was not interested in my history at all: 'Not in the syllabus, lad. Can't talk about it.' I became so incensed with Mr Brilliant's inflexible approach to history that, one day, I stuffed all his textbooks in my desk and attempted to set fire to them. I was brought before Mr Harris who, reluctantly, administered 'six of the best'.

But it was not just at school that I had problems. It was clear to me that I was not accepted on the streets. The walk to and from school was the most painful part of my day. The gangs of youths I encountered on my daily journey had discovered a new game – 'Paki-bashing'. I was the perpetual *guli* to their *danda*.[1] I made it a principle to fight back and frequently arrived home with cuts and bruises, and on notable occasions even with a broken nose and then a leg. I was learning that being British meant forgoing essential parts of one's anatomy. At school, they castrated chunks of your history. On the streets, they took lumps out of you. [...]

It was in response to this determined process of extraction that I began to learn about proactivity, the resistance that defines the nature of my Britishness. [...]

To be a conscious and conscientious Muslim today requires constant struggle against obscurantism, against chauvinistic interpretations, against legal opinions that have served their purpose in history, against traditional notions direly in need of transformation, against blind imitation, against the tyranny of out-of-context quotations and anecdotes. The challenge of being a Muslim today is the responsibility to harness a controlled explosion, one that will clear the premises of all the detritus without damaging the foundations that would bring down the house of Islam.

Perhaps this is the common link between my British and Muslim identity, two volcanic imperatives, with me the molten and merged lava flow they generate. When I examine my Muslim identity, it is like excavating through a series of volcanic strata, burrowing through overlaid layers that form the ground on which I now stand. My early schooling in Islam was through my mother, who taught me to read the Qur'an as well as the basic tenets and rituals. There is nothing special in this, it is so conventional one might even neglect to mention the fact. It is an experience repeated in households the world over, the Muslim world, that is. The intimacy of one's Muslim identity is its domesticity. As I learned from my mother, so I have watched my wife teach my children. Through this most resilient tradition we are always closing the distance between Islamic identity and ourselves, hopefully so that we can take it deep inside ourselves. [...]

In the classical Golden Age nurturing writers had been the strength of Islamic education and leadership. Now, there was nowhere and no one in the Muslim world I could think of to turn to.[2] So I reached out to my Maimonides.[3] I phoned Jerry Ravetz in Leeds. 'Get on the train, lad', he said, 'and we'll sort it out'. I met Jerry when he was the Secretary of the Council for Science and Society, a high-powered body that studied and published reports on the social and cultural problems of science. He had rung out of nowhere to invite me to join the Council's working group on 'the information explosion'. He was a reader in the History and Philosophy of Science at Leeds University. When I arrived we sat closeted for a few days while I poured out my problem and Jerry bobbled, bounced and flapped his hands, in characteristic fashion, as he engaged with my ideas. His advice was invaluable, but his enthusiasm was even more precious. Over the next year, in occasional meetings and by long-distance Jerry simply talked me through the process of writing the book. [...]

Together we all began wrestling with words to find expression for our ideas. In [the interdisciplinary philosophy journal] *Inquiry* we were tempered in a common fire and eventually found ourselves in riotous assembly on the same flight to Chicago. Aloft over the Atlantic Ocean we made a pledge to become a group; it took the rest of the flight to determine what the group should be called – one of our members is a linguist with a penchant for etymology. We never discussed the function of the group – that was self-evident: mutual support as the antidote to the isolation we had all endured. Ijmal, as we call ourselves, which means the beauty of synthesis, has been in existence for a decade. It is the most formally informal of groups, though it does have ground rules: every member must write. [...]

I am not a problem for *me*; the process I have been forced to undergo has not been a self-transformation, but a clarification and deepening understanding of the potential possibilities and unsuspected commensurabilities of all the heritages I am heir to. It is other people who have the problem. By profession other people are dedicated to the ideas that such composite self is impossible, or permissible only when fashioned in differently proportioned chemical recombinations, according to their recipe. There are fundamentalists and totalitarians on all sides whose definition of identity, nationality, culture, society, the nature and purpose of being deny ijmal, the infusion that sustains my *joie de vivre*. Whether it be right-wing Britain or left-wing British activism and the race relations industry; traditionalist or modernist Muslims; secularist or libertarian ideologists or squads of postmodern intelligentsia – it is they who cannot deal with my ease with myself. [...]

1 [*Guli Danda* is an outdoor game that originated in the South Asian subcontinent. The *guli* and *danda* are different kinds of sticks. The aim is to strike the *guli* with the *danda*.]

2 [In 1976 Sardar had approached the writer and activist Kalim Siddiqui (1931–96) for guidance on writing his first book based on his research of the *Hajj*. Siddiqui refused to help him.]

3 [Moses Maimonides (1135–1204), the Jewish scholar who synthesized Judaic, Islamic and Aristotelian ideas.]

Ziauddin Sardar, extracts from 'British, Muslim, Writer', in *Other than Identity: The Subject, Politics and Art*, ed. Juliet Steyn (Manchester: Manchester University Press, 1997) 63–81.

John Dewey
Democracy and Education//1916

[...] Exorbitant desire for uniformity of procedure and for prompt external results are the chief foes which the open-minded attitude meets in school. The teacher who does not permit and encourage diversity of operation in dealing with questions is imposing intellectual blinders upon pupils – restricting their vision to the one path the teacher's mind happens to approve. Probably the chief cause of devotion to rigidity of method is, however, that it seems to promise speedy, accurately measurable, correct results. The zeal for 'answers' is the explanation of much of the zeal for rigid and mechanical methods. Forcing and overpressure have the same origin, and the same result upon alert and varied intellectual interest.

Open-mindedness is not the same as empty-mindedness. To hang out a sign saying 'Come right in; there is no one at home' is not the equivalent of hospitality. But there is a kind of passivity, willingness to let experiences accumulate and sink in and ripen, which is an essential of development. Results (external answers or solutions) may be hurried; processes may not be forced. They take their own time to mature. Were all instructors to realize that the quality of mental process, not the production of correct answers, is the measure of educative growth something hardly less than a revolution in teaching would be worked. [...]

To charge that the various activities of gardening, weaving, construction in wood, manipulation of metals, cooking, etc., which carry over these fundamental concerns into school resources, have a merely bread and butter value is to miss their point. If the mass of mankind has usually found in its industrial occupations nothing but evils which had to be endured for the sake of maintaining existence, the fault is not in the occupations, but in the conditions under which they are carried on. The continually increasing importance of economic factors in contemporary life makes it the more needed that education should reveal their scientific content and their social value. For in schools, occupations are not carried on for pecuniary gain but for their own content. Freed from extraneous associations and from the pressure of wage-earning, they supply modes of experience which are intrinsically valuable; they are truly liberalizing in quality. [...]

Sensational empiricism represents neither the idea of experience justified by modern psychology nor the idea of knowledge suggested by modern scientific procedure. With respect to the former, it omits the primary position of active response which puts things to use and which learns about them through discovering the consequences that result from use. It would seem as if five minutes' unprejudiced observation of the way an infant gains knowledge would have sufficed to overthrow the notion that he is passively engaged in receiving impressions of isolated ready-made qualities of sound, colour, hardness, etc. For it would be seen that the infant reacts to stimuli by activities of handling, reaching, etc., in order to see what results follow upon motor response to a sensory stimulation; it would be seen that what is learned are not isolated qualities, but the behaviour which may be expected from a thing, and the changes in things and persons which an activity may be expected to produce. In other words, what he learns are connections. Even such qualities as red colour, sound of a high pitch, have to be discriminated and identified on the basis of the activities they call forth and the consequences these activities effect. We learn what things are hard and what are soft by finding out through active experimentation what they respectively will do and what can be done and what cannot be done with them. In like fashion, children learn about persons by finding out what responsive activities these persons exact and what these persons will do in reply to the children's activities. And the combination of what things do to us (not in impressing qualities on a passive mind) in modifying our actions, furthering some of them and resisting and checking others, and what we can do to them in producing new changes, constitutes experience. The methods of science by which the revolution in our knowledge of the world, dating from the seventeenth century, was brought about teach the same lesson. For these methods are nothing but experimentation carried out under conditions of deliberate control. To the Greek, it seemed absurd that such an activity as, say, the cobbler punching holes in leather, or using wax and needle and thread, could give an adequate knowledge of the world. It seemed almost axiomatic that for true knowledge we must have recourse to concepts coming from a reason above experience. But the introduction of the experimental method signified precisely that such operations, carried on under conditions of control, are just the ways in which fruitful ideas about nature are obtained and tested. [...]

John Dewey, extract from *Democracy and Education* (New York: Macmillan, 1916) 218–19.

Virginia Woolf
Three Guineas//1938

[...] The part that education plays in human life is so important, and the part that it might play in answering your question ['How in your opinion are we to prevent war?'] is so considerable that to shirk any attempt to see how we can influence the young through education against war would be craven. [...]

Let us then discuss as quickly as we can the sort of education that is needed. Now since history and biography – the only evidence available to an outsider – seem to prove that the old education of the old colleges breeds neither a particular respect for liberty nor a particular hatred of war, it is clear that you must rebuild your college differently. It is young and poor; let it therefore take advantage of those qualities and be founded on poverty and youth. Obviously, then, it must be an experimental college; an adventurous college. Let it be built on lines of its own. It must be built not of carved stone and stained glass, but of some cheap, easily combustible material which does not hoard dust and perpetrate traditions. Do not have chapels. Do not have museums and libraries with chained books and first editions under glass cases. Let the pictures and the books be new and always changing. Let it be decorated afresh by each generation with their own hands cheaply. The work of the living is cheap; often they will give it for the sake of being allowed to do it. Next, what should be taught in the new college, the poor college? Not the arts of dominating other people; not the arts of ruling, of killing, of acquiring land and capital. They require too many overhead expenses; salaries and uniforms and ceremonies. The poor college must teach only the arts that can be taught cheaply and practised by poor people; such as medicine, mathematics, music, painting and literature. It should teach the arts of human intercourse; the art of understanding other people's lives and minds, and the little arts of talk, of dress, of cookery that are allied with them. The aim of the new college, the cheap college, should be not to segregate and specialize, but to combine. It should explore the ways in which mind and body can be made to cooperate; discover what new combinations make good wholes in human life. The teachers should be drawn from the good livers as well as from the good thinkers. There should be no difficulty in attracting them. For there would be none of the barriers of wealth and ceremony, of advertisement and competition which now make the old and rich universities such uneasy dwelling-places – cities of strife, cities where this is locked up and that is chained down; where nobody can walk freely or talk freely for fear of transgressing some chalk mark, of displeasing some dignitary. But if the college were poor it would have nothing to offer; competition would be abolished. Life would be open and easy. People who love learning for itself would gladly come there. Musicians, painters, writers, would teach there, because they would learn. What could be of greater help to a writer than to discuss the art of writing with people who were thinking not of examinations or degrees or of what honour or profit they could make literature give them, but of the art itself?

And so with the other arts and artists. They would come to the poor college and practise their arts there because it would be a place where society was free; not parcelled out into the miserable distinctions of rich and poor, of clever and stupid; but where all the different degrees and kinds of mind, body and soul merit cooperated. Let us then found this new college; this poor college; in which learning is sought for itself; where advertisement is abolished; and there are no degrees; and lectures are not given, and sermons are not preached, and the old poisoned vanities and parades which breed competition and jealousy ...

The letter broke off there. It was not from lack of things to say; the peroration indeed was only just beginning. It was because the face on the other side of the page – the face that a letter-writer always sees – appeared to be fixed with a certain melancholy, upon a passage in the book from which quotation has already been made. 'Head mistresses of schools therefore prefer a belettered staff, so that students of Newnham and Girton, since they could not put B.A. after their name, were at a disadvantage in obtaining appointments.' The honorary treasurer of the Rebuilding Fund had her eyes fixed on that. 'What is the use of thinking how a college can be different', she seemed to say, 'when it must be a place where students are taught to obtain appointments?' 'Dream your dreams', she seemed to add. [...]

Virginia Woolf, extracts from *Three Guineas* (London: Hogarth Press, 1938); reprinted edition (Harmondsworth, Middlesex: Penguin Books, 1978) 27; 39–41.

Herbert Read
Education through Art//1943

The Purpose of Education

The thesis which is to be put forward in this book is: that art should be the basis of education. [...]

The purpose of education has at least two irreconcilable possibilities: one, that man should be educated to become what he is; the other, that he should be educated to become what he is not. The first view assumes that each individual is born with certain potentialities which have a positive value for that individual and that it is his proper destiny to develop these potentialities within the framework of a society liberal enough to allow for an infinite variation of types. The second view assumes that whatever idiosyncrasies the individual may possess at birth, it is the duty of the teacher to eradicate them unless they conform to a certain ideal of character determined by the traditions of the society of which the individual has involuntarily become a member. [...]

What is the Purpose of Education?

An answer to this question is implied in a libertarian conception of democracy. The purpose of education can then only be to develop, at the same time as the uniqueness, the social consciousness or reciprocity of the individual. [...]

Some such conception of education has been accepted by people of democratic faith for many years now, but like democracy itself, it is far from being consciously formulated or deliberately put into practice. It is not a specifically modern conception: in spite of the political limitations he placed on its application, Plato's theory of education assumes this principle of freedom. 'Avoid compulsion', he says, 'and let your children's lessons take the form of play. This will also help you to see what they are naturally fitted for.' But though there were earlier anticipations of many of its features, freedom as the guiding principle of education was first established by Rousseau. [...]

After Rousseau came Pestalozzi, Froebel and Montessori, all of whom contributed to the growth of freedom in education; but it is not until modern times, as in the works of John Dewey and Edmond Holmes, that we get something like a theory of education fully integrated with a democratic conception of society. [...]

What I have in mind is not merely 'art education' as such, which should more properly be called visual or plastic education: the theory to be put forward embraces all modes of self-expression, literary and poetic (verbal) no less than musical or aural, and forms an integral approach to reality which should be called aesthetic education – the education of those senses upon which consciousness, and ultimately the intelligence and judgement of the human individual, are based. It is only in so far as these senses are brought into harmonious and habitual relationship with the external world that an integrated personality is built up. Without such integration we get not only the psychologically unbalanced types familiar to the psychiatrist but – what is even more disastrous from the point of view of the general good – those arbitrary systems of thought, dogmatic or rationalistic in origin, which seek in despite of the natural facts to impose a logical or intellectual pattern on the world of organic life.

This adjustment of the senses to their objective environment is perhaps the most important function of aesthetic education, but there is another aspect we need to consider, which may profoundly modify our conclusions. The environment of the individual is not entirely objective: his experience is not only empirical. Within the individual are two 'interior courts' or existential states which can be externalized by the aid of the aesthetic faculties. One is somatic, and exists even in blind mutes: it is a store of imagery, derived not from external perception but from muscular and nervous tensions which are internal in origin. In itself such 'haptic' sensibility is perhaps not important, but the neglect of this element as it appears in aesthetic expression has led to much misunderstanding of those deviations from photographic naturalism which are found in primitive and modern art.

But deeper and more significant than these proprioceptive states are those levels of the mental personality which are *subconscious*. More or less detached features of this level enter into the foreground of our awareness in the form of images. These images appear with apparent casualness during states of day-dreaming, hypnosis or ordinary dreaming, and such imagery is a form of expression, a language, which can be 'educated'. It is one of the fundamental elements in all forms of artistic activity. We shall have to consider to what extent this imaginative activity as such should be encouraged by our methods of education. [...]

The Natural Form of Education

The wrangle over the timetable is as unnecessary as it is unseemly. Our aim is not two or more extra periods. We demand nothing less than the whole 35 into which the child's week is now arbitrarily divided. We demand, that is to say, a method of education that is formally and fundamentally aesthetic, and in which knowledge and manual ability, discipline and reverence, are but so many easy and inevitable by-products of a natural childish industry.

Obviously such requirements involve a reform of the educational system which is too revolutionary to be substantiated by the observations of one individual, and it is obviously not within my competence to say how such reforms would affect, say, the teaching of individual subjects like mathematics and geography. The integral education which I conceive is relatively indifferent to the fate of individual subjects, since its underlying assumption is that the purpose of education is to develop generic qualities of insight and sensibility, which qualities are fundamental even in mathematics or geography. [...]

From an active point of view the progression may be regarded as beginning with *play*, and as being, throughout the whole of the primary stage, nothing but a development of play. There is, of course, nothing very original in such a suggestion, and 'the play way' is a recognized method of education, especially in infant schools. But as I have already indicated, the conception of play on which these discussions and experiments are based is inadequate and sometimes superficial. At the lowest it becomes a pretence of 'not taking things seriously', and every subject is debased to a hilarious game in which the teacher becomes a histrionic buffoon. At its best the method tends to develop a form of sophistication which is only too evident to the child. The play method, if properly pursued, should not imply merely a lack of coherence and direction in teaching – that is playing at teaching, not teaching by play – *but to give coherence and to play is to convert it into art*, and it was for this reason that an objection was raised in the last chapter to the theoretical treatment of art as a form of play. Play is rather an informal activity capable of becoming an artistic activity and of thus acquiring significance for the organic development of the child. [...]

Herbert Read, extracts from *Education through Art* (London: Faber & Faber, 1943; reprinted 1970) 1–8; 220–23.

Black Mountain College[1]
Prospectus//1952

Black Mountain College is heretical because it has practised from its founding (1933) two of the simplest and oldest principles on which higher learning – when it has been higher – has rested:

I. that *the student*, rather than the curriculum, is *the proper* centre of a general education, because it is he and she that a college exist for.

II. that a faculty fit to face up the student as the centre have to be measured by *what they do with what they know*, that it is their dimension as teachers as much as their mastery of their disciplines that makes them instruments capable of dealing with what excuses their profession in the first place, their ability to instruct the student under hand.

Several things follow these two base principles, so far as the instruction at Black Mountain College goes. One characteristic, from the beginning, has been the recognition that ideas are only such as they exist in things and in actions. Another worth emphasizing (it is still generally overlooked in those colleges where classification into fields, because of curriculum emphasis, remains the law) is that Black Mountain College carefully recognizes that, at this point in man's necessities, it is not things in themselves, but what happens between things, where the life of them is to be sought.

The present faculty, herein presented, is a measure – both in their number (one to every two students) and in the range of their accomplishments as well as the disciplines offered – of what the standard of teaching and of life Black Mountain has tried to give students for nineteen years.

These are the present faces and facts. In offering them, the College takes pride in carrying before them some of the philosophy of teaching they represent as that philosophy got variously stated by the leader in the founding of the College, John A. Rice:

> Our central consistent effort is to teach method, not content; to emphasize process, to invite the student to the realization that the way of handling facts and himself amid the facts is more important than facts themselves. For facts change, while the method of handling facts – provided it is life's own free, dynamic method – remains the same. The law of a teacher at Black Mountain is to function as a working 'artist' in the teaching world, to be no passive recipient or hander-out of mere information, but to be and increasingly to become, productive, creative, *using* everything that comes within his orbit, including especially people.
>
> There is a technic to be learned, a grammar of the art of living and working in the world. Logic, as severe as can be, must be learned; if for no other reason, to know its limitations. Dialectic must be learned: and no feelings spared, for you can't be nice when truth is at stake. The hard, inscrutable facts of science must be learned, for truth has a habit of hiding in queer places. Man's responses to ideas and things in the past must be learned. But they are not all. There are subtle means of communication that have been lost by mankind, as our nerve ends have been cauterized by schooling. The arts, especially the performing arts, are more and more valuable in such restorations. For these nerves must be renewed, in both ourselves as faculty and in the students who come to us to communicate and to learn to communicate. To learn to move, at least without fear, to hear, see, touch, also without fear or at least without denials of first hungers, to be aware of everything around us (again, including especially people) – this is to start to

penetrate the past and to *feel* as well as mentally see our way into the future.

A good teacher is always more a learner than teacher, making the demand of everyone to be taught something. A man who never asks himself any questions had better not try asking others. In the centre of his being a teacher should be calm, quiet, *tough*. He must have in him the principle of growth; like the student, a sense of justice and a great capacity for dejection.

Teachers in a place like this, where education is taken seriously, should always bear in mind that they are the central problem, *that we would provide the students with a liberal education if we merely gave them the privilege of looking on while we educated ourselves.*

1 Although this text is unsigned, the writing style, layout and typography of the original strongly indicate that its author was Charles Olson. (Vincent Katz.)

'Black Mountain College Prospectus for Spring Semester, February 11 – June 7, 1952'; reprinted in *Black Mountain College: Experiment in Art*, ed. Vincent Katz (Cambridge, Massachusetts: The MIT Press, 2003) 202.

Vincent Katz
Black Mountain College: Experiment in Art//2003

[...] Perhaps, ultimately it was more about seeing than about an idea. When one looks at the work of the diverse talents that at one time or another composed Black Mountain College, an underlying factor seems to be the desire to see in a new way, free from previous restrictions. Looked at distinctly from the rhetoric that bound and binds so much artistic endeavour, the art is free to be seen afresh. When there is a use of abstraction, as there so often was in those days, maybe we can see it now as less an idea than a way of seeing.

During the 23 years of its existence, from 1933 to 1956, Black Mountain College, in southwestern North Carolina, was a magnet for artists establishing their professional identities. What was encouraged, what was engaged in at Black Mountain – both by student and by artist/teacher – was experimentation. People felt free there to undertake those activities that were geared towards finding new ways of doing, rather than learning and repeating the past. For artists who taught there, Black Mountain was a sojourn of great fertility, and like the shaman who goes on travels in quest of experience, these artists derived significant personal strength from their artistic voyages. Upon leaving Black Mountain, this personal power often translated into worldly power in the artist's career. At Black Mountain, relationships were forged or strengthened with fruitful and important repercussions. [...]

Albers was active as a designer of commercial textiles in her Black Mountain period and prolific as an author. Her texts, though not widely known, are some of the most perceptive from that period. Taking ideas from her mentor Walter Gropius, she went beyond his rigid adherence to the idea that architecture was the queen of the arts, under which all the others must be subsumed. She argued that marginalized crafts (and here she makes a subtextual critique of the Bauhaus' regulation of women to 'women's arts') had every chance of being great in the right hands. Anni had an early training in English that Josef lacked. When they first arrived, Anni was Josef's ears and voice, and many were enamoured of her clear style and throught.

'Life today is very bewildering', she wrote in 1937 in 'Work with Material', published as a *Black Mountain College Bulletin*. 'We have no picture of it which is all-inclusive, such as former times may have had. We have had to make a choice between concepts of great diversity. And as a common ground is wanting, we are baffled by them.' She goes on to analyse the role materials can play in providing personal strength. 'We have useful things and beautiful things – equipment and works of art. In earlier civilizations there was no clear separation of this sort.' By learning the qualities of and then experimenting with materials, one could create art:

> But most important to one's own growth is to see oneself leave the safe ground of accepted conventions and to find oneself alone and self-dependent. It is an adventure which can permeate one's whole being. Self-confidence can grow. And a longing for excitement can be satisfied without external means, within oneself; for creating is the most intense excitement one can come to know.[1] [...]

Art can be more than therapy; it can improve the world. Yet, to be fully engaging, it should be based on the manual interaction with materials, not simply an idea. [...] Seeing, in Albers' curriculum, developed from drawing:

> We cannot communicate graphically what we do not see. That which we see incorrectly we will report incorrectly. We recognize that although our optical vision is correct, our over-emphasis on the psychic vision often makes us see incorrectly. For this reason we learn to test our seeing, and systematically study foreshortening, overlapping, as the main form problems of graphic articulation, and distinction between, and the pronunciation of, nearness and distance. [...]

In the area of colour experimentation and theory, Josef Albers went beyond his Bauhaus experience. At Black Mountain, Albers developed the principles he later applied in his definitive series *Homage to the Square*. Part of the curriculum, the colour course, began with a systematic exploration of 'the tonal possibilities of colours, their relativity, their interaction and influence on each other, cold and warmth, light intensity, colour intensity, psychical and spatial effects.'[2] [...]

Overall, while at Black Mountain, Albers showed interest in a multiplicity of approaches, for example demonstrating that the geometric could be as free as freehand, and freehand as abstract as the geometric. Albers' conclusion to a text on the Graphic Tectonics summed up his attitude at the time: '... we cannot remain in a single viewpoint, we need more for the sake of free vision.' He was a meticulous planner and organizer, entirely devoted to his task as pedagogue, determined to provide the most varied and stimulating environment for the students – all this while being equally devoted and prolific in experimentation and achievement in his own art in various media. Albers painstakingly arranged for travelling exhibitions to come to Black Mountain, to borrow glass slide presentations on ancient and modern art, and, at least from 1944 on, made sure that the students were exposed to a variety of artistic viewpoints in the form of the artists invited to teach at Black Mountain. [...]

Elaine de Kooning later contrasted Josef Albers' and Willem de Kooning's methods of teaching:

> Albers preferred to talk to students as a group; Bill liked to talk to students one at a time. Albers' students sat at desks and worked cautiously on small, neat compositions; Bill's stood at easels painting boldly on large canvases. Albers presented his students with the same specific problems; Bill waited until they had evolved their own set of problems on canvas before discussing the range of options open to them. Since most of the students worked under both of them, the different approaches proved to be stimulating rather than mutually exclusive.[3]

When it came time for the de Koonings to leave, however, Albers had a stern talk with Willem. He had taught ten students, six of whom were leaving the school and moving to New York. He asked de Kooning, 'Do you know anything about this?' 'Sure', said de Kooning. 'I told them if they wanted to be artists, they should quit school and come to New York and get a studio and start painting.' [...]

1 Anni Albers, 'Work with Material', *Black Mountain College Bulletin*, no. 5 (November 1938); reprinted in Anni Albers, *Selected Writings on Design* (Middletown, Connecticut: Wesleyan University Press, 200) 6–7.

2 Josef Albers, 'Concerning Art Instruction', *Black Mountain Bulletin*, no. 2 (Black Mountain College, June 1934).

3 Elaine de Kooning, 'De Kooning Memories', *Vogue* (December 1983); reprinted in *The Spirit of Abstract Expressionism: Selected Writings* (New York: George Braziller, 1994) 207 ff.

Vincent Katz, extracts from essay in Katz, ed., *Black Mountain College: Experiment in Art* (Cambridge, Massachusetts: The MIT Press, 2003) 15; 31–4; 46–9; 110.

Hannah Arendt
The Crisis in Education//1954

[...] The extraordinary enthusiasm for what is new, which is shown in almost every aspect of American daily life, and the concomitant trust in an 'indefinite perfectibility' – which de Tocqueville noted as the credo of the common 'uninstructed man' and which as such antedates by almost a hundred years the development in other countries of the West – would presumably have resulted in any case in greater attention paid and greater significance ascribed to the newcomers by birth, that is, the children, whom, when they had outgrown their childhood and were about to enter the community of adults as young people, the Greeks simply called *oi veoi*, the new ones. There is the additional fact, however, a fact that has become decisive for the meaning of education, that this pathos of the new, though it is considerably older than the eighteenth century, only developed conceptually and politically in that century. From this source there was derived at the start an educational ideal, tinged with Rousseau-ism and in fact directly influenced by Rousseau, in which education became an instrument of politics; and political activity itself was conceived of as a form of education. [...]

Now in respect to education itself the illusion arising from the pathos of the new has produced most serious consequences only in our own century. It has first of all made it possible for that complex of modern educational theories which originated in Middle Europe and consists of an astounding hodgepodge of sense and nonsense to accomplish, under the banner of progressive education, a most radical revolution in the whole system of education. [...]

[W]hat makes the educational crisis in America so especially acute is the political temper of the country, which of itself struggles to equalize or to erase as far as possible the difference between young and old, between the gifted and the ungifted, finally between children and adults, particularly between pupils and teachers. It is obvious that such an equalization can actually be accomplished only at the cost of the teacher's authority and at the expense of the gifted among the students. [...]

These ruinous measures can be schematically traced back to three basic assumptions, all of which are only too familiar. The first is that there exist a child's world and a society formed among children that are autonomous and must in so far as possible be left to them to govern. Adults are only there to help with this government. The authority that tells the individual child what to do and what not to do rests with the child group itself. [...]

[B]y being emancipated from the authority of adults the child has not been freed but has been subjected to a much more terrifying and truly tyrannical authority, the tyranny of the majority. In any case the result is that the children have been so to speak banished from the world of grown-ups. They are either thrown back upon themselves or handed over to the tyranny of their own group, against which, because of its numerical superiority, they cannot rebel, with which, because they are children, they cannot reason, and out of which they cannot flee to any other world because the world of adults is barred to them. The reaction of the children to this pressure tends to be either conformism or juvenile delinquency, and is frequently a mixture of both.

The second basic assumption which has come into question in the present crisis has to do with teaching. Under the influence of modern psychology and the tenets of pragmatism, pedagogy has developed into a science of teaching in general in such a way as to be wholly emancipated from the actual material to be taught. A teacher, so it was thought, is a man who can simply teach anything; his training is in teaching, not in the mastery of any particular subject. This attitude, as we shall presently see, is naturally very closely connected with a basic assumption about learning. Moreover, it has resulted in recent decades in a most serious neglect of the training of teachers in their own subjects, especially in the public high schools. Since the teacher does not need to know his own subject, it not infrequently happens that he is just one hour ahead of his class in knowledge. This in turn means not only that the students are actually left to their own resources but that the most legitimate source of the teacher's authority as the person who, turn it whatever way one will, still knows more and can do more than oneself is no longer effective. Thus the non-authoritarian teacher, who would like to abstain from all methods of compulsion because he is able to rely on his own authority, can no longer exist.

But this pernicious role that pedagogy and the teachers' colleges are playing in the present crisis was only possible because of a modern theory about learning. This was, quite simply, the logical application of the third basic assumption in our context, an assumption which the modern world has held for centuries and which found its systematic conceptual expression in pragmatism. This basic assumption is that you can know and understand only what you have done yourself, and its application to education is as primitive as it is obvious: to substitute, in so far as possible, doing for learning. The reason that no importance was attached to the teacher's mastering his own subject was the wish to compel him to the exercise of the continuous activity of learning so that he would not, as they said, pass on 'dead knowledge' but, instead, would constantly demonstrate how it is produced. The conscious intention was not to teach knowledge but to inculcate a skill and the result was a kind of transformation of institutes for learning into vocational institutions which have been as successful in teaching how to drive a car or how to use a typewriter or, even more important for the 'art' of living, how to get along with other people and to be popular, as they have been unable to make the children acquire the normal prerequisites of a standard curriculum.

However, this description is at fault, not only because it obviously exaggerates in order to drive home a point, but because it fails to take into account how in this process special importance was attached to obliterating as far as possible the distinction between play and work – in favour of the former. Play was looked upon as the liveliest and most appropriate way for the child to behave in the world, as the only form of activity that evolves spontaneously from his existence as a child. Only what can be learned through play does justice to this liveliness. The child's characteristic activity, so it was thought, lies in play; learning in the old sense, by forcing a child into an attitude of passivity, compelled him to give up his own playful initiative. [...]

Whatever may be the connection between doing and knowing, or whatever the validity of the pragmatic formula, its application to education, that is, to the way the child learns, tends to make absolute the world of childhood in just the same way that we noted in the case of the first basic assumption. Here, too, under the pretext of respecting the child's independence, he is debarred from the world of grown-ups and artificially kept in his own, so far as that can be called a world. This holding back of the child is artificial because it breaks off the natural relationship between grown-ups and children, which consists among other things in teaching and learning, and because at the same time it belies the fact that the child is a developing human being, that childhood is a temporary stage, a preparation for adulthood. [...]

Hannah Arendt, extracts from 'The Crisis in Education' (1954), in Arendt, *Between Past and Future: Six Exercises in Political Thought* (New York: Viking, 1961); reprinted in *Philosophy of Education: An Anthology*, ed. Randall Curren (Oxford: Blackwell, 2006) 188–91.

George E. Hein
Constructivist Learning Theory//1991

Constructivism

What is meant by constructivism? The term refers to the idea that learners construct knowledge for themselves – each learner individually (and socially) constructs meaning – as he or she learns. Constructing meaning is learning: there is no other kind. The dramatic consequences of this view are twofold:

1 We have to focus on the learner in thinking about learning (not on the subject/lesson to be taught);
2 There is no knowledge independent of the meaning attributed to experience (constructed) by the learner, or community of learners.

Let me discuss the second point first because, although it appears radical on an everyday level, it is a position which has been frequently adopted ever since people began to ponder epistemology. If we accept constructivist theory (which means we are willing to follow in the path of Dewey, Piaget and Vigotsky among others), then we have to give up Platonic and all subsequent realistic views of epistemology. We have to recognize that there is no such thing as knowledge 'out there' independent of the knower, but only knowledge we construct for ourselves as we learn (Dewey, *Experience and Education*, 1938). Learning is not understanding the 'true' nature of things, nor is it (as Plato suggested) remembering dimly perceived perfect ideas, but rather a personal and social construction of meaning out of the bewildering array of sensations which have no order or structure besides the explanations (and I stress the plural) which we fabricate for them. [...]

The great triumph of Western intellectual history from the Enlightenment until the beginning of the twentieth century rested on its ability to organize the knowledge of the world in a rational way independent of the learner, determined by some structure of the subject. Disciplines were developed, taxonomic schemes established, and all these categories were viewed as components of a vast mechanical machine in which the parts could be explained in terms of their relationship to each other, and each part contributed to making the whole function smoothly. Nowhere in this description does the learner appear. The task of the teacher was to make clear to the learner the working of this machine and any accommodation to the learner was only to account for different appropriate entry points for different learners.

However, as I have indicated above, constructivist theory requires that we turn our attention by 180 degrees: we must turn our back on any idea of an all-encompassing machine which describes nature and instead look towards all those wonderful, individual living beings – the learners – each of whom creates his or her own model to explain nature. If we accept the constructivist position we are inevitably required to follow a pedagogy which argues that we must provide learners with the opportunity to: (a) interact with sensory data, and (b) construct their own world.

This second point is a little harder for us to swallow, and most of us constantly vacillate between faith that our learners will indeed construct meaning which we will find acceptable (whatever we mean by that) and our need to construct meaning for them; that is, to structure situations that are not free for learners to carry out their own mental actions, but 'learning' situations which channel them into our ideas about the meaning of experience. It is this tension between our desire as teachers to teach the truth, to present the world 'as it really is', and our desire to let learners construct their own world which requires us to think seriously about epistemology and pedagogy.

Principles of Learning

What are some guiding principles of constructivist thinking that we must keep in mind when we consider our role as educators? [...]

1 Learning is an active process in which the learner uses sensory input and constructs meaning out of it. The more traditional formulation of this idea involves the terminology of the active learner (Dewey's term) stressing that the learner needs to do something; that learning is not the passive acceptance of knowledge which exists 'out there' but that learning involves the learner's engaging with the world (Dewey, *Democracy and Education*, 1916).

2 People learn to learn as they learn: learning consists both of constructing meaning and constructing systems of meaning. For example, if we learn the chronology of dates of a series of historical events, we are simultaneously learning the meaning of a chronology. Each meaning we construct makes us better able to give meaning to other sensations which can fit a similar pattern.

3 The crucial action of constructing meaning is mental: it happens in the mind. Physical actions, hands-on experience may be necessary for learning, especially for children, but it is not sufficient; we need to provide activities which engage the mind as well as the hands (A. Henriques, 'Experiments in Teaching', 1990). (Dewey called this reflective activity.)

4 Learning involves language: the language we use influences learning. On the empirical level, researchers have noted that people talk to themselves as they learn. On a more general level, there is a collection of arguments, presented

most forcefully by Vigotsky (*Thought and Language*, 1962), that language and learning are inextricably intertwined. [...]

5 Learning is a social activity: our learning is intimately associated with our connection with other human beings, our teachers, our peers, our family as well as casual acquaintances. [...] We are more likely to be successful in our efforts to educate if we recognize this principle rather than try to avoid it. Much of traditional education, as Dewey pointed out, is directed towards isolating the learner from all social interaction, and towards seeing education as a one-on-one relationship between the learner and the objective material to be learned. In contrast, progressive education (to continue to use Dewey's formulation) recognizes the social aspect of learning and uses conversation, interaction with others and the application of knowledge as an integral aspect of learning.

6 Learning is contextual: we do not learn isolated facts and theories in some abstract ethereal land of the mind separate from the rest of our lives; we learn in relationship to what else we know, what we believe, our prejudices and our fears. On reflection, it becomes clear that this point is actually a corollary of the idea that learning is active and social. We cannot divorce our learning from our lives.

7 One needs knowledge to learn: it is not possible to assimilate new knowledge without having some structure developed from previous knowledge to build on. The more we know, the more we can learn. Therefore any effort to teach must be connected to the state of the learner, must provide a path into the subject for the learner based on that learner's previous knowledge.

8 It takes time to learn: learning is not instantaneous. For significant learning we need to revisit ideas, ponder them, try them out, play with them and use them. [...] If you reflect on anything you have learned, you soon realize that it is the product of repeated exposure and thought. Even, or especially, moments of profound insight, can be traced back to longer periods of preparation.

9 Motivation is a key component in learning. Not only is it the case that motivation helps learning, it is essential for learning. This idea of motivation as described here is broadly conceived to include an understanding of ways in which the knowledge can be used. Unless we know 'the reasons why', we may not be very involved in using the knowledge that may be instilled in us, even by the most severe and direct teaching.

George E. Hein, extract from 'Constructivist Learning Theory: The Museum and the Needs of People', paper for CECA (International Committee of Museum Educators) Conference (Jerusalem, 15–22 October 1991); reprinted in *Developing Museum Exhibitions for Lifelong Learning*, ed. Gail Durbin (London: The Stationery Office, 1996) 30–32.

Tamara Krikorian
Art Spaces and Social Contexts//1976

[...] In Scotland there has been little opportunity for people to discover contemporary work, apart from the collection at Inverleith House, Edinburgh [first site of the Scottish National Gallery of Modern Art, 1960–84]. The audience, confronted with the most up to date manifestations of the international art scene, and lacking any terms of reference, tends to dismiss them at a glance. Long-term planning is one immediate objective which should be put into force if the public are to gain more than a superficial understanding of contemporary art. The other objective should be the provision of activities and information with exhibitions; not just expensively produced catalogues with specialist essays by art historians, but talks, discussions, films, tapes and libraries of books and magazines, which would encourage the public to consider the objects seriously rather than treating them as decoration and parading up and down the galleries as if they were eighteenth-century drawing rooms.

A gallery/art centre/museum must be more than a space, if the gallery is not to become the art object described in Brian O'Doherty's 'Inside the White Cube' (*Artforum*, March 1976). In such a setting the objects lose their own value and simply become part of the internal decoration of the gallery. Eduardo Paolozzi's recent exhibition in Edinburgh intensified my feelings about this, as I realized that the work of an extremely intelligent artist could become anaesthetized in a cool white gallery space. This is an appalling distortion of an artist's work: no attempt is made to involve the public, and a whole generation, who are too young to remember the 1940s and 1950s, and the subsequent flowering of Pop, fail to realize that these shows are not just the exotic deliberations of a middle-generation establishment artist but have a serious social and historical context.

Education is not the only element in the provision of context. A space must be made inviting. Of all the spaces already mentioned, many of which have their special features and different ways of projecting themselves, the Aberdeen Art Gallery and Third Eye Centre seem to have overcome the dangers of a physical presence overriding the main activity. Aberdeen Art Gallery is housed in a splendid nineteenth-century monument to the granite millionaires, and contains an unusual collection of nineteenth- and twentieth-century British painting. Far from discouraging the historical connection, the director, Ian Mckenzie Smith, pursues a dynamic policy in bringing together a programme of events and exhibitions which not only complement the collection but further the knowledge of contemporary work. The gallery, quite unexpectedly for those coming from the south, has become a hub of activity and probably the most lively and well-attended provincial museum in Britain.

Far less physically conventional is Glasgow's Third Eye Centre [directed by] Tom McGrath. Glasgow is a working city, which has been appallingly neglected, particularly in relation to education and the arts. The main problem here is, therefore, that of establishing context; a basis for approaching 'art' without reaching down, but at the same time making the product attractive, not through packaging but by engaging the audience. In the twelve months that Third Eye has been open, the response has been surprising. It has attracted an amazingly mixed audience, whose attitude is refreshingly unpretentious and unprejudiced. They are given a swift-changing programme of both avant-garde and popular work. Bands play there almost every Saturday. Ethnic musicians play the fiddle in the café and local artists live in the bar. There is nothing awesome about this space. [...]

Tamara Krikorian, extract from 'Art Spaces and Social Contexts', *Studio International*, vol. 193, no. 983 (London, September/October 1976) 203.

Henry A. Giroux
Public Pedagogy as Cultural Politics//2000

[...] According to Stuart Hall, the educational force of culture redefines the politics of power, the political nature of representation and the centrality of pedagogy as a defining principle of social change; it also expands our understanding of the public reach of pedagogy as an educational practice that 'operates both inside and outside the academy',[1] expanding its reach across multiple sites and spheres. As a performative practice, pedagogy inhabits all of those public spaces where culture works to secure identities, does the bridging work for negotiating the relationship between knowledge, pleasure and values, and renders authority both crucial and problematic in legitimating particular social practices, communities and forms of power. It is precisely this legacy of both politicizing culture and insisting on the pedagogical nature of the political that makes Hall's work so important at the present time. If agency is negotiated, made and remade within the symbolic and material relations of power and enacted within diverse and changing historical and relational contexts, agency cannot be abstracted from the self-reflexive possibilities of pedagogy, nor can it be removed from the dynamics of cultural politics.

Of considerable importance to critical educators is Hall's theory of articulation for analysing how authority and power actually work in linking texts to contexts, ideology to specific relations of power, and political projects to existing social formations.[2] For educators this is an important insight and points to the centrality of context in shaping cultural pedagogy as a form of practical politics. Not only do political projects emerge out of particular contexts, but because contexts change as the relations between culture and power shift, such projects become practical only if they remain open, partial and incomplete. Central to Hall's work is the insight that public pedagogy is defined through its performative functions, its ongoing work of mediation and its attentiveness to the interconnections and struggles that take place over knowledge, language, spatial relations and history. At stake here is the call not only to link public pedagogy to practices that are interdisciplinary, transgressive and oppositional but also to connect such practices to broader projects designed to further racial, economic and political democracy, to strike a new balance and expand what Stuart Hall and David Held have called the 'individual and social dimensions of citizenship rights'.[3]

The concept of articulation does more than provide a theoretical rationale for 'the making of a relationship out of a nonrelationship or, more often, the making of one relationship out of another one';[4] it also reaffirms the political nature of cultural work that gives meaning to the resources that students bring with them to various sites of learning, while simultaneously subjecting the specificities of such meanings to broader interrogations and public dialogue. This is a crucial concept for any notion of public pedagogy. Central to such a project is the need to begin at those intersections where people actually live their lives and where meaning is produced, assumed and contested in the unequal relations of power that construct the mundane acts of everyday relations. Public pedagogy in this context becomes part of a critical practice designed to understand the social context of everyday life as lived relations of power.

At the same time, Hall has consistently insisted that cultural workers examine critically how meanings work intertextually to resonate with ideologies produced in other sites and how they work to legitimate and produce particular practices, policies and social relations. Educators cannot treat cultural texts as if they were hermetic or pure; such approaches often ignore how representations are linked to wider social forms, power and public struggles. Engaging cultural texts as part of a critical public pedagogy means refusing to limit our analysis of popular texts by focusing on either the polyphonic meanings at work in such texts or formalist strategies to decipher what is perceived as a text's preferred meanings. On the contrary, a critical public pedagogy should ascertain how certain meanings under particular historical conditions become more legitimate as representations of reality and take on the force of commonsense assumptions shaping a broader set of discourses and social configurations at work in the dominant social order. Hall's work has continually reinforced the necessity for educators to focus on representations as a mode of public exchange in order to explore, as Herman Gray attests, the ways 'these images, especially the historical and contemporary meanings they carry and understandings they express, are aligned and realigned with broader discourses'.[5] As public discourses, representations can be understood for the ways in which they shape and bear witness to the ethical dilemmas that animate broader debates within the dominant culture. This suggests a cultural politics that investigates how popular texts are articulated within structures of affect and meaning mediated by networks of power and domination bound to the specific historical, social and economic conditions of their production. [...]

Hall's writing has always refused to limit the sites of pedagogy and politics to those 'privileged' by the advocates of 'genuine' politics. Organizing labour unions, demonstrating in the streets for legislation to curb corporate crimes, and organizing workers to promote radical forms of social policy are important forms of political practice, but working in the schools, the television industry, law firms, museums, or in a vast number of other public spheres does not constitute for Hall a less reputable or less important form of political work. In fact, Hall has continually called for intellectuals to 'address the central, urgent and most disturbing question of a society and a culture in the most rigorous intellectual way we have available'.[6] He has urged cultural workers to take up this challenge in a variety of pedagogical sites, and in doing so has opened the possibility for working within dominant institutions, while challenging their authority and cultural practices. For Hall, the context of such work demands confronting a major paradox in capitalist societies – that of using the very authority vested in institutions such as schools in order to work against the grain of such authority. Such action is not a retreat from politics, as Todd Gitlin and others believe, but an expansion of the possibility of politics and critical agency to the very institutions that work to shut down notions of critical pedagogy, politics and social agency. Authority in this context pushes against the tendency to be complicitous and opens up the possibility of being resistant, transformative and contestatory. Within this discourse, public pedagogy and cultural politics are located 'on the dividing lines where the relation between domination and subordination continues to be produced, lines that extend into the academy itself'.[7] Hall's call for a cultural politics implies a public pedagogy in which learning becomes indispensable to the very process of social change, and social change becomes the precondition for a politics that moves in the direction of a less hierarchical, more radical democratic social order. [...]

1 [34] Stuart Hall, 'Race, Culture and Communications', in *Rethinking Marxism*, vol. 5, no. 1 (Spring 1992) 11.

2 [35] One of the most incisive commentaries on the meaning and importance of Hall's theory of articulation can be found in Lawrence Grossberg, 'On Postmodernism and Articulation: An Interview with Stuart Hall', *Journal of Communication Inquiry*, vol. 10, no. 2 (Summer 1986) 45–60.

3 [36] Stuart Hall and David Held, 'Citizens and Citizenship', in Stuart Hall and Martin Jacques, eds, *New Times: The Changing Face of Politics in the 1990s* (London and New York: Verso, 1990) 173–88.

4 [37] Grossberg, 'Cultural Studies: What's in a Name?', op. cit., 259.

5 [38] Herman Gray, *Watching Race* (Minneapolis: University of Minnesota Press, 1995) 132.

6 [39] Hall, 'Race, Culture and Communications', op. cit., 11.

7 [40] John Beverly, 'Pedagogy and Subalternity: Mapping the Limits of Academic Knowledge', in Rolland G. Paulston, ed., *Social Cartography* (New York: Garland, 1996) 352.

Henry A. Giroux, extracts from 'Public Pedagogy as Cultural Politics: Stuart Hall and the "Crisis" of Culture', in *Without Guarantees: In Honour of Stuart Hall*, ed. Paul Gilroy, Lawrence Grossberg and Angela McRobbie (London and New York: Verso, 2000) 139–47.

Roy Ascott
A Groundcourse for Art//1964

[...] No matter what our aspirations or intentions in art, we must prepare a discipline, a groundwork for creative activity. When I emphasize that my art and didactics are one, I am suggesting that the artist's discipline and experience can usefully be extended to the student. One can help him to win an outlook and to construct the groundwork for his own unique creative identity. But one artist is not enough. A wide diversity of artists and scientists, suitably co-ordinated, must confront the student. He, in turn, must be sufficiently uninhibited to respond. Out of the flux, a many-sided organism may evolve.

Such an organism, so to speak, is in the course of evolution at the Ealing School of Art in London. This two-year 'Groundcourse' is a microcosm of a total process of art education stretching from general secondary education to the graduate levels of professional art and design training, and it occupies the pivotal point in it. [...]

The first-year course has many facets. Empirical enquiry in response to precise questions is balanced by scientific study; irrational acts by logical procedures. At the core is a concept of power, the will to shape and change. Cybernetics and behavioural sciences are studied regularly.

The new student's preconceptions of the nature of art and his own limitations ('Art is Van Gogh'; 'Art is what my teacher said it was to get me through my art exam'; 'I am no good at colour'; 'I am the class clown'; 'I am thick, but good at patterns and posters') must first be severely shaken and opened up to his close scrutiny. His disorientation is contrived within an environment that is sometimes unexpectedly confusing, where he is faced with problems that seem absurd, aimless or terrifying. [...]

Perception studies examine the modes of human perception and their co-ordination and include the search for visual/plastic equivalents. Surface gesture, mark, colour and volume are investigated, always within some context. Example 1. Imagine you wake up one morning to find that you are a sponge. Describe visually your adventures during the day. 2. List the sense data of an umbrella or a hot water bottle. Visually restructure the parts to form a new entity. Ask your neighbour to identify it. [...]

In the workshop, the student acquires skills in joining, moulding, separating and transforming wood, metals and various transparent, reflective and flexible materials. Example 1. Make a sculpture in plaster of interlocking units, such that when a key piece is removed, the rest falls apart. Allot colours to the separate pieces (a) to indicate the key, (b) to facilitate reassembly. 2. Using only wood, sheet aluminium, string and panel pins, construct analogues of: a high-pitched scream, the taste of ice cream, a football match. Kinetic structures are built and studied. Concepts can be formed and developed by visual means. This might be seen as the third leg in the learning process, where, for some reason, verbal or numerical systems are inadequate. Unlike the latter symbolic systems, however, the visual ABC and syntax have to be reinvented for every problem. In visual terms, students set about analysing and inventing games, logical propositions, idea sequences and matrices. Visual polemic is induced, and codes are designed and broken. [...]

Concepts of behaviour, environment and identity find their way into practical classes. Example 1. Draw a man, machine or animal. Cut up the drawing into seven sections (e.g. arm, head, wheel, handle, etc.). Put the pieces with everyone else's in a box. Pull out another seven at random; logically construct a new entity. Draw the environment in which you might expect to encounter it. [...] 6. Entropy may be described as a constant drift in the universe towards a state of total undifferentiation; pockets of resistance are organizing continuously. Discuss this proposition, limiting yourself to six visual elements.

In this first-year course, the student is bombarded at every point with problems demanding total involvement for their solution. Ideas are developed within material limitations and in the abstract. For the teachers, the formulation of problems is in itself a creative activity; the above examples give a general indication of the kind of questions they have set.

In the second year, the situation changes radically. The general direction is programmed, but beyond that students must find their own problems. Students are set the task of acquiring and acting out for a limited period (ten weeks) a totally new personality, which is to be narrowly limited and largely the converse of what is considered to be their normal 'selves'. They design 'calibrators' to read off their responses to situations, materials, tools and people. They equip themselves with handy 'mind-maps' for immediate reference to their behaviour pattern as changes in the limitations of space, substance and state occur.

They form groups of six. These sexagonal organisms, whose members are of necessity interdependent and highly conscious of one another's capabilities and limitations, are set the goal of producing an ordered entity out of substances and space in their environment.

The limitations on individual behaviour are severe and unfamiliar. [...] The subsequent 'ordered entities' are as diverse as the composite personalities of the organisms they reflect. Totems, time machines, sense boxes, films, sexagonal cabinets and cages have been produced out of the flux of discussion and activity.

Students are then invited to return to their former personalities. They must make a total visual documentation of the whole process in which they have been engaged. They must search for relationships and ideas unfamiliar to art (e.g. spatial relationships are familiar). They use, at first, every possible expressive means: film, collage, graphic processes, wood, plaster, metal, cloth, glass, readymades, rubber, paint, and so on. They work on a huge scale at one point and in miniature at another, sometimes with kinetic structures, sometimes with static relationships.

In the process, and reflecting upon their previously contrived limitations of behaviour, they become aware of the flexibility of their responses, their resourcefulness and ingenuity in the face of difficulties. What they assumed to be ingrained in their personalities they now tend to see as controllable. A sense of creative viability is being acquired. [...]

1 Kenneth Adams, Anthony Benjamin, Adrian Berg, David Bindman, Dennis Bowen, Bernard Cohen, Harold Cohen, Noel Forster, B. French, N. Johnson, R.B. Kitaj, Stephen McKenna, J. Morris, J. Nerichov, George Popperwell, Peter Startup, William Suddaby, Brian Wall and Brian Wright.

Roy Ascott, extracts from the section 'A Groundcourse for Art' [on the unique course he initiated at Ealing School of Art, London, in 1961; students included Brian Eno and Stephen Willats], in 'The Construction of Change', *Cambridge Opinion* (January 1964); reprinted in Roy Ascott, *Telematic Embrace: Visionary Theories of Art, Technology and Consciousness*, ed. Edward A. Shanken (Berkeley and Los Angeles: University of California Press, 102–7.

Les Levine
The Great American Art Machine//1971

[...] The idea that we have any choice whatsoever, in a completely technological environment, is pretty ridiculous; we only assume we make a choice. However, most of the choices that we make are merely selections taken out of a precoded number of choices that society has already made for us. The society is clearly *pre-choiced*. [...]

There are two kinds of software: one is the very technical term, which is something a computer programmer needs to know; and the other is social software, which refers to the kinds of information in the environment that make us behave the way we do. The media environment is telling your brain how to operate; it is telling your body how to operate; it is telling you how to behave, what to look like, what to desire, what to look at, what to care about, what not to care about, what to be politically in favour of, what morally would be wrong, what would taste good, what doesn't taste good. In an environment that is constantly telling its inhabitants all these things, there is no such thing as individualism or personal property. If things become important to the general environment, the general environment will own them, and the individual will not. So the idea that the collector owns the artist's work is merely a hangover from a period in history when everyone viewed everything as property. The artist's work, whether it is owned by a collector or a museum, is always his work; it always will be owned by him no matter who has it in his possession. To assume we are individuals is very much beside the point. Of course, one could say, 'I want that automobile there in red, with white-walled tyres, and an air conditioner, etc.'

But you have to take into consideration that the company which makes that automobile has done market research to find out that someone who looks pretty much like you, who earns about the amount of money that you do, who wears the same clothes, who lives in the same kind of house, who has the number of children that you have, who is related to the number of people that you are, who vacations in the place that you vacation, who goes to see the movies that you go to, etc., will come in and say, 'I want that car in this colour with white-walls.' Our culture gives people an illusion of choice.

This tendency to be constantly involved in the idea of individual choices stems from the computer, unless you interact in a reasonably passive way.

Information has affected law. A smart lawyer realizes that evidence that is passed across an information retrieval system, such as television or newspaper, is just as valuable as evidence that is presented in court. So what is occurring in the courtroom now is a direct reflection of what occurs in the media. It is often possible actually to lose a case in a court room but win it in the media. If it is won in the media, it will be reversed in the courtroom. There is no way of unknowing information. In a society that is addicted to information, it is extremely dangerous not to put out information. In a society that demands to know everything, the man who remains quiet is guilty.

Now privacy is redundant; privacy only works in a society that is technically private. It is possible for the government to spy on a citizen at any time. It is possible for one firm to spy on another firm. If you live in a society that does not permit privacy, trying to be private is foolish. If you have sex in your living room, it shouldn't matter if everybody in the world can see you. Because if they wanted to, they could. Privacy becomes one-sided when you resist it. If you don't resist, then you become part of the working environment. The correct organic cell in the correct organic environment. You take the same attitude toward the government that they take toward you.

Now people say that computers are dehumanizing us; that there are too many machines. There are even people who blame the war in Vietnam on computers. Very few people have had any first-hand use of computers as an information retrieval system, as a surrogate brain, as an outside intelligence support, as a form of artificial thinking. We must realize that if everybody has computers, then it becomes possible for everybody to talk to everybody else. If you have a Telex terminal and you want to say, 'Screw you' on that terminal, everybody who owns a Telex terminal will get a printout saying, 'Screw you.' So that although companies do have the possibility to control you, if you are hooked into them you have the possibility to control back. Once we all have technological access, then we can talk to one another. The computer is going to bring about a new era of primitivism in art. The computer will in fact be the new folk art. [...]

Technology has had a greater effect on the cultural thrust than art. Technology has created technological man. It has created political change. It has created aesthetic change. It has created many levels of things that we thought art would. Probably the greatest reason that technology has taken over from art is because art was always technology anyway. The art of the cave painter was a technological art. It was an art of how to do it, how to image the society, how to present society with a working model of itself that would in fact be a 'conceptual tool', a valuable and useful device for the shaping of that society. Now we are coming back technologically to cave painting. We're now at a point where technology can present us with a working model of ourselves. [...]

Museums will probably undergo an enormously difficult period; it will become evident to them that there will be an enormous increased production from artists. And the collection of this production will cause real estate problems, will cause economic problems, and will also cause political problems. What it will probably be important for museums to be doing within the next few years will be bringing in the various underprivileged social groups in our society. Presenting the museum as a community cultural laboratory rather than as a place that sets up high standards and aesthetics.

The absurdity of formal art criticism is that it is pretty much umbilical to collecting. Formal art criticism must be judged as organized power. For all that formal art criticism hates commercialism, it always acts as a very straight commercial for the art it's talking about. In formal criticism when you say, 'Something is good', you're saying, 'buy it.' When you say, 'It is bad', you're saying, 'do not buy it.' So formal art criticism will find itself with the same problem that the collector finds himself in. People do not want to be told constantly what their taste should be anymore. Good taste, at this time, in a technological democracy, ends up as nothing more than taste prejudice. Expressing aesthetic authority over another human being is arrogant.

The artist must, without question, abdicate. He must realize that his work should not contain authority. It must in fact have the capability to succeed or fail as the viewer wants it. Thereby being much more supportive to the viewer. It must, in fact, be completely devoid of logic. The logical vacuum must be there so that the viewer applies his own logic to it and the work in fact makes itself before the viewer's eyes. So that it becomes a direct reflection of the viewer's consciousness, logic, morals and ethics. The work should act as a feedback mechanism to his own working model. [...]

Les Levine, extracts from 'The Great American Art Machine' (1971), in *New Ideas in Art Education: A Critical Anthology*, ed. Gregory Battcock (New York: E.P. Dutton & Co. Inc., 1973) 15; 23–8.

Adrienne Rich
Toward a Woman-Centred University//1973–74

[...] If the phrase 'woman-centred university' sounds outrageous, biased or improbable, we need only to try the sound of its opposite, the 'man-centred university' – not forgetting that grammar reveals the truth and that 'man', the central figure of that earlier renaissance, was indeed the male, as he still is. Or, as the catalogue of one 'co-educational' institution has it:

> Brandeis University has set itself to develop the whole man, the sensitive, cultured, open-minded citizen who grounds his thinking in facts, who is intellectually and spiritually aware, who believes that life is significant, and who is concerned with society and the role he will play in it.[1]

This is no semantic game or trivial accident of language. What we have at present is a man-centred university, a breeding ground not of humanism but of masculine privilege. [...]

A few male scholars have been examining the academic tradition from the point of view of its sexual bias. Walter J. Ong suggests that the very origins of academic style are peculiarly masculine.

> Rhetoric ... developed in the past as a major expression of the rational level of the ceremonial combat which is found among males and typically only among males at the physical level throughout the entire animal kingdom ... Rhetoric became particularly attached to Learned Latin, which the male psyche appropriated to itself as in extrafamilial language when Latin ceased to be a 'mother' tongue (that is, was no longer spoken in the home by one's mother). Latin, spoken and written for 1500 years with totally negligible exceptions only by males, became a ceremonial language institutionalizing with particular force the ceremonial polemic which set the style for all education until romanticism. For until the Romantic age, academic education was all but exclusively focused on defending a position (thesis) or attacking the position of another person – even medicine was taught this way.[2]

Ong remarks that 'the ancient art of rhetoric did not and could not survive co-education' – a statement that unfortunately is true only in the most literal sense.

A contemporary view is provided by Leonard Kriegel:

> ... my teachers at Columbia ... knew the value of reputation, and they would bank it with all the fierce pride of Wall Street lawyers ... The process of attaining a reputation was part of a Columbia graduate education, and we were exposed to it as soon as classes began. A man needed reserve and style and distance here; intelligence was not enough ...
>
> The 'name' professors, those faculty whose shoulders were burdened with the reputation of the department, possessed that distance and propriety. They possessed other qualities, too. Some of them possessed contempt for their students ... Two professors of modern drama duelled each other for students, insisted on declarations of allegiance, of commitment not to a critical perspective but to themselves ...

I soon found out that importance was measured not in terms of scholarship but of power within the department. The majority of graduate students ... were so caught up in the game, so victimized by their desire for careers, so willing to preserve a place at any cost at the side of some academic eminence, that their lives became mere extensions of the dehumanization of the university ... We emulated our models, working for the day when we, too, might claim professorial status for ourselves ... worshippers at the shrine of making it.

... For most of us, the academic world had promised a way in which we could ignore the lure of materialism. Unfortunately, we turned into the consenting victims of what we claimed to ignore. If a student wished to buy the academic world, then it followed that he had to buy the rest of America also.[3]

Certain terms in the above quotations have a familiar ring: *defending, attacking, combat, status, banking, duelled, power, making it.* They suggest the connections – actual and metaphoric – between the style of the university and the style of a society invested in military and economic aggression. In each of these accounts what stands out is not the passion for 'learning for its own sake' or the sense of an intellectual community, but the dominance of the masculine ideal, the race of men against one another. [...]

The early feminists, the women intellectuals of the past, along with educated men, assumed that the intellectual structure as well as the contents of the education available to men was viable: that is, enduring, universal, a discipline civilizing to the mind and sensitizing to the spirit. Its claims for both humanism and objectivity went unquestioned. One of the few voices to question this was that of Virginia Woolf, in her still little-read and extraordinary *Three Guineas*, an essay connecting war and fascism directly with the patriarchal system, and with the exclusion of women from learning and power. [...]

We need the university, with its libraries, laboratories, archives, collections, and some – but not all – of the kinds of trained thinking and expertise it has to offer. We need consciously and critically to select what is genuinely viable and what we can use from the masculine intellectual tradition, as we possess ourselves of the knowledge, skills and perspectives that can refine our goal of self-determination with discipline and wisdom. (Certainly we do *not* need the university to continue replicating the tradition that has excluded us, or to become 'amateur males'.) The university is by no means the only place where this work will be carried on; nor, obviously, can the university become more woman-centred and less elitist while the society remains androcentric. [...]

Women in colleges where a women's studies programme already exists, or where feminist courses are beginning to be taught, still are often made to feel that the 'real' curriculum is the male-centred one; that women's studies are (like Third

World studies) a 'fad'; that feminist teachers are 'unscholarly', 'unprofessional', or 'dykes'. But the content of courses and programmes is only the more concrete form of undermining experienced by the woman student. More invisible, less amenable to change by committee proposal or fiat, is the hierarchal image, the structure of relationships, even the style of discourse, including assumptions about theory and practice, ends and means, process and goal. [...]

The university cannot, it may be argued, become all to each; it cannot serve the education of young adults, train future specialists, provide a conduit for research and scholarship, and do all these other things you are suggesting. I have, I confess, thought long and hard on that side of the question. Part of my final resolution comes from the fact that we are talking about a process involving simultaneous changes both in society 'out there' and in the university, and that when the local or national community becomes able to develop strong and responsive centres such as I have been describing for all its citizens, the burden would not have to fall on the university. Ideally, I imagine a very indistinct line between 'university' and 'community', instead of the familiar city-on-a-hill frowning down on its neighbours, or the wrought-iron gates by which town and gown have traditionally defined their relationship. For centuries women were by definition people of the town, not of the gown; and still, there are many more of us 'down there'. [...]

1 [footnote 2 in source] *Brandeis University Bulletin* (Winter 1972–73) 11.

2 [3] Walter J. Ong, review of Brian Vickers' *Classical Rhetoric in English Poetry*, in *College English* (February 1972).

3 [4] Leonard Kriegel, *Working Through: A Teacher's Journey in the Urban University* (New York: Saturday Review Press, 1972) 43–4; 49–51.

Adrienne Rich, extracts from 'Toward a Woman-Centred University' (1973–74); reprinted in Rich, *On Lies, Secrets and Silence: Selected Prose 1966–1978* (New York: W.W. Norton & Company Inc., 1979) 125–36; 151–2.

Thierry de Duve
When Form Has Become Attitude – And Beyond//1993

[...] Two models, even though in reality they contaminate each other, divide up the teaching of art conceptually. On the one hand, there is the academic model; on the other, there is the Bauhaus model. The former believes in talent, the latter in creativity. The former classifies the arts according to techniques, what I would call the métier; the latter according to the medium. The former fosters imitation; the latter invention. Both models are obsolete. The academic model entered a deep crisis as soon as it began to deserve the derogative label of academicism. Its decadence was accomplished under the pressure of modern art, which is why no return to the past is thinkable lest the blackout is pronounced on all the art and all the artists of modernity. The Bauhaus model also entered an open crisis. That phenomenon is more recent but it isn't new, dating from the sixties, I would say. It, too, goes hand in hand with the art of its time ... [...]

Talent vs Creativity
The difference between talent and creativity is that the former is unequally distributed and the latter universally. In the passage from one word to the other, there is of course a complete reversal of ideologies, and it is not difficult to see that, historically, the progress of the ideology of creativity went hand in hand with that of the idea of democracy and of egalitarianism. [...]

Métier vs Medium
The difference between métier and medium is that the former has a historical existence and the latter a transhistorical existence. The Academy classified the fine arts according to the métier and everything the notion entails: specialized skills, artisan habits, sleights of hand, rules of composition, canons of beauty, in short, a specific tradition. Modernism classifies the arts according to the medium and everything this notion entails: particular materials, supports, tools, gestures, technical procedures and conventions of specificity. [...]

Imitation vs Invention
The difference between imitation and invention goes without saying. Whereas imitation reproduces, invention produces; whereas imitation generates sameness, invention generates otherness; whereas imitation seeks continuity, invention seeks novelty. The Academy was aware that artists worthy of the name invent. However, even though academic teaching spotted a sign of a student's

talent in his capacity to invent, it was not on his capacity to invent that it judged him, nor was it through stimulating invention that it claimed to educate him. Quite the contrary. It was through imposing on him imitation, invention's antithesis: the imitation of nature, of the Ancients, of the master. The Bauhaus model, by contrast, fosters invention, because every progress in its expression indicates a liberation of the student's creativity, an actualization of his artistic potential. [...]

Talent and Creativity vs Attitude

In the wake of the student upheaval of the late sixties no one was ready to admit the inequality of talent, out of fear of seeming irredeemably reactionary. But the May '68 slogan, 'all power to the imagination', didn't last very long, and soon creativity lost its aura, too. Philosophically speaking, the times were very suspicious of anything more or less resembling the old psychology of the faculties, and creativity, which is a neo-Romantic amalgam of the Kantian faculties of sensibility and imagination, became old hat. It had everything against itself: being universal, it could only be 'bourgeois'; being transcendental, it could only be 'metaphysical'; being natural, it could only be 'ideological'. But its greatest sin was that it could not be willed, and the most progressive art and art teaching of the seventies thought that art had to be willed, whether it aligned itself with some political programme bathed in revolutionary rhetoric, or whether it saw itself as the relentless critique of the dominant ideology. Anyway, it had become hard to suppose that creativity was the potential of mankind in general, and equally hard to hope that it could be instilled through propaganda or education (think of Joseph Beuys, in this context: he certainly represents the last great and tragic hero of the modern myth of creativity, immolating himself on the altar of both pedagogy and 'social sculpture'). Thus another concept took the place of creativity, that of 'attitude'. A concept that is a blank, actually: a sort of zero degree of psychology, a neutral point amidst ideological choices, a volition without content.

Of course, in order to be progressive – and how could art of any significance not be progressive? – attitude had to be critical. Lukács, Adorno, Althusser and others were called in to tell would-be artists that neither talent nor creativity were needed to make art but, instead, that 'critical attitude' was mandatory. And the fact that not just artists but all 'cultural workers' were thought to be in need of a critical attitude of course helped to shape a new, strongly politicized discourse about art and its relation to society, a discourse that, throughout the seventies and part of the eighties, became the dominant discourse, not in all art schools, admittedly but certainly in the most progressive, the most avant-gardistic or – why not say it? – the most fashionable ones. Even if you turn to less politicized aspects of the dominant discourse about art in those years you will see the central position of the notion of attitude confirmed. It is towards the end of the sixties that the concept of 'aesthetic attitude' surfaced in art theory, thanks to Jerome Stolnitz in particular, but also, I should say, thanks to Duchamp's growing reputation as the first conceptual artist, a combination of influences that greatly helped in pushing aside aesthetics while retaining the notion of attitude. Finally – and this, I believe, clinches it, if only symbolically – it was in 1969 that Harald Szeemann organized the famous exhibition 'When Attitudes Become Form', at the Kunsthalle in Bern. Both the date and the title coined for this exhibition are symptomatic, for it was then and there that conceptual art was acknowledged for the first time by a major art institution (MoMA was to follow before long with the 'Information' show, in 1970), providing a new model for advanced art soon to be emulated and disseminated by most art schools.

Everybody here, I'm sure, is familiar with what happened next. Linguistics, semiotics, anthropology, psychoanalysis, Marxism, feminism, structuralism and post-structuralism, in short, 'theory' (or so-called 'French theory') entered art schools and succeeded in displacing – and sometimes replacing – studio practice while renewing the critical vocabulary and intellectual tools with which to approach the making and the appreciating of art. [...] In those days attitude still had to be critical, which basically meant: critical of the social and political status quo. But soon the very success of these art schools began attracting students who went there because of the instant rewards they were seemingly able to promise them. For these students (with or without the conscious or unconscious complicity of their teachers, I can't tell), what had started as an ideological alternative to both talent and creativity, called 'critical attitude', became just that, an attitude, a stance, a pose, a contrivance. This phenomenon, of course, widely exceeds a few art schools; it even exceeds art schools in general, for it is rampant throughout the whole academic world, especially in the humanities. It can be summarized by saying that political commitment sank into political correctness. Meanwhile, what remains of the old postulates – the academic postulate called talent and the modernist postulate called creativity – on which to ground a plausible art curriculum is the poorest, the most tautological notion of all: that of an artist's attitude.

Métier and Medium vs Practice

Dividing the arts according to the medium rather than to the métier; reading art history in terms of 'a progressive surrender to the resistance of its medium' (Clement Greenberg); fostering the purity of the medium as a value in itself, are the three strong points of formalist criticism and modernist doctrine in art. As is well known, formalism and modernism have been under heavy fire since the mid sixties, first in America, soon after in England, and then in the rest of the Western world. Just as with Harald Szeemann's show, 'When Attitudes Become Form', let me choose a symbolic event to pinpoint this, an event all the more symbolic in that it happened in 1966 at an art school. John Latham was a part-time instructor at St Martin's, in London, when he borrowed Clement Greenberg's *Art and Culture* from the school's library and, with the complicity of Barry Flanagan, then a student at St Martin's, organized an event entitled *Still & Chew*, when a number of pages of the book were chewed by the participants and spat into a jar, then submitted to a complex chemical treatment. You know the aftermath of this performance (or was it a happening?): a year or so later, when asked to return the book to the library, John Latham returned it indeed, but in the shape of a jar containing the unspeakable, let alone unreadable, mixture. He was fired the next day.

Today, needless to say, he could do the same performance with the principal's blessing, and the librarian wouldn't even bother to reorder *Art and Culture*. Events, happenings and performances have long been absorbed into art schools, and even though most schools keep a painting studio, a sculpture studio, a printmaking studio, and so on, they have added to the list of 'mixed media' an 'interdisciplinary', or a 'free-for-all' studio – whatever the name – which definitely indicates that the teaching of art no longer rests on an aesthetic commitment to the specificity or the purity of the medium. By 1970 Clement Greenberg and Michael Fried were already the last art critics to uphold the idea that no art of significance could be done that sits in between media, and that if something is neither painting nor sculpture, then it is not art. Against them, a whole generation of conceptual artists were relying on Duchamp in order to maintain that the art was in the concept, that it was dematerialized, that it did not cling to any medium, above all not to painting. They fought against the medium but, of course, didn't rehabilitate the métier for all that. Just as with the word 'attitude', what was soon to replace both the métier and the medium was another magical word, 'practice'.

By 1975, the word 'practice' was widely in use among all the people who had been in touch with 'French theory', and since 'French theory', after all, originated in France, it is there, in the writings of the *Tel Quel* people, in particular, that it acquired a cluster of interesting meanings in the context of literature and art. One of its benefits was that it was charged with prestigious political connotations, Marxist, of course, and Althusserian. More important is that it is a general word not a specific one, or, to say this differently, that it puts the emphasis on the social, not on the technical, division of labour. Applied to painting, for example, it allowed us to conceive of painting not in terms of a specific skill (such as the Greenbergian flatness), but in terms of a specific historical institution called 'pictorial practice'. This is the way both the painters belonging to the *Support-Surface* group, and their arch-enemy, Daniel Buren, used the word in defence of painting. Other artists, who were defending interdisciplinarity against specificity, began speaking of 'artistic practice', or 'practices', depending on whether the generic was thought of as being one or plural. But the most interesting – i.e. symptomatic – phenomenon is that the word art itself (simply, art) became taboo. It was guilty of conveying some faith in the 'essence' of art, I mean, in the existence of some transhistorical and transcultural common denominator among all artistic practices. Our epoch being radically relativistic, it wouldn't allow such unorthodox belief. The orthodoxy of the times prescribed – and still prescribes – conceiving of art as being just one 'signifying practice' (that expression was coined by Julia Kristeva) among others.

I have just said: 'prescribed – and still prescribes'. In fact, I'm not so sure. One of the things I expect from this conference [Southampton, 1993] is that it may help me understand to what extent the orthodoxy of discourse (what I nastily referred to as political correctness) fails to hide the reality of anxieties, disappointments, shattered beliefs, which, I suspect, have a hard time expressing themselves without giving the impression (as I most probably do) of wanting to go backwards and resorting to nostalgia. I hope that the discussion will bring these difficulties into the open, but meanwhile I would like to stress that what was in the seventies an avant-gardistic discourse has, by now, been largely institutionalized. I know of at least one art school where the students have the choice of enrolling either in 'Communication' or in 'Artistic Practice'. As always, the magic of changing names is a symptom: the expression 'artistic practice' has become a ritual formula, conveying the vague suspicion that has come to surround the word art, while failing to designate referents in the world (that is, actual works) of which one could be sure that the word art has ceased to apply to them significantly.

Imitation and Invention vs Deconstruction

[...] The triad of notions, 'attitude–practice–deconstruction', is not the postmodern paradigm that supposedly substituted for the modern paradigm, 'creativity–medium–invention'. It is the same one, minus faith, plus suspicion. I tend to see it as a mere after-image, as the negative symptom of a historical transition whose positivity is not clear yet. As such it is quite interesting, and it can yield strong works of art. But for the teaching of art it is sterile. Once it is possible to put it down on paper, this means that its potential for negation has already become conventional (deconstruction is today's good taste), that its anguish is no longer of the kind that nourishes true artists (it is fake, because it is reconciled with the present); and that its suspicion is, unlike Descartes' doubt, not fruitful (it is aimed at the other and not at oneself). [...]

The modern paradigm hasn't ever ceased informing art teaching surreptitiously. It is therefore to this that we need to respond, analysing, again, the traits that opposed it to the paradigm that it superseded. This is why it is not without value to ask again if we must choose between talent and creativity, between métier and media, between imitation and invention, or if those oppositions themselves do not suggest their own resolution.

Talent, Creativity, Judgement

We must rehabilitate the notion of talent, and I don't think this needs to cause anyone big ideological heartbreaks, or that it necessitates institutional reforms. We should be able to rediscover, in a new way, the continuity that existed in the past from the humble artisan to the artist of genius. We should also gather the conviction that if art is not taught, judgement forms itself. What kind of judgement? Armed with the prestige of the humanities, critical awareness, suspicion and questioning nonetheless tend to finesse the kind of judgement which in art counts for more than anything else, and which is art teaching's first task to form, that is, aesthetic judgement. We never encourage students enough to make value judgements of the artworks we show them, and we never show them enough that we make such judgements ourselves. I would like to see the motto 'you will be judged on your judgement' as the ethos on which any art education is based. With this perspective, to have the *attitude of an artist*, a critical attitude, is to have, quite simply, judgement. Aesthetic judgement, what was once called taste and what today is both more and something else, gets taught. More precisely, it is formed. It is formed by being exposed to the judgements of others, it is formed as it is exercised, and it is exercised above all in relation to the art of others. As with the academic model, judgement is formed via contact with works of the past. These are no longer models to imitate through the exercise of talent, for imitation implies a stable tradition; much less are they foils against which to react to prove one's inventiveness and creativity; they remain examples to emulate. As with the Bauhaus model, judgement is formed in contact with the medium. But the medium, today, is embodied in works that are in museums, as part of our heritage. This means, very concretely, that everything is grist to the studio teacher's mill, whether the *métier* of Van Eyck or the medium of Mondrian, provided we historicize them.

Métier, Medium, Tradition

Speaking of *artistic practice* rather than métier or medium is to recognize the existence of art in general, for example, the art of choosing a readymade. No skill, no sleight of hand entered into Duchamp's choice of the bottle dryer, which, moreover, does not belong to any artistic medium. You can make art from anything and everything. The Bauhaus model was thus right to minimize craftsmanship and to be wary of an excess of technical skill. But if you can make art from anything and everything, you can also do so with oil painting or copper plate engraving. Why should we deprive ourselves of teaching means of expression which take a long time to master and whose apprenticeship has everything to gain from being guided by a practitioner? I have seen too many students fall back on readymade techniques because they lacked more traditional means. [...] If there's just one word we should rehabilitate, it's tradition. To reserve it for the academy, just as dadaism is in the museum, is to condemn ourselves to the infantile and avant-gardist vision of history that regrets or denounces the 'recuperation' of avant-gardes and values rupture for its own sake. It is also to perpetuate the modernist myth of the *tabula rasa* and prevent ourselves from seeing, in retrospect, that the continuity between modern art and the past takes precedence over the discontinuities. And finally, it is to cast away pre-modern tradition into a finished past, dead, where it is available to be pillaged but can no longer be formative of judgement. [...]

The word tradition means transmission, nothing else. It does not refer to any particular style that we deem – favourably or not, it doesn't matter – 'traditional'. It refers to the fact that for a long period, and through a succession of societies whose values possibly negate each other, artists have continued to practice. 'Tradition' is a name for the continuity of artistic practices in the *longue durée*, however numerous and violent may have been the formal ruptures. To a large extent, however, these ruptures were concomitant with changes in the *mode* of transmission, changes the 'traditionalists' do not perceive as such, regularly confusing them with the decline of tradition. There was a time when art was transmitted directly from master to apprentice in the studio. There was then a time when its transmission, enjoying the aura of a new intellectual prestige, was the exclusive prerogative of the Academies. It is now transmitted by art schools that have inherited the great educational utopias of modernity, no longer know very well what to do with them, and yet transmit a tradition regardless, albeit that of anti-tradition. An art school is thus a professional school which is distinguished from other professional schools in that transmission is the first 'material' to be transmitted.

Imitation, Invention, Simulation

The academic model, which taught respect for rules, was expected to accomplish the formation of an individual who gradually acquired the autonomy by which an artist is recognized. Building on the lessons of modern art, the Bauhaus model instructed this individual, in the discovery of rules, instead. Creativity as source would encounter the medium as target and confront it. From battling with constraints, one was expected to acquire a language. When the deconstruction of language and of rules are supposed to embody the new rule and provide a new language, paralysis grips all, students and teachers alike. Aimless disorder reigns, with Alexandrianism as background. And so we have recently seen the resurgence of the myth of personal expression, but as simulacrum. [...] Teachers settle in a relationship with each isolated student akin to that of analyst and analysand. [...] The teaching regresses beneath the Bauhaus model, even beneath the academic model. One believes in reviving the former intimate relation of master and apprentice, but it is a simulacrum. One forgets that the master transmitted a tradition while the teacher today, a false Socrates, practices maieutics without history. The cleverest students, the best perhaps, make a whole other argument, more instinctive than conscious. Since the Bauhaus model enjoins them to be creative purists and experimental innovators, they become impure appropriators and existential simulators. Here we are. It is this generation that has been landing on the art scene in the last few years.

The antidote to careers as simulators is teaching through simulation. This is anyway what we do in art schools – well, let's say it. Consider the art history course, which the Bauhaus model almost entirely eliminated and which is so needed today. Whatever we do, we never bring works into the classroom. Whatever we do, we send our students doing tourism in the past. Like any good tour operator whose brochure sells us the beaches of Bali, we can expect one thing: that upon viewing the slide show, the students will be curious enough to go and see the original. Now consider studio teaching. The degeneration of the Bauhaus model has revived a semblance of the old studio relationships: when professors of painting can no longer believe that they are teaching their classes the rudiments of a universal language, they fall back on individual demands. But they are no longer masters, they are facilitators, communicators, information providers, psychologists who must steer their patients through their desires. And their students are no longer apprentices; they are the teachers' passengers.

Tourism is the dominant model of our culture. It turns time into space and cancels the latter in the ubiquity of the image. For production in the symbolic, it substitutes consumption in the imaginary. The world is a museum where the imaginary museum has preceded us – it's banal to reiterate this, so long after Valéry, Benjamin and Malraux. What is curious is that the education system still hasn't registered it. Great consumer of audio-visual techniques, it pretends not to have anything but an instrumental relation to them, which leaves it unscathed. And it is precisely by being blinkered to the fact that cultural transmission happens in the mode of simulation – in other words, in *Flash Art* rather than at the museum – that educators, whose mission is to transmit culture, have morphed into the welcoming hosts of a great cultural Disneyland. Hello young people, let us guide you to the realm of simulation.

I'm joking? No. What I want to say is this: through simulation, we will transmit to you [the art students] everything in artistic culture that is transmissible. Simulation is a method for apprenticeship, not a goal. We will not teach you how to pretend to be an artist, we will teach you to act as if you were this artist, then another, as if you belonged to this culture, then another, to this epoch, then another; we will teach you to simulate so that you assimilate. Simulation is of course a form of imitation. Where it differs is that it requires no faith in mimesis but merely *suspension of disbelief*. Simulation is the game of 'as if' in which you put yourself in the shoes of someone whose culture is not, or is no longer, ours at present, but remains ours in the past or will become ours through hybridization. Parody and pastiche are merely nihilist modes of simulation, the only ones available as long as official culture has not recognized its positivity. Unlike imitation, simulation does not put a brake on invention, it situates it outside the formal register. Its role is not to discipline but to awaken dormant meanings whose source is not in the individual's creativity but in the simulated tradition.

Thierry de Duve, extracts from paper presented at the conference 'The Artists and the Academy: European Perspectives on Today's Fine Art Education' (University of Southampton, 1993), in Stephen Foster and Nicholas de Ville, eds, *The Artist and the Academy: Issues in Fine Art Education and the Wider Cultural Context* (Southampton: John Hansard Gallery, 1994) 23–40. The last part of the text published here (from 'Talent, Creativity, Judgement' on) was not included in *The Artist and the Academy*, and is here adapted by the author (trans. Ian Farr) from the earlier version, *Faire école (ou la refaire?)* (Dijon: Les Presses du Réel, 1992).

Carol Becker
The Art of Crossing the Street//1999

We, the School of the Art Institute of Chicago, called our class *The Art of Crossing the Street*. In the original description of this class we asked the question: 'How can artists cross the street without leaving their art behind?'

We envisioned a pilot programme, still subsidized in part by the List Foundation, that would use three faculty members and a series of visiting artists. We imagined a two-semester sequence, the first semester the more theoretical one, using the three-hour seminar format, and the second semester a six-hour studio format, both team-taught. The students who had participated in the Headlands conference, most of whom were already student leaders, were invited to serve as teaching assistants and were part of the discussions designed to choose the reading material, the sequence of topics for discussion, and the visiting artists. [...]

The enrolment in the first class was almost fifty students, half of them freshmen, although there were many upper-level students who wanted to take the class as an elective and had been waiting 'for years' to study the issues of artist as citizen. The idea was to keep the class together as a unit when there was a visiting artist/scholar/writer/intellectual and then to split the class into smaller groups when there was a discussion about the readings. This proved to be the biggest structural problem: because there were so many presenters and so much to discuss with the group as a whole, we did not break the large group into smaller units often enough. Unfortunately, having too many large sessions left only the most gregarious students confident enough to speak.

The teaching team (students and faculty) chose the books that would be required reading and envisioned the division of the units. Basic units included the possibilities and challenges of community work; the reality of artists' lives; the work of engaged artists, with a focus on Fred Wilson, Bill T. Jones and Mierle Laderman Ukeles; South Africa – postcolonialism, the National Artists Coalition, artists in struggle. There were many visiting artists and arts activists who spoke to the group or to the larger school community about their work and about how they came to be who they are and do the work they do. These guests included poet Roberto Bedoya, Director, National Association of Artists' Organizations; Claudia Bernardi, painter and forensics expert; Rick Lowe, Director, Project Row Houses; Nayland Blake, photographer; and Bill T. Jones, dancer and choreographer.

The students were asked to write four papers analysing various lectures, exhibitions or other events they attended with the class. They also were asked to interview someone whose work and life they admired. Some students did projects and used these as the subject of their papers. Certain of these projects directly affected the school community, while other students went into the city and worked as volunteers in churches, Head Start programmes, community centres – sharing their skills in computing, writing, art making.

Perhaps the most moving papers were those written about a visit students made to meet Zolo Agona Azania, a prisoner on death row in Michigan City, Indiana. Zolo allegedly killed a police officer, although he denies this accusation. He has spent most of his adult life in prison, where he has become a painter, initially instructed by a fellow inmate. As a result of their encounter with Zolo, the students were moved to observe and then write eloquently about their own situations – in particular, how much freedom and privilege they actually have, how many possibilities and opportunities their own lives provide. Others expressed an understanding of how loved and cared for they have been and still are. They were struck by Zolo's good-naturedness in the face of his impending death. He never expressed anxiety about his situation to them; rather, he seemed inordinately joyful. [...]

During the first semester I lectured on the role of artists in South Africa, focusing on how the term political was defined in relationship to art-making during the apartheid years. I explained the sophistication and breadth of the National Artists Coalition, an organization formed by thousands of South African artists, many of whom were in the ANC, to help develop a policy for arts and culture so that when the ANC came to power, the position of artists would be secured, free and supported by the new government. I pointed out that even those who have worked closely with the ANC were not certain that any government ultimately could be trusted to give art its rightful place without the intervention of artists' voices. History has proven them to be correct, and these same artists are now grappling with the complexity of post-apartheid conditions. As part of a class entitled *Art and Politics in the New Southern Africa*, Lisa Brock, Valerie Cassel, Marilyn Sward and I took sixteen students to South Africa and Zimbabwe in January 1998 on a study trip. Some students who had been in *The Art of Crossing the Street* class participated. And some from the South Africa class were inspired to take the second half of *The Art of Crossing the Street*.

The spring semester of the course has been structured around a six-hour studio format. Three faculty members have been assigned once again, and this time they are all artists who have worked in collective, collaborative, community-based contexts. One is a visiting professor from South Africa, sculptor Andries Botha; another is video artist Maria Benfield, who has done intensive neighbourhood street video making with gang members and inner-city youth; the third artist/faculty member is Michael Ryan, who has worked in the student affairs department at the School and has helped students to coordinate the student galleries and exhibition spaces. There have also been many guest lecturers and a new selection of readings, as well as serious debate and discussion about collective practice.

In the class we have presented artists and thinkers who have found ways to treat the entire society as a suitable site for the presentation of their work. Dan Peterman, for example, one of our visiting artists, had moved his studio into a recycling centre in order to be close to the materials he uses for his sculptural installations and to reflect his concern for ecological issues as manifested in his art-making. To further integrate himself into the community, he has also set up a bicycle repair shop adjacent to his work space. Neighbourhood youth now come together there to fix their bicycles and, once they learn the skills and help others, they can earn credit towards acquiring a bicycle or bicycle accessories. This communal bike shop is only one way Peterman hopes to get to know his community and ultimately to achieve his goal of making the work he wants, as he wants, from the materials he wants, and to do so within the society, engaging people at all stages of the work's development. Not all artists can function in such public ways. Not all need to. The challenge for students is to ask themselves what their goals are and how to achieve them. [...]

After watching videotapes from Henry Sayre's series of artists' tapes entitled *A World of Art: Works in Progress*, it became important for students to note, for example, that Guillermo Gómez-Peña (included in Sayre's series), who has used pirate radio as a format for his cultural interventions, is now doing 'legitimate' radio spots on National Public Radio. He uses some of the same techniques he developed for alternative systems, while reaching a new, wider audience.[1] [...]

To experience the methodologies of many artists who are not afraid of asking difficult questions, and who have been able to answer them successfully for themselves, helps students imagine their own futures courageously without being immobilized by the contradictions in US society. They need to learn that consciousness can lead to action, that there are artists who experiment in form and content and take their inspiration from their interaction with the world. They will, of course, also have ample opportunity to learn about more traditional forms of art-making in their other studio and art history classes. [...]

1 Henry Sayre's *A World of Art Works in Progress* is a ten-part video series produced by Sayre. [...] The artists included are Judy Baca, Beverly Buchanan, Goat Island, Guillermo Gómez-Peña, Hung Liu, Lorna Simpson, Milton Resnick, Mierle Laderman Ukeles, Bill Viola and June Wayne.

Carol Becker, extracts from 'The Art of Crossing the Street', *Art Journal*, vol. 58, no. 1 (New York: College Art Association, Spring 1999) 11–15.

Why go to college. Or, as a man said, it
is too far away.

Why go.

If I don't get there, this year
anyhow I know some of the names, I know
what it might have been like, say, or

you say.

Robert Creeley, from 'An Ode (for Black Mountain College)', undated

INDISCIPLINE

Paul Dash
Foreday Morning//2002

[...] In 1957 my parents found the cash to send for my brothers and me. The Atlantic crossing took eleven days. [...]

Within a few weeks places were found for Gerald and me at Cowley St John Secondary Modern School[1] on the Cowley Road [in Oxford]; we hadn't taken the eleven-plus exam and so were not eligible for grammar school.[2]

The curriculum was basic. There were only twelve staff teaching the 'three Rs' [reading, writing, arithmetic], PE, art, history, geography, music, metalwork, woodwork and general science. For us in the B stream it was dire. We did arithmetic, as opposed to maths. We didn't do English literature; teachers didn't introduce us to authors, either contemporary or classical. I had always wanted to learn a foreign language, regarding that ability as a key indicator of a sound education. Attending a school which didn't set homework, which set the level of mathematics below that I had been used to at primary school in Barbados, and not having the opportunity to study a foreign language were all a huge disappointment.

My form mistress was one of the school's few female teachers, Mrs Harris. From the outset I was made to sit at the front, away from the other children, and just a few paces from her desk. There was nothing between her and me but the polished parquet flooring. I was very conscious of my blackness, aware of every action I took. [...]

One afternoon in my second week at the school, Mrs Harris instructed us to take pens, rulers and pencils from our desks in preparation for a history lesson. As I lifted my desk lid and collected what was needed, the wooden ruler slipped from my hand and fell to the floor. This simple incident, an innocent everyday occurrence in almost every classroom, led to what was one of the most humiliating and painful experiences in my childhood. Watching the ruler fall was like a slow-motion scene from a movie, every millisecond registered, my panic magnified in dreadful anticipation. I froze in my seat, desk lid still open, my head out of sight of Mrs Harris. When the ruler fell on the parquet floor the clatter reverberated round the room. Being painfully shy and nervous in this new envirnment, the last thing I wanted was to draw attention to myself. What I craved was to disappear, be rendered invisible. But I was under the watchful eye of Mrs Harris. She represented all that I had come to fear in whites as figures of authority, and, worst of all, in her I sensed a loathing, a profound dislike of me, which undermined my confidence.

What followed surpassed my worst fears. I glanced over the rim of my desk lid, but Mrs Harris was already moving towards me. She fell on me in half-crazed violence and hate, hitting, kicking and snarling. She slapped my head, punched my shoulders and chest, kicked my bare shins. This was no mere scolding but a symbolic beating to death, an act of annihilation, a violation of my right to be. My Barbadian upbringing, my ingrained respect for teachers and awe of whites, combined to paralyse me, to make retaliation or even evasive action impossible.

I sat through the afternoon lessons like a loyal but brutalized puppy, still strangely respectful of my teacher, as I had been brought up to be. By the end of the day Mrs Harris was worried: I was still weeping inconsolably. She found a handkerchief, wiped away my tears and begged me not to tell my parents. Her fear was palpable, and I was confused. But she needn't have worried.

The day after my beating I was back in school as usual. Though she tried not to show it, I could tell Mrs Harris was relieved that the matter had apparently been taken no further. Our relationship settled into one of tolerance; she tolerated me and I despised her while accepting her authority. [...]

Cowley St John put a cap on my learning as it did on the learning of other children there. There was no nurturing, no introduction to new layers of learning which would have moved our thinking on in a structured way, no follow-up, no extension, no expansion of an idea or concept, just a shutting-down of potential.

I regularly found myself walking with children who attended Cheyne Grammar School. All the children had satchels, in which they carried their homework and books.

To this day I balk at the whole idea of grammar-school education, because there are bound to be many children who, like me, feel excluded, failures merely because of the school they find themselves in. Many years later I was a head of department at a school where a former Cheyne student was also head of department. We sat together at meetings, chaired by the headteacher, and I couldn't help thinking about the past and seeing it in the light of the present.

As an eleven-year-old, I brooded on this inequality, and grew more and more anxious. Instead of turning in on myself and allowing myself to be defeated by exclusion, I vowed to overcome my serious social and educational disadvantages by self-education. [...]

John Goodgame was often in trouble and frequently caned. He got his come-uppance after he broke the window of a house near the school; The headmaster, Mr Clibborn, convened a special assembly and in front of the whole school slippered John Goodgame across the backside, with all the force he could muster. It was a nasty beating of real viciousness. John was never the same person after that. [...]

One of the ordinary classrooms doubled as an art room and Mr Goodwill, who taught us English, doubled as art teacher. The room was badly furnished for art and we had to keep it clean for the English classes. [...] I painted to my heart's content, as there was no firm theme or project around which our activities were planned, refining my technique and creating a body of work with growing skill and assurance. I began to look forward to Friday afternoons in the art room with greater and greater excitement; I couldn't wait to get in there and settle into work. The smell of powder paint was as sweet as anything in God's creation, the clink of brushes in water-jars harbingers of deep pleasure. Watching an image build on the sugar paper, making decisions, being in charge, was most enjoyable. I lost myself totally in my art. By the age of fourteen my reputation for art in the school was established. Mama bought me artist's materials, initially cheap paints, then squirrel, ox-hair and other watercolour brushes. Few trips went without a purchase. She bought little sketchbooks into which I put different images, branching out from my usual street scenes. She bought small tubes of watercolour. I didn't take any of these materials to school.

I started painting at home scenes based on my idea of Caribbean life. The work I did in school I liked for the pleasure of doing it. The work I made at home was my private world, a world I couldn't share with my teachers or anyone outside of the family. It was a world which constituted me, one too private for such exposure.

Art, I had discovered, was a subject which allowed one freedom to roam. That discovery was arguably the single most important thing I gained from the school. My talent had been recognized by Mr Goodwill, and through him I discovered what ability I had and it raised my self-esteem. The experience could, in that regard, be likened to that of someone with a disability who is thought to be without a mind, without the capacity to formulate simple views or make even the most basic communication with those around them. Then one day they gain access to a computer and their life is transformed: they find a voice, and the world discovers they have a mind. [...]

[In 1964], at the age of 18, I took my GCEs [General Certificate of Education][3] and gained the qualifications I needed to enter the school of art. I applied to the School of Art to do a foundation year, which I hoped would lead to a Diploma in Art and Design and [I was] offered a place. I felt as though I was walking on air.

That autumn I duly enrolled at the school, and started work in earnest under the guidance and supervision of Len McComb,[4] without doubt the finest teacher I have ever known, of any subject. I had applied for a grant and got a full one. For the first time in my life I had real money in my pockets. It was without doubt the most enriching and purposeful year in my career at art college. [...]

Nothing could have been better than making work at home in my shared bedroom. This was a magical world, cut off from the rest of the art environments to which I had grown accustomed. I created paintings which spoke for me without worrying about modernism or breaking new ground. I merely painted for the love of painting. [...]

When I applied to Chelsea School of Art I knew nothing whatever about the college. I hadn't spoken to Len McComb about it. As far as I was concerned, the college was comparatively near Oxford, and it was an art college, and that was it.

Chelsea was a huge disappointment. The lecturers took little direct interest in me, or my work. The world I had created as a young man in Oxford disintegrated, but there was nothing to take its place. Constructivism and Minimalism were the flavour of the moment. This was light years away from what I wanted to do.

While in Oxford, I hadn't engaged in any theoretical debates about art-making: where we are today and should be tomorrow. I just lived the style of 'the artist' and produced work I enjoyed, work which spoke to me at that time. The concept of breaking new ground didn't occupy my mind in any way. In that respect going to Chelsea was a traumatic experience, because the students and certainly the staff favoured avant-garde work. The tension between those two diametrically opposed positions almost destroyed me; the only thing that kept me going was my own passion for making work. [...]

In my third year at Chelsea I met John La Rose, one of the chief architects of the Caribbean Artists' Movement (CAM). He recruited me into the movement and I met Andrew Salkey, Wilson Harris, Ronald Moody, Eddie Brathwaite, Beryl McBernie, Ann Walmsley, Errol Loyd and others. I was greatly uplifted by the experience of being with people from middle-class West Indian backgrounds who had been steeped in literature and reading, and had been taught to analyse text and extract meaning from a wide range of sources. These very able people lived in a different world from mine.

Being a member of CAM was liberating. It was almost as if I had been imprisoned for many years, and then suddenly set free. [...]

1 [British secondary modern schools were set up in 1944 for all children who were tested at the age of 11 and did not reach scores in the top 25 per cent. By the 1970s in England they had mostly been replaced by comprehensive schools which were non-selective, although some English counties continue to operate a selective system (see Henry Ward in this volume, 110–11.]

2 [Grammar schools at this time were entitled by the 1944 Education act to select pupils from the top 25 per cent of 'eleven-plus' exam results and offered a highly academic curriculum.]

3 [At that time secondary modern pupils were not eligible for the GCE exam to enter any type of further education. Dash had to go to a college to study for GCEs before he could apply to study art. Later, secondary moderns offered the less valuable CSE exams but uptake was low.

4 [The painter and sculptor Leonard McComb, RA.]

Paul Dash, extracts from *Foreday Morning* (London: Black Amber Books, 2002) 113–216 [n.b. numerous ellipses within each extract have been left unmarked, with the author's permission].

Caroline Benn
Common Education and the Radical Tradition//1992

[...] Commitment to greater human equality is a central feature of [the Left's radical tradition in education] – and one of its basic constituents is common education: all members of a society educated together. Common education's first objective is a broad and balanced learning experience that develops all human beings to their full capacities, its second to act cohesively on those who live together to create one society. Its origins are in the seventeenth-century reforms of Bishop Comenius who was faced with social havoc caused by wars between Christian sects in the wake of the Reformation. Before this time the different denominations controlled formal learning, but Comenius proposed a new education system: common to all, regardless of religious affiliation. As well as learning together, everyone in his system also proceeded in steps – or grades – from earlier to later years, and from lower to higher forms of enlightenment. Most modern education systems descend in part from these proposals.

That everyone could be equally well educated was – and remains – a revolutionary idea. For this reason common education has always been opposed by conservatives and elitists who fear it will lead to changes in class and productive relations in favour of new social groups. Their counter-proposals always favour different types of education according to a person's social or economic level (and lately, innate 'intelligence'), their motives no less political than those behind common education. Lately, opposition has also come from those who resist mass production in education as leading to state manipulation; patently also a social concern. One modern educator – Ivan Illich – even blamed Comenius' original plan for the compulsory schooling systems which he believes strangle genuine education in all advanced nations today, where the institution has come to define the purpose of education rather than the other way around. However, Illich's main complaint – that 'no matter how much each generation spends on schools, it always turned out that the majority ... were certified unfit for higher grades of enlightenment and had to be discarded' – is exactly the starting point of those who have advocated common schooling in modern times.

That the majority should have the same rights as an elite minority to enjoy the full range of education available to each generation was an idea that dawned in the industrial revolution, as artisans were struggling to understand their political and class predicament in early nineteenth-century Britain. Soon Chartists and other reformers were asking for common schools – to break down class barriers and give the majority 'better opportunities', as Richard Cobden put it. When the 1870 Act brought universal basic education, the radical tradition, now augmented by a socialist movement and the 'new unionism' of workers in the skilled trades, immediately sought to advance it in a common direction. Thus Keir Hardie, at an 1896 International Socialist Congress, successfully moved for the same educational provision for everyone without regard to any individual's test score or exam qualifications, while a Trades Councils and Cooperative Societies' representative, appearing before the Bryce Commission investigating secondary education in 1894, made another of common education's basic demands: that the system be organized on the basis of age divisions rather than those of social class. Neither demand was likely to be conceded by the bourgeoisie (let alone the old aristocracy), who feared the surge of equality – and demand for public services – that universal basic education would foster. Indeed, the forces of elitism were already hard at work to mitigate the latest reforms by devising new types of segregation. [...] At the upper end of the middle class, professional parents were busy starting new private enterprises, their own 'public' schools. Some of these had been founded specifically as common schools – in the cases of Winchester and Eton as fourteenth- and fifteenth-century neighbourhood schools for poor children without clerical backing, to help them compete with the well to do of the day. In the nineteenth century this practice of 'enclosing' once-common institutions for the use of elite groups – so closely paralleled by the enclosure of the common land going on at the time – was even more pronounced in the case of the much larger group of endowed schools. These had often been established by religious bodies specifically to provide free, local education for the poor. The Endowed Schools Commission of 1867, reviewing their operation, made several key changes in response to the growing claims to education of the bourgeoisie – all entirely at the expense of the working class. These included empowering such schools to charge fees.

Dividing Schools and Minds

For the majority of the working class it was a case of starting all over again, as it so often is in the drama of common schooling, where a new divided system replaces an old, and has to be countered anew. In the late nineteenth century pressure for change came particularly on behalf of skilled workers' children for the kind of education which the middle classes took for granted for their sons (daughters everywhere had a much harder struggle). This led to 'scholarships' for the poor – provided they were few in number, industrious, capable of passing tests, and working strictly out of individual ambition to advance in the existing system – in other words, 'deserving'. Radicals opposed this idea of education as a privilege, a 'ladder' for the few; they believed it was a right for all, and should be a 'broad highway', an extension of basic common schooling to promote the collective advance of working-class communities. The heart of it was a growing belief in the educability of everyone. They had to face not only traditional elitism from the middle and upper classes, but from their own ranks as well. Most Fabians, for example, were strongly in favour of a segregated education for Labour's own aristocracy of leaders. They supported the establishment of local grammar schools brought in by the 1902 Education Act: mirror-image public schools offering classical education to the less affluent. It was at this precise date, as Brian Simon and David Rubinstein point out, that divisive 'differentiation of the types of school ... was built into the national system' in Britain (*The Evolution of the Comprehensive School*, 1969). It was also at this point that radical reformers began the lengthy task of combating the determinism inherent in the concept of 'intelligence' – a formidable new criterion that was to regulate educational opportunity for at least half a century.

From the Ministry of Education, men like Cyril Burt, the high priest of IQ, set the new determinist view: 'intelligence ...is inherited ... not due to teaching or training ... uninfluenced by industry or zeal ... (and) measured with ... ease.' Segregation was justified by science in the form of the IQ test, claimed to be value free, fair, and nothing to do with social status or wealth.

Meanwhile, however, a divisive secondary system had been entrenched in Britain after the 1944 Act at a time when countries with educational histories very similar to Britain's were beginning to move away from crude academic selection. Ironically, it was the work of a supposedly 'reforming' British Labour government, which, despite protests from its own supporters, insisted not only on retaining the old system of different 'types' of schools, but adding to it a national IQ test at 11-plus. It assumed that a radical remit had been discharged with the introduction of a new Secondary Modern School for the majority and the abolition of fees for grammar schools – illustrating the way partial reforms can often prolong inequalities rather than end them. Behind this failure to reform radically in 1945 was the same powerful civil service and educational establishment. [...]

Comprehensive Reform

Those who opposed this elitist orthodoxy were the supporters of comprehensive education – as common schooling had come to be called in Britain after the Second World War. [...] Secondary schools saw first hand what talent had been unable to show itself at an earlier stage, and primary schools, watching comprehensive primary education developing so successfully, wanted it extended, abolishing altogether the hated examination that decided children's futures at the absurdly early age of eleven. They were opposed by the majority of teachers in the prestige areas of secondary education, the grammar and public schools, who supported selection. So too did the media, particularly influential journals like the *Times Educational Supplement*, whose editorials for most of the

1950s and 1960s were intensely anti-comprehensive. As for the universities, only one vice-chancellor ever supported the comprehensive cause, and even as late as the 1970s the principals of all Oxford colleges signed a letter deploring the comprehensive change.

Yet by the 1970s, common secondary schooling was well established, having accelerated after 1945 when Labour local authorities like Middlesex and London, defying a Labour government, applied to develop comprehensive schools rather than a divided system. [...]

The Counter-Reformation

This change bred a counter-reformation which did not begin in 1979, when a Conservative majority was elected, but long before. [...] Nationally, most Labour leaders and education ministers, though committed to a degree of social mixing, privately believed in the limited availability of intelligence and the necessity of protecting an academic elite – if not in grammar schools, at least within the comprehensives. Their comprehensive reforms were consequently strictly limited to external structural reorganization. [...]

Although discussion was constant in all comprehensives about the forms of grouping, curriculum and assessment most appropriate to a common school, lack of guidance from the top meant that some new schools carried on the old divided system under a new roof, while others sought to develop new forms of education that enhanced learning and had social impact. [...]

The consolation for radical reformers was in having won so many of the arguments, but to secure developments in practice, forward planning was required, particularly after 14-plus. This had already occurred in Scandinavian countries through twenty-year rolling programmes of comprehensive legislation that saw an ordered change-over, with streaming abolished and education and training curricula reformed and extended to the age of 18 by the late 1970s. Comprehensive development was also proceeding in almost all of the rest of Europe, both eastern and western – as well as in Japan from 1945, and, after the Cultural Revolution, in China as well.

The two world giants, the USA and the USSR, had legislated for comprehensive systems after the First World War to bring social cohesion to their diverse populations – and to raise mass standards in anticipation of technological change. [...] In Britain the training system was still rudimentary – largely confined to apprenticeships, mostly going to white males, while the percentages staying on in education after school-leaving – or going on to higher education – were nearly the lowest of all the major industrial nations.

But Labour left office in 1979 without taking decisive legislative action on this major reform. In 24 years of Labour governments from 1924 there had been no major Labour Education Act. For a Party committed to change through the Parliamentary process rather than extra-Parliamentary action, this legislative abdication is highly significant, and points yet again to a radical educational tradition in Britain that has repeatedly lacked translation into positive political action at the top. Behind it is a failure by Labour to formulate change – in terms of the values and objectives of egalitarian social change – a failure that was to loom all the larger as Conservatives swept through the 1980s enacting legislative change in every corner of the education and training system – pursuant to a well defined and articulated political ideology of elitism and market-led restructuring. [...] As Brian Simon noted, when commenting on the objectives of ministry mandarins controlling these draconian reforms, their most significant, if inadvertent, comment on why this 'change' was needed, was that education had to teach people 'to know their place once more'.

Mirror-Image Politics

[...] Common education's next great historic advance must involve tackling the selective processes that divide and oppress in the occupational structure. This will force us to look at the kind of society that education and work are both supposed to serve – in short, rediscovering education's social and political purposes. These purposes will be forced upon society in any case, as, on a daily basis, through the educational services and elsewhere, we seek to redistribute resources to mediate the world's economic and cultural diversity, and to negotiate the planet's social and environmental welfare. Only a common education service can hope to educate for success in these crucial tasks. Far from being over, as elitists prematurely conclude, it is more than possible that common education's greatest contribution is yet to come. [...]

Caroline Benn, extracts from 'Common Education and the Radical Tradition', in *Rethinking Radical Education: Essays in Honour of Brian Simon*, ed. Ali Rattansi and David Reeder (London: Lawrence & Wishart, 1992) 142–62.

Paulo Freire
Pedagogy of the Oppressed//1968

[...] In the banking concept of education, knowledge is a gift bestowed by those who consider themselves knowledgeable upon those whom they consider to know nothing. Projecting an absolute ignorance onto others, a characteristic of the ideology of oppression, negates education and knowledge as processes of inquiry. The teacher presents himself to his students as their necessary opposite; by considering their ignorance absolute, he justifies his own existence. The students, alienated like the slave in the Hegelian dialectic, accept their ignorance as justifying the teacher's existence – but, unlike the slave, they never discover that they educate the teacher.

The *raison d'être* of libertarian education, on the other hand, lies in its drive towards reconciliation. Education must begin with the solution of the teacher-student contradiction, by reconciling the poles of the contradiction so that both are simultaneously teachers and students. [...]

Dialogue is the encounter between men, mediated by the world, in order to name the world. Hence, dialogue cannot occur between those who want to name the world and those who do not wish this naming – between those who deny others the right to speak their word and those whose right to speak has been denied them. Those who have been denied their primordial right to speak their word must first reclaim this right and prevent the continuation of this dehumanizing aggression.

If it is in speaking their word that people, by naming the world, transform it, dialogue imposes itself as the way by which they achieve significance as human beings. Dialogue is thus an existential necessity. [...]

Paulo Freire, extracts from *Pedagogia do oprimido* (Santiago de Chile, 1968; first trans. 1970); trans. Myra Bergman Ramos, *Pedagogy of the Oppressed* (New York and London: Continuum, 1994) 53; 69.

Allan Kaprow
Success and Failure when Art Changes//1994

In the late 1960s, an educational experiment called *Project Other Ways* took place under the wing of the Berkeley, California, Unified School District. Educator Herbert Kohl and I were its stewards, assisted by a Carnegie Corporation grant. Its purpose was to bring the arts into a central role in the public schools' curricula. To do this, the project acted as an agency which drew together school administrators, teachers and their students with young poets, storytellers, sculptors, architects, photographers, happeners and even athletes who saw their sport as art.

Participation was more informal than strict; membership varied from individuals to teachers and their classes (K through 12). Some attended only workshops while others were committed to semester projects. We were located in a storefront not far from the Berkeley high school, which made us pleasantly accessible to passers-by, but much of our work extended out into the city's classrooms and the everyday environment.

At the time, Berkeley, along with nearby Oakland and San Francisco, was the scene of massive social upheaval, and armed forces were everywhere. It is important to mention this because our activities rarely addressed the conflict directly, yet they reflected its paranoias and powerful energies, as well as the surge of utopian fervour that fuelled it. Most of our efforts, in fact, focused on learning staples such as reading, writing, maths and community studies, and we believed that the arts could foster them. But no one could ignore the tension and the smell of tear gas, and our experiments sometimes approached the edges of social boundaries.

For example, there was a sixth grade class in one of the Oakland schools whose kids were considered unteachable illiterates. I forget the official label but it was enough to sentence them to permanent societal rejection. Their days in school (when they showed up) were largely a matter of disciplinary supervision, not education. Some of them came to our storefront with their teacher one afternoon. We had just been given a number of cheap Polaroid cameras and film, and I invited the kids to take a walk with me and snap pictures of anything they liked. On the way, they took pictures of each other making faces, of their shadows, of helicopters in the air, of army tanks and cops; but mostly, they seemed to prefer graffiti on the sidewalks and walls of buildings. I wondered why, if they were illiterate, they were so interested in words, especially sexual ones.

So I said let's take photos of the graffiti in men's and women's public toilets. The kids thought that was a great idea, especially if the girls could go into the men's toilet stalls and vice versa. We went around town to filling stations and motel restrooms and shot off dozens of film packs, most of which didn't come out. But of those that did, it was clear that the kids understood four-letter words and related descriptions around certain drawings. Illiterate? Not quite.

Kohl and I saw the germ of an idea in what had just happened. We covered the walls of our storefront offices with large sheets of brown wrapping paper, provided felt-tip pens, paints and brushes, staplers and rubber cement. We invited the kids back the following week and put on a table the photos they had taken. They were asked to make graffiti, using the photos and any drawings they wanted to make, like the graffiti they had seen on our tour. At first they were hesitant and giggled, but we said there were no rules and they wouldn't be punished for dirty words or drawings, or even for making a mess. Soon there were photos all over the walls. Drawn and painted lines circled and stabbed them, extending genitalia and the names of locals they obviously recognized. These names, like Huey (probably Black Panther Huey Newton, then under arrest), Bobo (an area gang leader), and César (César Chávez, farmworkers' labour leader), were painted in large letters. Sometimes opposition names would be followed by verbs like 'sucks' and other equivalents.

Their own names and images began to appear in the next days, often with the help of our staff, occasionally by helping one another. Later on, the kids were encouraged to tell stories about what they had done and what they saw on other parts of the walls. The better writers were asked to print the stories at the appropriate places. These were usually no more than two- or three-word labels (like much public graffiti), rarely complete sentences. But after a week, a guarded enthusiasm replaced shyness and a core of active literacy began to emerge.

Kohl heard that the school system's textbook depository was discarding outmoded Dick and Jane early reader books, and that we could have as many as we wanted. The thought was to have our small group rewrite and re-illustrate them. If any young people could possibly have been interested in the primers' stereotyped narratives in those years of social challenge, they could only have been the sons and daughters of patently sexist and racist parents. But there didn't seem to be many of them willing to speak out in Berkeley then, and that was one of the reasons the city was getting rid of the books. Our assumption was that the kids' sensitivity to these biases (the majority were black or Hispanic) would provide us the openings for frank discussion, and would make attractive the prospect of wholesale revision of the texts. We were right.

Dick and Jane were transformed into monsters with wildly coloured hair. Images were cut out and replaced by drawn ones. Pages were reordered to create time reversals. And the text became a parody of 'Run, Spot, run!', as 'Run, man, fuzz!' seemed suddenly more real. One of the kids was helped in typing the texts on the office typewriter, while others hand-lettered the books. A small exhibit of the results was shown to the school officials, who were impressed enough to consider reclassifying the students.

Was the experiment a success? It depends on our criteria. Conventionally, in our culture, something is either art or it's something else; either a poem or a telephone call to a relative. But *Project Other Ways* was intent on merging the arts with things not considered art, namely training in reading, writing, maths, and so on. Significantly, the innovative art movements of the day provided the models for our objectives. The Japanese Gutai, Environments, Happenings, Nouveau Réalisme, Fluxus, events, noise music, chance poetry, life theatre, found actions, bodyworks, earthworks, concept art, information art – the list could go on – confronted publics and arts professionals with strange occurrences bearing little resemblance to the known arts.

The identity problem these movements caused in arts circles (that is, what exactly were these new creatures, and how should we deal with them?) was nothing compared with the potential confusion we could sense lying a short distance away in the education community. We at *Project Other Ways* were privileged in this regard, by grant money and experience as artists, to play and change as we saw fit, where in the average classroom it would have been almost impossible. Educational philosophy and teacher training would have to be radically revised. We said so, and were under no illusions that the task would be easy.

If the new arts were bewildering to many within their own arts circles, they shared two conditions. One was that the borders between the arts and the rest of life were blurred. The other was that their makers wanted them to be still known as art. And in order to be considered art, they had to be acknowledged and discussed within the arts' institutional frameworks.

So the artists saw to it that this connection with the machinery of validation was solidly maintained. Their work was widely promoted as art, in the form of photo documents, recordings, and descriptive texts, by galleries, new music and dance impresarios, collectors and arts journals. Although I personally intended our educational experiment at the project to be art at the same time as it was a way to increase literacy, and some students and colleagues heard me say so, the work was never published or exhibited. Thus, by the rules of the game at the time, it failed to count as art.

Today, twenty-five years later, the story is about to be printed in an art book. The art frame will descend upon it. Does it become art at last? And if so, is it good art? A complicating factor is that in my own thoughts and writings about Happenings and their progeny in the sixties, I placed a strong emphasis on identity ambiguity: the artwork was to remain, as long as possible, unclear in its status. By this standard, the experiment at *Project Other Ways* was good art (up to now, to me at least), as long as I kept the story mere hearsay among friends. My guideline was simple: one shouldn't rush too quickly to label life as art; it may deaden the game.

Has enough time elapsed to allow the story of the event to become useful gossip today – useful because it could act as permission for others to leave straight art for the art/life game? Hard to answer. Or, instead, have I devalued the game by casting it in the cement of art history, that is, as nothing but art? Maybe. Being merely art, the potential influence it might have on public education, and on art itself, can be shelved indefinitely.

As a safeguard against this possibility, suppose that right here I withdraw all art status from a past event that I once designated art. [...]

Most artists, of course, are less keenly interested in ambiguity of identity and purpose than I am. Open-endedness, to me, is democratic and challenges the mind. To others, it is simply waffling and irresponsible. [...]

The late artist Robert Filliou once said that the purpose of art was to reveal how much more interesting life is. The task for contemporary experimental artists may well be to probe that paradox, day by day, again and again. Then, perhaps, their gift to the public could be the mystery of tying a shoelace.

Allan Kaprow, extracts from 'Success and Failure when Art Changes', in *Mapping the Terrain: New Genre Public Art*, ed. Suzanne Lacy (Seattle: Bay Press, 1994) 152–8.

Suzanne Lacy
Activism in Feminist Performance Art//2006

[...] Derived from the historical trajectory of visual arts, feminist performance artists were left with the dilemma of explaining the social justice intentions in their work to a largely indifferent profession. Visual art performance had evolved as a series of reactions: to the object, to the museum, to the market system, to the subjects seen as appropriate for art, and to the identity of the maker. The goal was not the emancipation of the polis *per se*, but of artists and even art itself. For Allan Kaprow, the 'un-artist' was a counter-model to the over-mythologized artist (e.g. Jackson Pollock) and to art as commodity. His claim was to undermine a hierarchy of ideas, to produce innovation for the sake of art.

Augusto Boal established a clear paradigm of difference between his work and traditional theatre while retaining enough of its aesthetic inheritance to situate himself clearly in the trajectory of theatre scholarship. Boal reconfigures recognizable elements of theatre with activist agendas: 'The theatre has to be ... regained, reclaimed, from the bourgeoisie which has preserved theatre in its own likeness as a closed system' (interview with Charles Driskell, *Latin American Theater Review*, Fall 1975). [...]

His social justice goals were configured as aesthetic strategy itself, and it is here that feminist performance art finds common ground with Boal. [...]

[Throughout the 1990s] I collaborated with scores of Oakland artists and youth to produce performances and installations on public schooling, health care, criminal justice and public policy issues. Our strategies included reflection on core issues (community policing, schooling, neighbourhood safety, youth leadership and civic participation), skill building (public speaking, computer literacy, writing, video and photography), and workshops on team building, mentoring and anti-racism. [...] Youth opinion also led us to focus on police-youth relations in *Youth, Cops and Videotape* (1995), a training videotape for the police, and *No Blood/No Foul* (1996), a highly-publicized basketball-game-as-performance between police and youth to support the passage of Oakland's first Youth Policy.

Then in 1999, dozens of black, red and white cars with headlights blazing converged on the rooftop of the City Center Garage. In the spotlight of these beams, 100 police officers met in small groups with 150 local youth to talk candidly and intensely about crime, authority, power and safety. An audience of 1,000 community members roamed freely between cars witnessing the spontaneous dialogue of youth and police exploring realities and stereotypes. Named after the police radio code for 'emergency, clear the air waves', *Code 33* was a three-year performance project to explore institutional intervention through visual performance art concepts, to practically reduce police hostility towards youth, and to provide youth with a set of skills and a public context more conducive to civic inclusion.

By the time we produced *Code 33* we had developed a model which included an extensive workshop period prior to a large public installation or theatrical event. For two years before the rooftop event, activities in different neighbourhoods were constructed to serve a need but configured as 'acts' within the whole 'performance': weekly youth leadership team meetings; youth presentations before Neighbourhood Crime Prevention Councils; art workshops for 350 probation and high school students; a prototype youth-police training series aired on local television; collaboration with non-profits and mentoring groups; and an artist team who designed the *Code 33* performance.

Our model was derived from process-based and media-critical visual arts theories and grew out of strategies that had continually evolved since 1970s feminist performance art. Here again, Kaprow's ideas were important in the transition from single event to complex and layered community performance. Kaprow emphasized art's meaning-making capacities. His focus on process could be extended such that all parts of a community-based artwork, including preparation and follow-up, were part of what I later termed an 'expanded performance'. Activities in *Code 33* were framed as components of (in Kaprow's terms) the entire life-like performance.

Although this work was not influenced by Boal's, and my own mentorship by Kaprow places me squarely in his visual arts lineage, *Code 33*'s deep structures bear an uncanny resemblance to Boal's Legislative Theatre. Speaking of this work, Boal suggests: 'It should be understood that rehearsals are already a cultural political meeting in themselves ... every exercise, every game, every technique is both art and politics' (*Legislative Theatre* [1998] 48). Boal and Kaprow share this and other aesthetic ideas, particularly those having to do with expanding boundaries of art, and relate to the times from which they drew their inspiration. While Kaprow clearly gives permission to include all subject matter as relevant, it is in Boal's work that we find evidence of a highly refined aesthetic of social justice in operation, one that informs and deepens the critique of feminist performance art.

The Public Gaze and the Politics of Perception

[Boal's] Theatre of the Oppressed and feminist art share a focus on the act of perceiving and the politics of perception. An often-related tale told by youth in *Code 33* goes like this: a black teenager is walking down a street and approaches a middle-aged white woman who involuntarily clutches her purse as she hurries past him. Knowing they are objects of a frightened, disapproving and racially charged gaze, youth often respond with aggressive boisterousness. One youth spoke with frustrated helplessness: 'They say, "Oh, he black, he rob, he kill." What can I do? I'm only sixteen years old. If nobody won't help me, I might as well do it.'

Boal, too, gives an example of the relationship of the gaze to oppression, one he observed in the Satrouville mental hospital: 'I was surprised at the expressions in [the nurses'] faces which changed according to whom they were looking at. When their eyes met mine, they were polite but when they looked at a kid, they became authoritarian, severe and tough.' ('Une expérience à Sartrouville', unpublished [1988] 22). He speculates on the personal impact of this intimidating intimate gaze.

> Let's assume that ... I was taken for a sick person. How long would I have been able to stand it? ... I am not saying that these kids became sick because of the [gaze of the] nurses ... They all had their own families' histories prior to being

> there which included ... alcoholic parents, poverty, overcrowded homes, dirty neighbourhoods, drugs, physical abuse ... They certainly did not need to be hurt by a simple gaze in order to be where they were. But this way of looking at people struck me in a powerful way. (Ibid.)

When I began working on the Oakland projects, it was in part because of the image publicly projected by groups of youth who walked from high school to a bus stop near where I worked. I was curious: who were these young people with their hooded sweatshirts, baggy pants and loud theatrical street discourse? The perceptual effect was an attractive one – textural, colourful and sonorous, with a group synergy that clearly excluded me. I was vaguely aware of increasingly ominous images in the early 1990s California mediascape: youth as unwed mothers, truants, drop-outs, addicts and criminals.

After a year volunteering in an Oakland high school, a shift occurred in my perceptual field. As crowds of youth walked by I no longer visually noted grey hooded sweatshirts but found myself unconsciously peering inside the hoods: was it one of the students from our class? Similarly, after a year of working as an artist with police officers, long enough to know several by name, I noticed another unbidden perceptual shift. Whereas earlier a black and white police car registered in my awareness by the pattern of its colour, calling forth a furtive re-examination of my recent actions, now the car's appearance was a signal to peer into the window in an attempt to recognize and identify its occupants. My looking was refined and individuated by intimacy.

For five weeks during the development of *Code 33*, after-school sessions of intensely moderated encounters between 18 youth and 12 police officers explored their stereotypes of each other, developing an underlying fabric of relationship that carried over into their encounters on the street. In participants' evaluations, both youth and police stressed the shift in their perception of the other. [...]

This personal/political positioning links Legislative Theatre and *Code 33*-type works; in both there is a metaphoric situating of the individual such that his or her body, or presence, challenges stereotypical perceptions and categories. In *Code 33*, actors and spectators represented themselves as individuals in the context of social stereotypes portrayed daily in Oakland newspapers. Suspecting that my shifts in perception of youth and police might be shared, to some degree, by an audience, *Code 33* presented the community with a more intimate access to real people in the process of trying to understand each other.

Legislative Theatre, too, restages and reinvents mediated images in a public setting, thus forcing the audience through steps in the politics of perception, toward intimacy:

> The aesthetic space is the creation of the audience: it requires nothing more than their attentive gaze in a single direction for this space to become 'aesthetic', powerful, 'hot', five-dimensional ... the objects no longer carry out their usual daily signification but become the stuff of memory and imagination ... [E]very tiny gesture is magnified, and the distant becomes closer. (*Legislative Theatre*, 71–2)

The significance of a civic site selected as a stage is not only based on geography and metaphor (in this case, the rooftop garage overlooked City Hall, source of policy for the city's youth, and the rooftop's height represented street life elevated to theatrical status) but on significance provided by the rapt gaze of the audience. Who the audience is and what experiences they bring to the event – whether activists protesting against police abuse, families of policemen, teachers, children, the elderly, African-American, Latino, white or South-east Asians, politicians, students or businessmen – provides aesthetic texture and political significance to this gaze. [...]

As with Legislative Theatre, the drama of *Code 33* relied upon real people assuming the roles they played in life, with legitimate stakes in the event. Performers traversed roles: some policemen and policewomen dropped their impenetrable façade and expressed vulnerability and fear, some youth offered advice to officers. Boal discusses the importance of transitive roles:

> The frontier between the actor and the spectator is no longer impassable because there is an exchange of duties ... It is the stable division of functions which has been transformed, as neither the actor nor the spectator plays the same role throughout the event ... the double role of all theatrical work has been preserved as the action always takes place under the control of a critical gaze. (Boal, cited in Banu, 'Augusto Boal and the Project of a Self-Managed Theatre', *International Theatre Yearbook* [1981] 6)

Of course not all performers experienced the transition between power and vulnerability. Very real power difference was always there ready to erupt at any sign of disturbance.

Visual and theatre artists working in communities struggle with a continuing quest to make their work effective and relevant. What they often cannot deliver is ongoing public policy and institutional change. [...]

Suzanne Lacy, extracts from 'Activism in Feminist Performance Art', in *A Boal Companion*, ed. Jan Cohen-Cruz and Mady Schulzman (London and New York: Routledge, 2006) 95–100.

Pierre Bourdieu and Alain Darbel
The Love of Art//1969

[...] The deliberate neglect of the social conditions which make possible culture, and culture to become nature, a cultivated nature with all the appearances of grace and talent but nevertheless learned and therefore 'deserved', is the condition for the existence of the charismatic ideology, which allows culture and especially 'the love of art' to be given the central place they occupy in the bourgeois 'sociodicy'. The heir of bourgeois privileges, not being able to invoke rights of birth (which his or her class historically denied the aristocracy) or the rights of nature, a weapon in the past levelled against nobiliary distinctions which would run the risk of backfiring against bourgeois *'distinction'*, or the ascetic virtues which allowed the first generation of entrepreneurs to justify their success by their merit, can call on cultivated nature and naturalized culture, on what is sometimes called 'class', by a sort of Freudian slip, on 'education', in the sense of a product of education which seems to owe nothing to education, on '*distinction*', a grace which is merit and a merit which is grace, an unacquired merit which justifies unmerited attainments, namely heritage. In order for culture to fulfil its function of legitimating inherited privileges, it is necessary and sufficient that the link between culture and education, at once obvious and hidden, should be *forgotten* or *denied*. The unnatural idea of a culture given at birth, a cultural gift bestowed on certain people by nature, supposes and produces a blindness to the functions of the institution which ensures the profitability of the cultural inheritance, and legitimates its transmission by hiding the fact that it fulfils this function. The school is in fact the institution which, by its positively irreproachable verdicts, transforms socially conditioned inequalities in matters of culture into inequalities of success, interpreted as inequalities of talent, which are also inequalities of merit. [...]

Pierre Bourdieu and Alain Darbel, extract from *L'Amour de l'art: les musées d'art européens et leur public* (Paris: Les Éditions de Minuit, 1969); trans. 'The Love of Art', in *Art in Modern Culture: An Anthology of Critical Texts*, ed. Francis Frascina and Jonathan Harris (London: Phaidon Press, 1992) 178.

Jacques Rancière
The Ignorant Schoolmaster//1987

An Intellectual Adventure

[...] Among those who wanted to avail themselves of him were a good number of students who did not speak French; but Joseph Jacotôt knew no Flemish. There was thus no language in which he could teach them what they sought from him. Yet he wanted to respond to their wishes. To do so, the minimal link of a *thing in common* had to be established between himself and them. At that time, a bilingual edition of *Télémaque* was being published in Brussels.[1] The thing in common had been found, and Telemachus made his way into the life of Joseph Jacotôt. He had the book delivered to the students and asked them, through an interpreter, to learn the French text with the help of the translation. When they had made it through the first half of the book, he had them repeat what they had learned over and over, and then told them to read through the rest of the book until they could recite it. This was a fortunate solution, but it was also, on a small scale, a philosophical experiment in the style of the ones performed during the Age of Enlightenment. And Joseph Jacotôt, in 1818, remained a man of the preceding century.

But the experiment exceeded his expectations. He asked the students who had prepared as instructed to write in French what they thought about what they had read:

> He expected horrendous barbarisms, or maybe a complete inability to perform. How could these young people, deprived of explanation, understand and resolve the difficulties of a language entirely new to them? No matter! He had to find out where the route opened by chance had taken them, what had been the results of that desperate empiricism. And how surprised he was to discover that the students, left to themselves, managed this difficult step as well as many French could have done! Was wanting all that was necessary for doing? Were all men virtually capable of understanding what others had done and understood?' (Félix and Victor Ratier, 'Enseignement universel: Emancipation intellectuelle', *Journal de philosophie panécastique*, no. 5 [1838] 155) [...]

The revelation that came to Joseph Jacotôt amounts to this: the logic of the explicative system had to be overturned. Explication is not necessary to remedy an incapacity to understand. On the contrary, that very incapacity provides the structuring fiction of the explicative conception of the world. It is the explicator who needs the incapable and not the other way around; it is he who constitutes the incapable as such. To explain something to someone is first of all to show him he cannot understand it by himself. Before being the act of the pedagogue, explication is the myth of pedagogy, the parable of a world divided into knowing minds and ignorant ones, ripe minds and immature ones, the capable and the incapable, the intelligent and the stupid. The explicator's special trick consists of this double inaugural gesture. On the one hand, he decrees the absolute beginning: it is only now that the act of learning will begin. On the other, having thrown a veil of ignorance over everything that is to be learned, he appoints himself to the task of lifting it. Until he came along, the child has been groping – blindly, figuring out riddles. Now he will learn. He heard words and repeated them. But now it is time to read, and he will not understand words if he doesn't understand syllables, and he won't understand syllables if he doesn't understand letters that neither the book nor his parents can make him understand – only the master's word. The pedagogical myth, we said, divides the world into two. More precisely, it divides intelligence into two. It says that there is an inferior intelligence and a superior one. The former registers perceptions by chance, retains them, interprets and repeats them empirically, within the closed circle of habit and need. This is the intelligence of the young child and the common man. The superior intelligence knows things by reason, proceeds by method, from the simple to the complex, from the part to the whole. It is this intelligence that allows the master to transmit his knowledge by adapting it to the intellectual capacities of the student and allows him to verify that the student has satisfactorily understood what he learned. Such is the principle of explication. From this point on, for Jacotôt, such will be the principle of *enforced stultification*. [...]

The experiment seemed to him sufficient to shed light: one can teach what one doesn't know if the student is emancipated, that is to say, if he is obliged to use his own intelligence. The master is he who encloses an intelligence in the arbitrary circle from which it can only break out by becoming necessary to itself. To emancipate an ignorant person, one must be, and one need only be, emancipated oneself, that is to say, conscious of the true power of the human mind. The ignorant person will learn by himself what the master doesn't know if the master believes he can and obliges him to realize his capacity: a circle of *power* homologous to the circle of powerlessness that ties the student to the explicator of the old method (to be called from now on, simply, the Old Master). But the relation of forces is very particular. The circle of powerlessness is always already there: it is the very workings of the social world, hidden in the evident difference between ignorance and science. The circle of power, on the other hand, can only take effect by being made public. But it can only appear as a tautology or an absurdity. How can the learned master ever understand that he can teach what he doesn't know as successfully as what he does know? He cannot but take that increase in intellectual power as a devaluation of his science. And the ignorant one, on his side, doesn't believe himself capable of learning by himself, still less of being able to teach another ignorant person. Those excluded from the world of intelligence themselves subscribe to the verdict of their exclusion. In short, the circle of emancipation must be *begun*.

Here lies the paradox. For if you think about it a little, the 'method' he was proposing is the oldest in the world, and it never stops being verified every day, in all the circumstances where an individual must learn something without any means of having it explained to him. There is no one on earth who hasn't learned something by himself and without a master explicator. Let's call this way of learning 'universal teaching'. [...]

The Ignorant One's Lesson

[...] This is the first principle of universal teaching: one must learn something and relate everything else to it. [...] The Old Master would say: such and such a thing must be learned, and then this other thing and after that, this other. Selection, progression, incompletion: these are his principles. We learn rules and elements, then apply them to some chosen reading passages, and then do some exercises based on the acquired rudiments. Then we graduate to a higher level: other rudiments, another book, other exercises, another professor. At each stage the abyss of ignorance is dug again; the professor fills it in before digging another. [...] The same nature that opens up a career in science to all minds wants a social order where the classes are separated and where individuals conform to the social state that is their destiny.

The solution to this contradiction is found in the ordered balance of instruction and moral education, the dividing up of the roles that fall to the schoolmaster and to the father of the family. Using the light of instruction, the first chases away the false ideas the child receives from his parental milieu; the second, by moral education, chases away the extravagant aspirations the schoolchild would like to extract from his young science and take back to his life condition. The father, incapable of drawing on his own experience to further his child's intellectual instruction, is, on the other hand, all-powerful in teaching him, by word and example, the virtue of remaining in his condition. The family is at once the nucleus of intellectual incapacity and the principle of ethical objectivity. [...]

Reason between Equals

[...] We know that improvisation is one of the canonical exercises of universal teaching. But it is first of all the exercise of our intelligence's leading virtue: the poetic virtue. The impossibility of our *saying* the truth, even when we *feel* it, makes us speak as poets, makes us tell the story of our mind's adventures and verify that they are understood by other adventurers, makes us communicate our feelings and see them shared by other feeling beings. Improvisation is the exercise by which the human being knows himself and is confirmed in his nature as a reasonable man, that is to say, as an animal 'who makes words, figures and comparisons, to tell the story of what he thinks to those like him'. The virtue of our intelligence is less in knowing than in doing. 'Knowing is nothing, *doing* is everything.' But this doing is fundamentally an act of communication. And, for that, '*speaking* is the best proof of the capacity to do whatever it is.' In the act of speaking, man doesn't transmit his knowledge, he makes poetry; he translates and invites others to do the same. He communicates as an *artisan*: as a person who handles words like tools. Man communicates with man through the works of his hands just as through the words of his speech: 'When man acts on matter, the body's adventures become the story of the mind's adventures.' And the artisan's emancipation is first the regaining of that story, the consciousness that one's material activity is of the nature of discourse. He communicates as a *poet*: as a being who believes his thought communicable, his emotions sharable. That is why speech and the conception of all works as discourse are, according to universal teaching's logic, a prerequisite to any learning. The artisan must speak about his works in order to be emancipated; the student must speak about the art he wants to learn. 'Speaking about human works is the way to know human art.' [...]

The Emancipator and His Monkey

The duty of Joseph Jacotôt's disciples is thus simple. They must announce to everyone, in all places and all circumstances, the news, the practice: one can teach what one doesn't know. A poor and ignorant father can thus begin educating his children: *something must be learned and all the rest related to it, on this principle: everyone is of equal intelligence.*

They must announce this principle and devote themselves to its verification: speak to the destitute person, make him talk about what he is and what he knows; show him how to instruct his child; copy the prayer that the child knows by heart; give him the first volume of *Télémaque* and have him learn it by heart; respond to the demand of those who want to learn from the master of universal teaching *what he doesn't know*; finally, use all possible means of convincing the ignorant one of his power. A disciple in Grenoble couldn't persuade a poor and elderly woman to learn to read and write. He paid her to get her consent. She learned in five months, and now she is emancipating her grandchildren. [...] And education is like liberty: it isn't given; it's taken. [...]

1 [François Fénelon's *Télémaque* (*c.* 1695) was one of the most popular prescribed texts for teaching in the eighteenth and nineteenth centuries. Constructed as a continuation of Book IV of the

Odyssey, where Telemachus learns that his father Ulysses is detained on Calypso's isle, it functions as a 'pedagogical' fable, prefiguring Enlightenment ideas.]

Jacques Rancière, extracts from *Le Maître ignorant* (Paris: Fayard, 1987); trans. Kristin Ross, *The Ignorant Schoolmaster: Five Lessons in Intellectual Emancipation* (Stanford: Stanford University Press, 1991) 1–2; 6–7; 15–16; 20–21; 35; 64; 101; 107.

Jimmie Durham
Amusing Personal Anecdote//1988

I was actually taught opposites in school. That was in Arkansas, where everything is clear, in about my fifth year in school. (I think I must have been 11 years old by the European system of counting.) I had previously been taught that the correct way to say 'possum' was 'opossum', so I imagined that we probably said 'posits', and I listened to adults to see if I could hear that word and show off my new knowledge.

The teacher said that black was the opposite of white, sweet was the opposite of sour, and up was the opposite of down. I began to make my own list of opposites: the number one must be the opposite of the number ten, ice was the opposite of water, and birds were the opposite of snakes.

But I soon had problems, because if snakes and birds were opposite, where could I put the flying rattlesnake, which we saw every evening as the rattlesnake star? I theorized that in special circumstances things could act like their opposites. If grey is the blending of the opposites white and black then the flying rattlesnake could be seen as a grey bird. That worked out well because our most common bird was the mockingbird, which everyone knows likes to eat pokeberries to get drunk – an activity closer to snake behaviour than to bird behaviour. I said to my family, 'What is the opposite of a mockingbird?' 'A mockingbird, ha ha ha.' They didn't get it.

Much later in life some African friends made me study Marx and Engels, wherein I learned that progress is simply a matter of opposites pushing against each other. The cop pushes me, I push the cop; the cop puts me in jail where I have time to plan my next move and strengthen my resolve. My opposite, the cop, is unaware that he has played a part in my development and in the overall scheme of human liberation. I give him a superior smile, which heightens the dialectical struggle.

The moral: dialectically we are far beyond the stage when your folks came over and pushed my folks. We have now reached the stage where I get paid real money for writing these words because some of your artists try to steal our images. Ha, ha, sucker, I win! [...]

Jimmie Durham, extract from 'The Search for Virginity' (1988), in Jimmie Durham, *A Certain Lack of Coherence: Writings on Art and Cultural Politics*, ed. Jean Fisher (London: Kala Press, 1993) 154–5.

Elliot W. Eisner
Evaluation and Assessment: Conceptions in Search of Practice//1996

1 Art education historically has embraced a set of educational aims that appear inimicable to the aims reflected in the use of standardized achievement tests. The result has been a paucity of such devices in the field.
2 Although the virtual absence of standardized achievement tests provides no tradition that needs to be abandoned in order to be innovative, attitudes among art educators towards assessment in the visual arts may still be less than enthusiastic.
3 The different functions of assessment need to be appreciated so that a single approach does not, by fiat, define how assessment is to occur and for what purposes.
4 The subject matters of assessment as well as its functions differ. Programme content and teaching practices as well as student outcomes should be regarded as critically important commonplaces for assessment. [...]

Elliot W. Eisner, extract from 'Evaluation and Assessment: Conceptions in Search of Practice', in *Evaluating and Assessing the Visual Arts in Education: International Perspectives*, ed. Doug Boughton, Elliot W. Eisner, Johan Ligvoet (New York: The Teachers College Press, 1996) 7.

Dennis Atkinson
Art in Education: Identity and Practice//2002

[...] The discursive norms stated by SCAA [the National Curriculum School Curriculum and Assessment Authority, England, 1996] are: *working towards*, *achieving* and *working beyond* the expectation of practice, which in this particular case is concerned with recording responses, through observation of the natural and made environment. These three categories establish a normative framework in which students' art practice is assessed, positioned and regulated, but no definitions of what constitutes a particular norm of *working towards*, *achieving* or *working beyond* are provided. But as we read on, and consider the assessment comments for each of three paintings, what the norm consists of becomes clearer.

The SCAA assessment comments focus upon the student's ability to record what is seen, and, significantly, the term *accurate* is employed as a key assessment criterion. The painting considered to be working towards the expectation of practice at this key stage is described:

> Information about the shapes of buildings and machinery which feature in the environment has been observed and recorded, but greater analysis is needed in order to represent this accurately. (Sir Ron Dearing, Foreword, *Consistency in Teacher Assessment: Exemplification of Standards* [1996] 8.)

The painting viewed as *achieving* the expected standard is described:

> The shapes of building and other objects in the environment have been selected, analysed and represented with some accuracy, technical skill and attention to detail which indicates first-hand observation. (Ibid., 9.)

The painting assessed as *working beyond* the expected standard is described:

> There is detailed and accurate analysis of the buildings and their surroundings. The shapes of buildings and details of the setting have been selected, recorded and organized into a coherent form. (Ibid., 10.)

The frequent use of the term *accuracy* and other terms, *observation* and *technical skill*, is telling and I believe that it is this deceptive word which constitutes the norm according to which the paintings are assessed. Further, it is according to this *accuracy* that each student's pedagogized identity as a subject of art practice is produced. What does this term imply in the context of the student's art practice, which is concerned with recording observations of the natural and made environment? I suggest in the context of this specific drawing and painting activity it implies that drawing and painting as practices of observation and representation are concerned with the depiction of accurate views (and that this is achievable). A further implication is that vision is assumed to be a universal process in which data from the external world are received unmediated and that the ability to render this unmediated information rests upon the individual student's skill. The term *accurate* implies, I suggest, that it is possible to produce a representation that directly corresponds to a particular view. Thus this term invokes what I have called earlier a particular discourse and practice of visuality in which each student's art work *becomes visible and regulated as art practice*. Variation in the standards (of accuracy) achieved by each student rests upon their varying ability as determined by this specific discourse and practice of visuality.

An interesting issue here is that it is well understood by many people that observational painting and drawing does not mirror reality, yet there is still a tendency, as the use of the words *accurate, technical skill* and *observation* demonstrate, to act as though that is its purpose. The term *accurate* establishes a conterminous relation between a visual representation and a prior observed reality and simultaneously a normative structure of representation within which the three paintings are positioned. Once we acknowledge that an *accurate visual representation* of perceptual experience is not possible, we might also begin to consider how the term *accuracy* is being used. I suspect that rather than invoking a prior reality which can be used as an assessment yardstick, it invokes an established and valued representational system. Thus the term *accuracy* is not concerned with the depiction of optical truth but with the ability to conform to a particular semiotic practice. Crucially then the term *accuracy* is a key discursive figure which designates a student's painting practice not simply and directly for other individuals such as other students and teachers, but primarily for the symbolic and normative order of a particular representational system in which the three paintings are inserted in order to achieve meaning. [...]

The approach to assessment of students' artwork I have just described can therefore be understood as a specific discursive practice in which particular norms of practice are established and according to which students' practices are positioned, regulated and understood. Such assessment practices are constituted by powerful codes of recognition through which student's artwork is made visible. The immanence of power in such discursive practices is often difficult to detect because of our tendency to comprehend such practices as based upon natural capacities or facilities. But it is through the consecration of particular forms of art practice and the subsequent consecration of particular students of practice (often those seen to possess artistic talent) that relations of power in the pedagogic context constitute specific pedagogized identities in the field of art education.

Power-Knowledge

Foucault employs the term *power-knowledge* to describe how knowledge is imbued with power in fields of practice. Manifestations of power-knowledge can be seen in the relations developed between teachers and students where particular forms of practice and knowledge are desired. Such relations can also be found in the construction and imposition of curriculum content and practices by government who then assess teachers' competence according to government standards. One view of knowledge and power is to regard them as separate entities whereby knowledge is viewed as a search for truth that is taken to exist in particular fields of practice. Power, on the other hand, is often regarded as a kind of possession used to dominate others particularly in institutional contexts or organizations such as the state. Foucault's integration of power-knowledge invokes the idea that the acquisition, transmission or use of knowledge, (particularly disciplinary knowledge of pedagogic or curriculum discourses which constitute different teaching sites) implicate forms of power. [...]

To understand this idea it is important to remember [...] the idea that discourses constitute truths as opposed to revealing truths. The fact that a particular discourse of assessment in art education leads to the production of pedagogic identity means that the knowledge which constitutes this practice is imbued with power. [...]

Dennis Atkinson, extracts from *Art in Education: Identity and Practice* (Dordrecht: Kluwer Academic Publishers 2002) 102–5.

Dennis Atkinson
Pedagogy of the Event//2009

[...] Michel Foucault's later work moved from exploring the subject as an effect of discourse towards seeing the formation of the subject *in relation to norms*, and it is in and through such *relations* that the self as a human process comes to be viewed as an act of poiesis, a creative and aesthetic process which incorporates a process of critique. This critical position in relation to normalizing frameworks provides a basis upon which we might begin to question the parameters of teaching and learning in which pedagogized subjects are produced. Such critical practice introduces a question of ethics, in that the critique of normalizing frameworks is, by implication, a critique of self, in that the self is organized/recognized and constituted within such frameworks. However, this critique, I would argue, is precipitated through disturbances, or events, in practice, and I think it is towards such disturbances that Judith Butler alludes when she comments:

> With the help of Foucault's self-criticism, it may be possible to show that the question of ethics emerges precisely at the limits of our schemes of intelligibility, [those sites] where we ask ourselves what it might mean to continue in a dialogue where no common ground can be assumed, where one is, as it were, at the limits of what one knows yet still under the demand to offer and receive acknowledgement: to someone else who is there to be addressed and whose address is there to be received. (Butler, *Giving an Account of Oneself* [2005] 21–2, my parentheses.)

In pedagogic relations it is not uncommon to have experiences in which what happens cannot be understood within established frameworks when we assume common ground but which in fact is not secure. Extending Foucault's writing to this kind of situation, where teachers begin to question how they respond to learners when the latter do not conform to established frameworks of understanding, suggests that teachers are in a sense putting themselves at risk, becoming unrecognized within the normalizing frameworks that govern their practice. Is the teacher in such a situation risking his or her identity and professional standing by contravening the norms that govern '*the scene of recognition*' anticipated by other professionals (inspectors, etc.) who want or need to feel reassured? Is the teacher in such situations indirectly asking the question who he or she is? Is she entering the not-known? Does this state involve a questioning of the domain of the thinkable (Rancière)?

Consequently what kind of forms of address should a teacher as a reflective practitioner find appropriate in relation to such 'insecure' or 'uncertain' pedagogical relations? In such relations it does not seem appropriate to take a reflective or reflexive stance towards the self in terms of a current or future ontology but rather to ask the question, 'Who are you?' This posits the notion that there is a subject in the pedagogic relation who the teacher probably does not fully comprehend. Here the relation to the other disrupts the self. This seems to indicate a tension between representation and 'what happens'.

If in a pedagogical relation the learner is fantasized through the norm, the Other of the norm, then the learner becomes a surrogate identity (she produces what the teacher expects). If the pedagogical encounter begins from the question, 'who are you?' then a different relation seems to emerge and it is possible to turn this question into, 'How does the other learn?'

Pedagogy against the State

The notion of risk-taking has often been put forward by educators in order to promote creative and individual approaches to learning (e.g. Swift and Steers, *A Manifesto for Art in Schools*, 1999). The idea of learners being encouraged to take risks in their specific learning context suggests a pedagogy that is not totally controlled by specified learning outcomes. It suggests a flexible teaching-learning space that attempts to accommodate unpredictable or unexpected directions in learning. Encouraging learners to take risks in their practice, by implication, suggests that teachers themselves are also taking risks in that they have to be able to 'let things happen'; they have to be able to facilitate these learning pathways without a clear sense of outcome. But how can we understand the idea of risk-taking? Is it possible to provide a theoretical basis upon which to enhance our understanding of this concept that takes us beyond the prosaic idea of 'taking a chance' and thereby provide pedagogy with a more substantial theoretical underpinning of this concept?

I believe that we can develop this line of enquiry by thinking about real learning arising through an event which involves a movement into a new or changed ontological state. Learning can thus be conceived as a problem of existence as it involves this ontological evolution. If real learning, as I call it, involves a disruption of established states of pedagogical knowledge and practice through which learners are recognized but through which such recognition may also be constraining, then a pedagogy commensurate with such disruption is required, a pedagogy which I call *pedagogy against the state*, or perhaps, a *pedagogy of the event*, in order to expand our grasp of what it is to learn and lead to the possibility of forming new and more effective learning communities.

Immanent to such pedagogy is therefore a movement against itself. The ethical imperative for pedagogy therefore is concerned with maximizing the power of learning; it is not focused on what we are and should be, that is to say on some transcendent position towards being, but upon the potentiality and 'unknown' of becoming. An ethics of the unknown, an ethics of becoming. [...]

Dennis Atkinson, extract from transcript of 'Pedagogy of the Event', paper presented at symposium: 'On Not Knowing: How Artists Think' (Cambridge, England: Kettles Yard, 29 June 2009).

Rebecca Sinker
On the Evolution of a Peer-Led Programme//2008

Tate Forum was set up in 2002 as a peer-led youth advisory group [which involves] young people, aged 13 to 25, through a range of different events and projects. It was developed at Tate Britain, building on peer-led youth groups first established in 1988 at Tate Liverpool. [...] The six month projects for young people are funded through Study Support and, recently, through the John Lyons Charity. For several years we have also worked with Children's Services teams in Westminster and Harrow, to develop creative opportunities for looked-after children (LAC) and young people leaving care, as well as with the Cardinal Hume drop-in centre for young homeless people.

The other programmed drop-in activities and events are for a broad audience of young Londoners, marketed through the Young Tate website, e-bulletins, MySpace, local radio spots, club flyers, schools and colleges. [...]

The present Tate Forum structure consists of bi-weekly, two-hour evening meetings [facilitated by staff at Tate Britain, London] throughout the year when members meet and plan projects and events. [...] Members take an active part in youth programme development and production. Those over 16 are also invited to become involved in other departmental events such as Late at Tate or Education Open Evenings, for which they are paid.

Over the year Tate Forum plan a number of short, public events, programmed for young audiences, including artists' talks, creative art workshops and online projects. Devising, marketing, running, documenting and evaluating the projects is the responsibility of the young people, in consultation and with support from the Youth Curator and other relevant members of Tate staff.

In terms of being peer-led, Tate Forum has largely migrated from rung 6 to the current structure between rungs 7 and 8 on Hart's ladder of youth participation:

1 Manipulation
2 Decoration
3 Tokenism
4 Young people given assigned role but informed
5 Young people consulted and informed
6 Adult-initiated projects or programmes, shared decisions with young people
7 Young people-initiated and directed, supported by adults
8 Young people-initiated projects or programmes, shared decisions with adults

In several cases the early members of Tate Forum have grown with and shaped the programme's evolution. [...]

> We're young, we need help or we want inspiration, we could go to the Tate and come back feeling like we've got a lot of work done, and process it for Art [General Certificate of Secondary Education] and it was really helpful. But it also helped with stuff outside of art ... it was a real eye-opener to a world outside of art and how there are other types of art than just paintings ... we learned that art isn't just whatever you would say was a painting, a drawing or a sculpture – art is whatever you make it to be because art is an expression of yourself. (Sean Labode)

The structure of Tate Forum as a peer-led group based in a gallery, offered freedom from a formal model of art education for Charlotte Allen, who loves art but hated the way it was taught in school. She prefaced this by stating, 'My family are not artistic in any shape or form.'

> I've lost interest in art in the classrooms, I don't see why I have to be in a classroom to draw or do anything, why do I have to be regimented? Why do I have to do what my teacher says when surely art is an opinionated subject? ... I see coming here as what I think art should be – it shouldn't be in the classroom, it should be in galleries, it should be outside ... that's what I think is the problem with art in schools. [...]

As Nivek Amichund says, 'I think I have a different mindset because I'm not an artist ... I don't think art is only for artists.' Nivek joined the group in order to meet more people of his own age. Arriving in Britain from South Africa in 2004, he took work as a gallery assistant (because he needed a job.) He wasn't interested in art and hadn't studied it – in fact it was taken off the curriculum in his school in South Africa and was not valued as an educational subject or a profession. But Nivek has taken an active role in Tate Forum, and subsequently in Tate's 'Visual Dialogues' project. He clearly sees Tate Forum as a door to other opportunities, as well as valuing the social aspect of the group, 'I saw I'd get free training in public speaking, learn about organizing events and marketing, getting to know the right people, Tate Forum does all of that, it opens up the doors ...' [...]

Rebecca Sinker, extracts from 'On the Evolution of a Peer-led Programme', *Engage*, no. 22, ed. Karen Raney (London, 2008) 25–8.

Carmen Mörsch
Take the Terror out of Error//2009

[...] In 'Queering Gallery Education', an article written for the journal *Ästhetik & Kommunikation* prior to this letter [to participants], I had speculated whether power relationships at Documenta 12 could be temporarily shifted. I found it a risky but nonetheless promising venture to promote the interaction between local interest groups and the gallery education team by inviting specific groups that some educators in particular, and/or the institution as a whole, thought they could learn from.

These 'special' invitations aimed at inverting the paternalistic approach of gallery education, which emphasizes targeting subjects supposedly 'excluded' from the art world: instead of 'introducing' those 'excluded' from the exhibition, it is the institution itself which, isolated as it is from so many different realities, needs to be carefully familiarized with the latter. A further gesture of reversal lay in the effort to address specific segments of the public sphere – among them some of the smallest and most unlikely – rather than abandoning the exhibition to the large numbers of 'interested' visitors who could be relied on to come.

Although these attempted reversals maintained a critical position in regard to an almost unrecorded history of gallery education – that of audience development – they could do little to change the underlying paradox: the question of how to plan in advance with a particular interest group in mind, without cementing any identity ascriptions. [...] [T]his dilemma is unsolvable, for it generates a conflict that is fundamentally at the heart of gallery education. Finding a possible answer to it depends on the degree of collaboration with those who accept the invitation. How such cooperation actually unfolds determines whether paternalism, emancipation or even indifference will prevail. Most of the time, all three aspects are at play – negotiating between them is part of what the job is all about. [...]

At the beginning, my wish to initiate gallery education projects at Documenta 12 along these lines bore enormous expectations. The projects I considered paradigmatic were embedded in an institutional context in which programmatic and controversial discussions had been taking place for many decades, and in which a great deal of money and energy had been invested. In particular, I thought of the three-year research project Tate Encounters of the education department at Tate Britain, whereby a group of visitors, gallery educators and researchers use a variety of media and methodologies to examine ways in which narratives of Britishness are constructed in the Tate displays. Or consider the

Turner Contemporary in Margate, which, as the museum undergoes const… is already involved in an educational programme that foresees the participa… of diverse audiences. And there are also London's Serpentine Gallery, the Photographers Gallery, and Camden Arts Centre, all of which feature a gallery education programme run independently of exhibition activities, if not the art world market, and in which – at least in my opinion – some of the most interesting activities have taken place. This doesn't mean I had indulged in the illusion that we could reproduce these examples, for they developed out of completely different economic, historical, cultural and political conditions. Rather, what interested me about the prospective Documenta 12 projects was the possibility that – combined with the activities of the Documenta 12 advisory board – they might showcase future avenues for the development of gallery education in coming Documenta exhibitions. But it was precisely this need to set an example that exerted an unavoidable pressure, under the circumstances. There was no institutional funding for the projects. [...]

I would like to mention what I had least expected while reading through your texts [invited in response to the programme]: the effect made on me by the way in which project participants expressed themselves. The sound files for *Urban Ghosts* or the texts from the *Kassel Apollo meets Documenta 12* reader, the contributions in brochures such as *Personal Lives* or the radio and video recordings of the different project discussions in the exhibition, all provoked an unexpected emotional response in me, like a kind of gallery education 'punctum'. What remains, after my analytically trained eye identifies and removes clichés and familiar phraseologies, is the unambiguousness of the relevance of your projects to those who were willing to participate in them, no matter how difficult it was for me to endure some of their reactions. Besides your reflections and your more than fulfilled aims, this significance and urgency answers all allegations of paternalism, instrumentalism, of reproducing the symbolic order, or of reinforcing hegemonic and neoliberal conditions. It responds to these allegations without dismissing them. It simply provides an alternative to a paranoid reading.

In a 2003 collection of essays entitled *Touching Feeling: Affect, Pedagogy, Performativity* by the queer and literary theorist Eve Kosofsky Sedgwick, I found, for the first time, a different proposal for a structure of thought which, while not attempting to replace a decades-old critical theory, an almost uncontested practice of paranoid reading, or a 'hermeneutics of suspicion', invites us to consider these and other readings of reality as lying alongside one another – and to ponder readings that don't only engage in indisputably necessary practices of exposure. In fact, the title of this letter (I know, most letters don't have a title) comes from one of Sedgwick's essays. I find the political dimension of her proposal very convincing, and I draw a connection here to your projects. She the practice of exposing hidden connections, on which critical grounded, nor proposes to replace it with affect or some kind of l immediacy. Instead, she considers existing or dominant relations eless advocating a collective and supportive agency, without singling out the practice of exposure as the only possible practice. On another level, she points to the structural similarities between the uncovering of repression and repression itself. Thus, Sedgwick questions whether there is any possible criticism of the phallus without re-erecting it. Here I am reminded, again, of the power relationships within the gallery education team, brought about by different commands of discourses and power of definition, and abilities to articulate a critique of power relationships. How to avoid this in the future is a question that I often ponder. I believe that each accusation of 'instrumentalism' entails an act of victimization, for it implies that the people involved do not know what they are getting into, that they can neither stand for their own rights nor gauge the real situation, and thus are less smart than the responsible ones. Many of your projects casually demonstrate that the people involved do not articulate themselves as a weak counterpart; they prove the uncontrollability, the resoluteness and self-interest of subjects and groups.

Carmen Mörsch [co-organizer, with Ulrich Schötker, of the educational mediation concept for Documenta 12], extracts from 'Take the Terror out of Error', a letter to participants, in *Documenta 12: Education 1*, ed. Wanda Wieczorek, et al. (Berlin and Zürich: Diaphanes, 2009) 101–6.

Luis Camnitzer
Art and Literacy//2009

[...] Interestingly, at least in the languages I know, when one talks about alphabetization there is always the mention of reading and writing, in that order. Ideologically speaking, this prioritized order not only reflects the division between production and consumption, but subliminally emphasizes the latter: ignorance is shown more by the inability to read than by the inability to write. Further, this order suggests that alphabetization is more important for the reception of orders than for their emission. [...]

Educational institutions expect everybody to be able to learn how to read and write. It would follow that, if everybody has the potential to use reading and writing for expression, everybody should also have the potential to be an artist.

Yet in art the assumption is different. Everybody may be able to appreciate art, but only a few are expected to produce it – not all readers are writers. [...]

Forty years ago, I was invited to organize the art department in a US university. I refused on the grounds that art is not really 'art' but a method to acquire and expand knowledge. Consequently, art should shape all academic activities within a university and not be confined to a discipline. I recognize that my position reflected a form of art-imperialism, and this is something I still adhere to. As in all imperialisms, my position was not necessarily based on solid information and I used aggression as a tool for persuasion. Predictably, I was defeated, and shortly after was condemned to solitary confinement in the art department I had so proudly rejected. Yet I am unrepentant: I continue to operate with poorly informed opinions, I continue to be aggressive, and, to be sure, I will continue to be defeated.

My imperialism is based on a generalist view of art in which everything (including the 'rest') can be seen as art. I also believe that the social structures that divide us into producers and consumers – those that ensure our lives conform to the laws of the market instead of seeking a collective wellbeing – should be demolished. These were the views we developed as students during the late 1950s while I was in art school in Uruguay.

They clarified claims surrounding the ownership of knowledge, how that ownership is distributed, and who benefits from it. Even if these issues are normally considered to be outside the scope of art, it is on their account that the use of language and the means of engaging illiteracy become interesting to art. [...]

Both art education and alphabetization have in common the dual and often contradictory mission of facilitating individual and collective cultural affirmation and expression on the one hand, and of being necessary tools to cement and expand forms of consumption on the other. Consequently, education is not only an ideologically fractured field, but one in which each of its ideologies assumes its own particular pedagogical approach to apply to all fields of knowledge, overcoming all irresolvable contradictions. When reasonably progressive, such pedagogies assume that one can ensure the stability and smoothness of the existing society while at the same time forming critically questioning, non-submissive, creative individuals. This approach takes for granted that education will create good, accepting citizens who play by the rules, but who will also be subversive individuals attempting to change that society. In a conservative pedagogical approach, the latter part of the mission will simply be ignored.

As it is, the educational system emphasizes good citizenship during the early stages of formation and postpones any potential subversion until the postgraduate level. Speculation and imagination are allowed only after becoming a good citizen. In order for actual subversion to take place, it would first have to address the earlier parts of the educational process. This explains why alphabetization takes place at the beginning of the educational voyage while true art-making is placed at its end, or is indeed postponed until after formal education is over.

The tension that emerges from this built-in stability/instability contradiction creates two main divisions in how education is approached: between 'integralism' and 'fragmentalism', on the one hand; and between tutorial education and massive education, on the other. [...]

A real education for an artist consists of preparation for a pure research of the unknown. In a strong art education, this starts at the very beginning. But as institutional education in other areas is organized to convey only known information and to perpetuate conventional habits, these are two pedagogies in fundamental conflict. Where, then, should the fight against illiteracy be placed? Should alphabetization be handled as a subject for training or as a tool for discovery?

The question may be too schematic. In art, pure discovery leads to amateurism, while pure training leads to empty professionalism – good preparation ultimately seeks a balance between them. [...] In other words, we need a pedagogy that includes speculation, analysis and subversion of conventions, one that addresses literacy in the same way as any good art education addresses art. This means putting literacy into the context of art. By forcing art to focus on these things, in turn, the art empire itself will also be enriched.

Luis Camnitzer, extracts from 'Art and Literacy', first presented as a paper at the First International Meeting on Education, Art and Functional Illiteracy, Rio de Janeiro, 1–3 December 2008; published in *e-flux journal*, no. 3 (February 2009) www.e-flux.com

Henry Ward
Opening the Box//2010

Welling School is a specialist visual arts college in the borough of Bexley on the outskirts of London. The school is large, with over 1600 students aged 11-18, and is non-selective in an area that still operates the grammar school system. The vast majority of our students come to us having failed their 11 plus exam. The visual arts faculty has built a reputation for pioneering the use of contemporary art practice in the classroom, and making use of the school's gallery.

I teach on the principle that all students are already artists. Billy, a 17-year old student, made a work using footballs: he would climb on top of the school roofs to find the footballs that had ended up on the roof, and he cast them into concrete. I saw them as a sort of monument to something lost. I don't think Billy understood how poignant this is for an adult: I couldn't make a work like this now.

Our teaching is responsive to each group of students, each situation. Sometimes we create installations that provoke students to reflect on their work, which leads to profound shifts in their work that they sustain over a long period.

The school bought interactive whiteboards which generated an enormous amount of cardboard from their boxes. We had an impending Ofsted inspection, so, testing the idea of inspection, I created a shanty town of eight or nine separate studios with the boxes and allocated them to the students. I couldn't see any of the students in the class, and there was no point in writing anything on the board because they couldn't see it. A GCSE student made a tunnel to make it really, really private, and the privacy really worked. From a playful project, putting kids in boxes, students made significant developments in their work.

The Ofsted inspector said, 'Don't mind me', and she got down on her hands and knees and crawled into these big boxes and talked to the students. She thought it was fantastic, 'real work'.

One of the most frustrating things about being an art teacher is trying to maintain your own practice and being in the classroom as a practitioner. One thing is possibly to embrace what you do in classroom as practice in its own right, although there is a downside to this. There's no switch off.

Henry Ward, from a talk given at 'Two Words Four Talks', Welling School's Biannual Arts and Education Conference (Welling, Kent, England, 2010).

Michael Archer
Educating Art Away from Life//2010

How does art practice fit into the current structuring of education? It is all very well to insist that art students are already making art, but you have to be careful not to make that claim in bad faith. Whatever students do has to be understandable to some extent within the framework not of the gallery but of the art school. Which is to say, it's fine to agree that it's art, but it is going to be assessed according to a set of criteria printed in a course handbook. If you want to believe that these two things are straightforwardly reconcilable, or that they are the same thing, or that you can ignore one aspect in favour of the other, then you're probably doing a lousy job as a tutor. The difficulty from the tutor's perspective is that for him or her, too, there are increasing pressures to treat the demands of art and the requirements of educational assessment as one and the same thing. Over a number of years art practice has been forced to claim itself as a legitimate form of research activity. This shift, from seeing one's activity as practice, to describing it as research, is one that has been driven not by art but by educational institutions and, beyond them, the government mechanisms that control their funding streams. It's no longer the case that you are a professional who supplements your income by teaching in an art school, you now find yourself within the art school in order to behave as a professional artist. What you do, whatever its motivation, its form, its character, its ambition, has to be made understandable in educational terms. You log everything you've produced within the period of each REF (Research Excellence Framework) assessment of the university. All the art you've made, the exhibitions, are understood as research outcomes so that they (i.e. You) can be assessed. It's perfectly possible to say 'for the purposes of this exercise we will call what I do research' but, inevitably, it becomes understood in those terms and people find themselves behaving accordingly. It is risible, it is pernicious, and it is the reality within which we work.

In Britain, and increasingly elsewhere, this idea of art practice as research has been embedded through the introduction of the Ph.D. Questions are raised about what a Ph.D might be for an artist. It presents an artist with a professional trajectory: you do a Foundation course, a BA, a Masters, and then you do a Ph.D, and part of your Ph.D requirement is that you do some teaching, so that when you finish your Ph.D you are absolutely qualified to carry on working as an artist in an academic environment. This does little to nourish art.

A positive thing is that students do comprehend and work with and against this practice/education dichotomy. Last term one of the students talked to me about what he was going to do as his presentation to the convenor (group crit). He'd made some films, and he could easily show and discuss these, but he also had this big bag of stuff that he really wanted to talk about. In the end we were in the room, the walls were bare, and he had someone ripping up white-tack into little balls and he just spent the time sticking this stuff up. And it was everything. It was concert tickets, drawings he'd made when he was in primary school, pictures he'd pulled out of magazines when he was twelve. It was his whole life, his whole education, his education into being the art student that he is. He was absolutely engaged with this question as to how it is that the individual comes through this set of personal experiences which, by definition, are absolutely unique, and ends up in this place thinking about this social thing called art practice. How might he contribute to it and what sense could he make of it? And in turn what could we do, faced with all of this which was also readable in relation to our own obsessions and experiences? He's thinking very hard about the relation between art education and art practice and what the distinctions might be. But all the time, he's wanting not to find himself separate from everything going on outside the walls of this place. Because if there's any point in coming in through the door, it's only because when you go back out again something's going to happen that might be slightly better.

Michael Archer, from conversation with Felicity Allen at Goldsmiths, University of London (11 August 2010).

Claire Gibb
Room 13 Art Studio//2010

'Room 13' art studio in Fort William, Scotland, was set up by a group of young artists in 1994. They ran the studio as a business, with a dedicated studio bank account and elected office bearers. They employed an Artist in Residence, bought in equipment and supplies, staged exhibitions, took on commissions, sold photographs, stationery and artworks to generate funds and occasionally applied for grants to fund their ongoing activities. [...]

Coming across a group of children in a primary school,[1] who are running their own studio, making work and conversing on an intellectual level beyond anything one has experienced or anticipated within one's own education is a humbling experience. For me as a sixteen-year-old, the discovery of Room 13 offered an environment so compelling that I immediately abandoned my intention to go to Art College. I could see that the potential to learn and develop as an artist in the real world context offered by Room 13 was and still is far greater.

My own experience with Room 13 spans that of student, adult artist and practitioner. Working under the direction of subsequent student management teams, I have been fortunate to be involved in the process by which Room 13 has gone on to establish an international network of student-run art studios, serving an expanding community of young artists which extends from the original studio in Scotland to include inner city schools in London, Los Angeles, Mexico City and Mumbai; community spaces in South Africa, Canada and Holland; rural village schools in India and an orphanage in Nepal.

Each Room 13 studio is founded on business principles and facilitates the work of young artists alongside a professional adult artist in residence.

The achievements are nothing short of remarkable for a group of pre-teens and perhaps for this reason Room 13 is frequently hailed as a 'groundbreaking' and 'innovative' initiative. Yet the children themselves are entirely unremarkable. Their achievements are a consequence of the timely application of principles that are ancient, and align more fully with the renaissance model of apprenticeships than any modern day ideas of progressive or liberal education.

Rob Fairley, who was selected by the students of Caol Primary School to be their first Artist in Residence, determined the ethos of Room 13 and set the standard by approaching the children of the school as artists and intellectual equals. Taking them and their work seriously, he fostered their expectations and instigated a studio culture which thrived on intense discussion and critical discourse. He avoided any formal instruction, challenging the students instead to make work of their own volition and with serious intent, while he provided advice on the materials and techniques that would help them realize their ideas. [...]

[Room 13] provides an arena in which fulfilment and achievement do not lie in the future, as the reward for years of successful studying and passing of exams, but are constantly present. [...]

The key to the broad educational relevance of Room 13 lies in the fact that the students run their studio as a business. The skills required to run a competent business are precisely those covered by core curriculum subjects.

In the process of managing the studio, the students must undertake a range of tasks: conducting meetings, writing letters, maintaining accounts, ordering and organizing materials; arranging and fulfilling commitments; negotiating; planning; problem-solving; corresponding, sharing life experiences and trading physical goods with contemporaries around the globe. [...]

These tasks are disseminated widely and involve many more students than the elected management team.

In this way, the studio provides a functional interface between the classroom and the expression of curriculum learning in a real world context. [...]

> The self-confidence that children get from what they do is unbelievable. Kids who struggle in other areas no longer feel failures and they feel able to have a go at difficult areas of the curriculum that they would otherwise decide were hard and boring. Through Room 13 we get to see the whole personality of the child, not just the bit that performs academically.[2] [...]

Using students' own questions and observations as the starting point, the Room 13 Artist in Residence and teaching staff work together to guide them in making connections that will significantly enhance their understanding of the tools that the curriculum provides.

Room 13's great strength is in the fact that it adheres to a simple concept which may be adapted to fit into any educational environment, thereby offering every child the opportunity to get the best out of the education that is freely available to them. This is one brand of elitism that does not require a parental decision to seek an alternative to mainstream schooling. In fact, many of the schools in which Room 13 thrives are situated in economically deprived, socially disadvantaged areas. [...]

1 [In Scotland, up to the age of twelve.]

2 [footnote 11 in source] Jennifer Cattenach, Head Teacher, Caol Primary School, Fort William, cited in article by John Crace, *Guardian Education* (18 June 2002).

Claire Gibb, extracts from 'Room 13 Art Studio', previously unpublished text (2010).

Allan Sekula
School is a Factory//1978–80

Our schools are, in a sense, factories in which the raw materials are to be shaped and fashioned into products to meet the various demands of life. The specifications for manufacturing come from the demands of the twentieth-century civilization, and it is the business of the school to build its pupils to the specifications laid down.
– Ellwood Cubberly, [American] *Public School Administration* (1916)

[...] This essay is a deliberate provocation, less an intervention from some fictitious 'outside' world than an argument from within.

In the 'developed' world, school and media bring a formidable play of forces to bear upon the self, transforming and supplanting the more traditional patriarchal authority that emanated from religion and family in the epochs of feudalism and entrepreneurial capitalism. Both mass schooling and mass media are developments intrinsic and necessary to the corporate capitalist world order that emerged in the very late nineteenth and early twentieth centuries. In the United States, the decade after the First World War saw the triumph of a new national culture, a 'business' culture, reproduced through compulsory education and promulgated by mass circulation periodicals, radio and the movies. These forces sought to organize people as atomized 'private individuals', motivated en masse by the prospect of consumption, thus liquidating other dangerously oppositional forms of social bonding based on class, sex, race and ethnicity.

We have been led by the champions of corporate liberalism to believe that schooling and the media are instruments of freedom.

Accordingly, these institutions are seen to fulfil the democratic promise of the Enlightenment by bringing knowledge and upward social mobility within reach of everyone, by allowing each individual to reach his or her limits. This ideology hides the relentless sorting function performed by school and media. Both institutions serve to legitimate and reproduce a strict hierarchy of power relations, tracking individuals into places in a complex social division of labour while suggesting that we have only ourselves to blame for our failures. School and the media effectively situate most people in a culture and economy over which they have no control, and thus are mechanisms by which an 'enlightened' few promote the subtle silencing of the many.

School and the media are inherently discursive institutions, sites within which discourse becomes a locus of symbolic force, of symbolic violence. A communicative relation is established between teacher and student, performer and audience, in which the first part, as the purveyor of official 'truths', exerts an institutional authority over the second. Students and audience are reduced to the status of passive listeners, rather than active subjects of knowledge. Resistance is almost always limited only to the possibility of tuning out. Domination depends on a monologue of sorts, a 'conversation' in which one party names and directs the other, while the other listens deferentially, docilely, resentfully, perhaps full of suppressed rage. When the wholly dominated listener turns to speak, it is with the internalized voice of the master. This is the dynamic of all oppressions of race, gender and class. All dominating power functions semiotically through the naming of the other as subordinate, dependent, incomplete as a human being without the master's discipline and support. Clearly, such relationships can be overthrown; the discourse of domination finds its dialectical antagonist in a discourse and practice of liberation. Like home, factory, prison and city streets, school and the media are sites of an intense, if often covert, daily struggle in which language and power are inextricably connected.

Most of us who have managed to develop a professional relation to the traffic in words and images (as artists, writers or teachers) share, often unequally and competitively, in a *symbolic privilege* which situates us above whole populations of the silenced and voiceless. This role, the role of cultural mouthpiece, normally partakes in the privileging and accreditation of its own status and that of its patrons and employers, while suggesting that culture exists for everyone, or for its own sake. A contradiction has developed between the bureaucratic and professional organization of all cultural work and the Janus-faced mythology of culture, which suggests, on the one hand, that mass culture is popular and democratic, while arguing, on the other, that high culture is an elite activity, an Olympian conversation between genius and connoisseur. High culture is increasingly no more than a specialized and pretentious variant of mass culture, speaking to an audience composed of the upper class and the intermediary strata of professionals and managers (and especially those professionals and managers whose business is culture). The star system prevails in both SoHo and Hollywood: all culture becomes publicity, a matter of exposure.

But artists and intellectuals do not control the interlocking apparatuses of culture and education. Increasingly they are the functionaries and employees of corporate and state institutions: primarily as teachers and grant recipients. The ideology of autonomous professionalism serves to legitimate and defend career interests while, particularly in the case of artist-teachers, building on a hollow legacy of Romantic individualism. Although the myth of the lonely oppositional path retains its redemptive ideological force, artists are forced into a dreary upwardly-mobile competition for visibility, with reputation translating into career-capital. Those who refuse or fail are officially invisible, without voice. (I once heard a well-known artist characterize less well-known artists, generally, as lazy.) [...]

Very few teachers acknowledge the constraints placed on their would-be *auteurs* by a system of educational tracking based on class, race and sex.

Thus most of us who teach or make art, or go to school with a desire to do these things, are forced to accept that a winner's game requires losers. One can either embrace this proposition with a social-Darwinist steeling of the nerves, or pretend that it is not true while trying to survive anyway. Otherwise we might begin to work for a method of education and a culture based on a struggle for social equality. [...]

An Open Conclusion

The celebration, by ruling class commissions, of universal art education, of art education as the 'Fourth R' in a revamped, redecorated system of schooling, must be questioned when the same ruling class is promoting educational cutbacks at the same time. When functional literacy rates are declining, what does it mean to promote a massive shift of educational attention to the development of the aesthetic faculties? This plan reads like a technocratic perversion of the liberating pedagogy envisioned by the German Romantic poet Schiller in his 1793 letters *On the Aesthetic Education of Man*. The aestheticism encouraged by the cultural bureaucrats of the 1980s stops short of a necessary integration with critical consciousness. Rather, what seems to have taken shape in these plans is a technocratic vision of a society of expressionist *units*, playing happily as consumers (of less and less) in a world in which political life is increasingly limited to a spectacle of representation. The task of progressive teachers, artists, and students is to critique this vision and combat its further realization, while preserving the awareness that utopian aesthetic possibilities must be struggled for as intrinsic to a genuinely democratic future, but cannot be achieved in a society governed by a mechanical and world-threatening lust for profit and control.

Allan Sekula, extracts from 'School is a Factory' (1978–80); reprinted in *The Impossibility of Art Education*, ed. Geoff Cox, Howard Hollands and Victoria de Rijke (London: Camerawork, 1999) 81–4 [footnotes not included].

Pen Dalton
The Gendering of Art Education//2001

[...] Although the rhetoric of progressive pedagogy was tied in with notions of freedom and self-agency, choice and self-expression, it was in progressive pedagogies that some of the most rigid, formulaic and static systems of art teaching have been established. [...]

Copying, attempts at fine detail or realism and the use of drawing instruments, rulers or optical devices were not encouraged. Gentle persuasion was employed to approve appropriate child art practice and discourage undesirable art – cartoon drawings, drawings of sex or copying commercial illustrations of fashion or war – that children, left to their own devices, were apt to 'fall into'. Such work was removed, it received little praise or simply was not put on the classroom walls. A genre of school art emerged that had a specific 'look': a gender-neutral 'Child Art'. [...]

A theory of recapitulation, in which the growth of the individual (ontology) was seen to parallel the development of the human species (phylogeny) seemed to provide an explanation for gradual change, growth and developmental progress. Education was structured in stages to guide children through what was thought to be their natural ontology. [...]

The work of Jean Piaget is significant in this context because it was his well-defined account of cognitive development in the twentieth century that brought Darwinian developmentalism up to date and offered modernist education its clearest scientifically legitimized sequential structuring paradigm. [...] Cross-cultural studies have suggested that the stages of artistic development based on the classic studies of Piaget and Inhelder, upon which so many drawing systems and notions of Child Art are based, are not universal or fixed. Erica Burman suggests that developmental psychology has to be regarded now as a historically and socially specific practice, as 'a paradigmatically modern discipline, arising at a time of commitment to narratives of truth, objectivity, science and reason'. [...]

The Russian psychologist Lev Vygotsky, who was working at about the same time as Piaget, also produced a developmental scheme but he questioned its forward moving and biologistic metaphors. He suggested that cognitive growth is sometimes retrogressive, it can stand still or move backwards and repeat some events. Cognitive development does not occur as an unfolding of a pre-existing inner nature, but grows as a result of social interactions, with the body, with languages, tools and technologies. [...]

Psychologist Valerie Walkerdine, who worked within Lacanian and Vygotskian theories, has questioned the psychological practices through which the rational is produced as masculine in her study of mathematics education. She demonstrated, in her detailed and convincing studies, that the meanings and pleasures of the intellect and rationality are continually constructed through discursive narratives of pedagogy, through the things that children and teachers do and say and the symbolic materials they use. Reason, she argues – its superiority, its social status, the potential pleasures and its rewards of control and mastery – is not *in* the child to be drawn out and nurtured but is *produced* as the climax of a narrative of mathematical discourse which involves a consequent denial of the feminine. [...]

Creativity has a privileged place in art education and, like other discourses, has gendered connotations. Psychology in art education has constructed a major discourse of creativity which, following on the experimental work of the psychologists Sherrie Turkle and Seymour Papert, I shall refer to as the 'planning' mode. [...] Turkle and Papert, in their investigation of the different ways that children engage with computers, have described a specific and culturally dominant model of creativity which involves linear, developmental and sequential thinking. In this model of creativity, basic rules and existing precedents are mastered through research, and innovative thinking proceeds through logically ordered processes of adjustment and empirical testing. Prototypes are constructed and if not successful are discarded on the way as 'natural wastage'. The final outcome is a new and original idea or a product which has developed out of, but is different from the old. These 'planners', Turkle and Papert suggest, enjoy a high level of abstraction, hierarchy and structure and they have found that boys and scientists are often, but not always, most successful as planners. This description of creativity is similar to the logical, deductive and sequential thinking processes that Liam Hudson produced in his notion of 'convergent' thinkers. [...]

The narrative of the creative process in modernist art education was similarly represented: first children observed, examined and drew the growth and structure of natural forms, noting accurately how different elements were constructed. Then they freely played with different ideas, colours and materials, if possible making prototypes; they then tried out different samples, adapting and modifying them in relation to other external factors such as the nature of materials, the target audience and the time available. They then selected the best idea from the options they made, treating the rejected models as 'natural wastage' and bringing the final product (the painting, the pot, the embroidery) to a finished state, testing and evaluating it against the original aims. This creative process is the process of evolution, scaled down and encoded in processes for producing art. [...]

Traditional psychology has produced other models of creativity which appear to be in opposition and subordinate to the planning mode, associated with play, with 'concrete' thinking and earlier modes of learning. These models have been called 'combinatory' or 'bricolage' creative modes. Combinatory creativity is recognized as a form of creativity that involves a broader, eclectic approach rather than a linear approach. It collects and gathers heterogeneous information and ignores boundaries. It recombines existing ideas and genres in unorthodox ways. It corresponds to Hudson's notions of 'divergent' thinkers. Divergent thinkers, traditional psychology suggests, are less original and less creative than 'convergent' planners. It appears to allow individuals to become 'too creative', to bring in 'irrelevant' or trivial concerns:

> In terms of requirements for an act of originality, the divergent thinking tests leave a lot to be desired . . . The responses frequently serve no useful purpose and often display flights of fancy bordering on the grotesque, the sadistic and trivial. What we have are two operational definitions of short term thinking styles: one, the divergent kind relying on ideational fluency in open-ended problems; the other, convergent thinking favouring those who like homing in on one solution.[1] [...]

Turkle and Papert in recent years have argued for the privileging of this notion of divergent/ bricolage thinking:

> The bricoleur resembles the painter who stands back between brushstrokes, looks at the canvas, and only after this contemplation, decides what to do next. For planners, mistakes are missteps; for bricoleurs they are the essence of a navigation by mid-course corrections. For planners, a programme is an instrument for premeditated control; bricoleurs have no goals, but set out to realize them in the

> spirit of a collaborative venture with the machine ... While hierarchy and abstraction are valued by the structured programmers' planners aesthetic, bricoleur programmers prefer negotiation and rearrangement of their materials.[2]

They suggest that the skills and values of bricolage – cooperation, play, concrete application of ideas, negotiation, the breaking of boundaries – have been neglected in education and are today as, if not more, important than older planning modes. [...]

Education is increasingly drawing its occupationalist educationalist ideologies from new relations and art practices found in the powerful image of global corporate culture and consumption to replace the 'old fashioned' masculine legitimizing discourses of science, industry and productivity. [...]

Business and arts education are finding reciprocal power and legitimizing authority in each other's practices. The Getty Education Institute for the Arts, which supports American Discipline Based Art Education, vigorously promotes this relationship. [...]

Some art courses in higher education in Britain are shifting their educational priorities in line with new business imperatives: the aims of the five key skills at Camberwell College of Art, for instance, and those of Birmingham Institute of Art and Design, are the same as those promoted by the Confederation of British Industry (CBI): 'Initiative, self-motivation, creativity, communication and teamwork'. These are now considered the necessary skills for arts graduates 'in a flexible labour market'. As Turkle and Papert have observed, the paradigm of economic man in the modern era was the rigorous, analytical scientist. The paradigm of postmodern economic man is the playful, creative, risk-taking, entrepreneurial artist. [...]

1 [footnote 48 in source] D. Child, *Psychology and the Teacher* (London: Cassell, 1973) 6th edition (1997) 276–97.

2 [50] S. Turkle and C. Papert, 'Epistemological Pluralism: Styles and Voices within the Computer Culture', *Signs* (Autumn 1990) 128–57.

Pen Dalton, extracts from *The Gendering of Art Education* (Milton Keynes: The Open University, 2001) 66–76; 110–11.

Henry A. Giroux
Youth in a Suspect Society//2009

[...] Central to the pedagogy of commodification is the notion that 'adults are never cool – they are boring, often absurd, sometimes stupid – and when they try to be cool they are pathetic.' There is more at work in this strategy than anti-adultism; there is a shrewd attempt to open a space free of adults that marketers and advertisers can tap into without having to deal with the mediating influence of the adult gaze. There is also an attempt to replace parental authority with the authority of the market, especially when it comes to the matters of commerce and commodification. The Nickelodeon motto 'Kids Rule' has nothing to do with either empowering kids or taking their voices seriously. On the contrary, it represents both a departure from the panoptic, disciplinary obsessions of traditional institutions of socialization and a new attempt to refashion 'pastoral power' and guidance for children under the omnipotent gaze of advertising, rather than religious institutions, schools and family. [...] Entire companies are now organized to do research on young people, gather information and sell it to client corporations, making it all the more difficult for children and youth to resist the ever-growing and changing ads, products and ideas aimed at turning kids into commodities. [...]

YMS Consulting's mission statement is a particularly clear expression of a business venture that employs the rhetoric of childhood commodification with no apparent ethical misgivings about selling children as markets to corporations, asserting (without irony) that they enrich the lives of young people. It states:

> Our mission is to be the most up to date and insightful 'Hub' of Information, Expertise and Advice for all those who seek to responsibly market to today's youth and their families. Simply put, our goal is our clients' success – especially when it results in the enrichment of the lives of the young people and their families who become the consumers of our clients' products and programmes.[1]

Kids are now hired to use their friends to gain information about what is cool and trendy, information that is later used to sell products to a larger teen demographic. Within this type of pedagogy, kids are not merely commodified. They also learn quickly that duplicity and deception are perfectly acceptable in a world in which manipulation translates into free products such as films, toys and concert tickets. [...] Kids are under intense pressure to keep up with trends, learning quickly that under the regime of market sovereignty their value, if not their dignity and identity, rests on what they accumulate rather than who they are. With alarming candour, Nancy Shalek, president of a reputable advertising company, revealed one element of the neoliberal ideology that drives her pursuit of the youth market. She claims without apology that 'advertising at its best is making people feel that without their product, you're a loser. Kids are very sensitive to that. If you tell them to buy something, they are resistant. But if you tell them that they'll be a dork if they don't you've got their attention. You open up emotional vulnerabilities and it's very easy to do with kids because they're the most emotionally vulnerable.'[2] [...]

Even [American] public schools, which have a civic responsibility to nurture the critical intellect, social responsibilities and civic capacities of young people, have been colonized by various corporate industries. Not only do they influence student diets but they also inundate kids with commercialized curricula and relentless ads that undermine their physical well-being and mental health. For example, Channel One Network gets inside of public schools by offering financially strapped districts borrowed television equipment in exchange for mandatory daily viewing by students of twelve minutes of soft news and advertisements. It has been estimated that the 'Channel One News reaches more than 7 million secondary-school children in 11,000 schools', an audience that is 50 times larger than the MTV teen audience. [...]

There is yet another type of disposability at work in consumer culture – the erosion of the childhood imagination, the slow death of the ability of young people to imagine a future outside of the lure of commodities, and the wearing away of any viable notion of human solidarity, social responsibility and critically engaged citizenship. As the public domain is transformed into the ruins of a homogenizing 'corporate monoculture', debate, critical dialogue, dissent, judgement and thoughtfulness, all of which are central to any substantive democracy, become suspicious, if not scorned, activities. [...] We need a new politics that makes education central to the struggle for democracy, one that is not limited to schools and that is willing to enlist and actively mobilize artists, intellectuals, academics and others in the struggle for a public able and willing to confront a reactionary state and a consumer society through multiple levels of resistance. Zygmunt Bauman illuminates this issue with razorlike precision:

> Adverse odds may be overwhelming, and yet democratic (or, as Cornelius Castoriadis would say, an autonomous) society knows of no substitute for education and self-education as a means to influence the turn of events that can be squared with its own nature, while that nature cannot be preserved for long without 'critical pedagogy' – education sharpening its critical edge, 'making society feel guilty' and 'stirring things up' through stirring human consciences.

The fates of freedom, of democracy that makes it possible while being made possible by it, and of education that breeds dissatisfaction with the level of both freedom and democracy achieved thus far, are inextricably connected and not to be detached from one another. One may view that intimate connection as another specimen of a vicious circle – but it is within that circle that human hopes and the chances of humanity are inscribed, and can be nowhere else.[3] [...]

1 See 'About Us: The YMS Mission' (undated). Corporate website for YMS Consulting (http://www.ymsconsulting.com/about_us.htm)

2 Cited in Juliet B. Schor, *Born to Buy* (New York: Scribner, 2005) 21.

3 Zygmunt Bauman, *Liquid Life* (London: Polity Press, 2005).

Henry A Giroux, extracts from *Youth in a Suspect Society* (New York: Palgrave MacMillan, 2009) 27–66.

Paul Clements
The Rehabilitative Role of Arts Education in Prison//2004

[...] There has been a massive increase in the prison population of England and Wales from 42,000 in 1992 to 70,000 in 2002. [...] The 'new medical model' of prison education [based on cognitive behavioural therapy] has been implemented since the late 1980s. [...] At HMP Brixton the curriculum in 1996 included 43 weekly classes in arts subjects, whereas by 2001 this accounted for ten. Furthermore, such classes were run only if they included a basic and key skills curriculum. Arts classes had been replaced with classes entitled 'Firmstart with Pottery' and 'Basic Skills through Art', amongst other instrumental agendas. [...]

Anders Lustgarten, a creative writing tutor, has condemned the systematic eradication of creative courses in drama, art and culture. He ridicules 'statistics as the surrogates of success. Annual intake a thousand men, annual productivity a thousand certificates, result (irrespective of what's taught, to or by whom), education', because they fail to recognize quality and value.[1] But his greatest wrath is reserved for the lowest common denominator qualifications that are unlikely to override the stigma of criminalization for prospective employers. In contrast, he explains his involvement in prison drama, and how during the rehearsal schedule he could visibly assess the changes and gradual empowerment of prisoners through their involvement in a production of *Accidental Death of an Anarchist* at HMP Wandsworth. [...]

Tom Inglis [in 'Empowerment and Emancipation', 1997] analyses the two concepts of empowerment and emancipation in terms of how power relations and structures affect the field of adult education. He challenges the commonly held view that emancipation can be attained through personal transformation and questions the concept of empowerment altogether. He cites the need for value which is central to humanity and overcoming organizational self-interest. For him empowerment involves 'people developing capacities to act successfully within the existing system and structures of power', which has traditionally been one of the aims of lifelong education but increasingly been appropriated by business, management and industrial training.[2] Empowerment can therefore be perceived as a subtle and pervasive means of organizational manipulation.

Emancipation, on the other hand, is concerned with changing the system by critically analysing, resisting and challenging the structures of power beyond merely individual concerns. The more psychological emphasis on empowerment, in terms of the realization and reconstruction of the self, recognizes education in terms of unblocking and unlocking capacities in response to the effects of power, not confronting this process. Inglis suggests that there is a need to discover a pre-social and authentic self, which is very different from a process of self-realization and empowerment which has shifted the focus onto the individual and ignored any analysis of power and the structures that operate to control that individual. His distinction between working within the system (empowerment) or changing that system (emancipation) is crucial to understanding the function of the arts that transgress this boundary. [...]

The social psychologist Erich Fromm argued that students need to establish their own individuality and satisfy inner psychological conditions to free themselves from unjust external authority. [...] Disempowered individuals lack spontaneity, which encourages a feigning to authority and compulsive automaton-like behaviour. Alternatively, this leads to mimicking authoritarianism. Powerlessness and insecurity help design a very isolated individual, which Fromm recognized requires the challenge of spontaneity:

> Spontaneous activity is not compulsive, to which the individual is driven by his isolation and powerlessness; it is not the activity of the automaton, which is the uncritical adoption of patterns suggested from the outside. Spontaneous activity is free activity of the self and implies, psychologically, what the Latin root of the word *sponte* means literally: of one's free will.[3] [...]

He referred to those artists as spontaneous whose thinking, feeling and acting are expressions of themselves. But there is a danger that spontaneity may unlock other aspects of character which can be antithetical to such objectives. Fromm did not espouse anarchy, distinguishing between rational and irrational authority, of which the latter can be usurped through a more spontaneous nature. Here rational authority is never in conflict with the true needs of the individual that concern liberation and self-discovery. He asserted that:

> There is nothing of which we are more ashamed than of not being ourselves, and there is nothing that gives us greater pride and happiness than to think, to feel and to say what is ours. This implies that what matters is the activity as such, the process and not the result. In our culture the emphasis is just the reverse.[4] [...]

1 [footnote 20 in source] Anders Lustgarten, 'Notes from the Underground', *Prison Report*, no. 55 (2001).
2 [22] Tom Inglis, 'Empowerment and Emancipation', *Adult Education Quarterly*, vol. 48, no. 1 (1997) 4.
3 [29] Erich Fromm, *The Fear of Freedom* (1942) (London and New York: Routledge and Kegan Paul, 1977) 223.
4 [30] Ibid., 226.

Paul Clements, extracts from 'The Rehabilitative Role of Arts Education in Prison: Accommodation or Enlightenment?', *JADE* (Journal of Art and Design Education), vol. 23, no. 2 (2004) 170–76.

Joanna Fiduccia
Mike Kelley: Educational Complex Onwards//2008

Educational Complex (1995), marks a breakthrough in Mike Kelley's career, though not as one might expect. An architectural maquette combining all the schools the artist ever attended, it initiated Kelley's work on Repressed Memory Syndrome, the pop-psychology notion that critics had grafted onto his earlier exhibitions. But if *Educational Complex* triggered the body of work presented at Wiels [in Brussels], it also managed to bracket the autobiographical sincerity behind any art-therapeutic revelation. Kelley's 'breakthrough' consisted of rendering his own liberally falsified biography as a foamcore campus, punctuated with the 'dark zones' of repressed memories. After the critics mistook Kelly's formal compositions for psychological afflictions, Kelley wilfully misconstrued a psychological syndrome as an aesthetic model, preserving its paradigm while fabricating its traumas. Perhaps that is why, despite the outmodedness of RMS,

Kelley's exhibition 'Educational Complex Onwards: 1995–2008' still proves so engaging: set loose in Kelley's oeuvre, trauma restores the classical notion of content to the art experience.

The 'dark zones' of *Educational Complex*, occluded sections of the model corresponding to sites of putative abuse, reappear in *Repressed Spatial Relationships Rendered as Fluid # 1–6* (2006), a set of industrial mobiles. Each mobile dangles blocks of Plexiglas or brushed steel, representing traumatic hot spots like gyms and faculty bathrooms. A speaker appended to one mobile sibilates with white noise, possibly echoing a shower room, that pitiless incubation chamber of high school neuroses. In Kelley's work, these neuroses come backed by reimagined torments, no less dreadful for being clichés. In the series *Timeless/Authorless* (1995), grisly tales of abuse are presented as enlarged newspaper clippings, illustrated by yearbook photos. The abuse tales alternate with restaurant reviews of exotic cuisine. Beside the conventional arousals of food writing, abuse testimony comes to seem equally predictable – a mere narrative zone to be stuffed with graphic filler.

On the second floor, *Sublevel* (1998), exhumes one zone of *Educational Complex* by enlarging its model of the CalArts basement (viewed by crawling under *Educational Complex* and lying on a child-size mattress). This waist-high labyrinth of plywood, whose inner surfaces are encrusted with lambent flesh-pink crystals, presents an eroticized visualization of the basement as both a site of abuse and the symbolic hub of the subconscious. A tunnel snaking under the structure leads to a metal chamber containing a card table and a shelf of obscure objects. This eerie antechamber has the restive quality of an empty stage. [...]

The exhibition evolves into a complete aesthetic experience, drawing you in with the lure of access to a hidden imaginary and spitting you out by way of aggressive spectacle. In doing so, it re-educates the viewer about art's function – being, in this case, neither to reveal nor to heal, but to traumatize. By the end, as with his 1988 installation of the same name, Kelley ensures that you 'pay for your pleasure'.

1 [*Pay For Your Pleasure* was an installation conceived for The Renaissance Society and the city of Chicago. The work comprised 40 banners painted with portraits and quotes from writers, artists and thinkers that addressed similarities and differences between criminal and creative activity, and, at the centre, a painting made in prison by John Wayne Gacy, the notorious Chicago serial murderer of the 1970s. The installation provoked questions about the institutions and desires responsible for criminality, incarceration and celebrity.]

Joanna Fiduccia, review of 'Mike Kelley: Educational Complex Onwards 1995–2008' at Wiels, Brussels, *Artforum* (November 2008).

SHE CAME FROM GREECE SHE HAD A THIRST FOR KNOWLEDGE; SHE STUDIED SCULPTURE AT SAINT MARTIN'S COLLEGE; THAT'S WHERE I CAUGHT HER EYE; SHE TOLD ME THAT HER DAD WAS LOADED; I SAID IN THAT CASE I'LL HAVE A RUM AND COCA-COLA; SHE SAID FINE AND IN THIRTY SECONDS TIME SHE SAID; I WANT TO LIVE LIKE COMMON PEOPLE; I WANT TO DO WHATEVER COMMON PEOPLE DO; I WANT TO SLEEP WITH COMMON PEOPLE; I WANT TO SLEEP WITH COMMON PEOPLE LIKE YOU; WELL WHAT ELSE COULD I DO – I SAID I'LL SEE WHAT I CAN DO; I TOOK HER TO A SUPERMARKET I DON'T KNOW WHY BUT I HAD TO START IT SOMEWHERE, SO IT STARTED THERE I SAID PRETEND YOU'VE GOT NO MONEY; SHE JUST LAUGHED AND SAID OH YOU'RE SO FUNNY; I SAID YEAH? WELL I CANT SEE ANYONE ELSE SMILING IN HERE; ARE YOU SURE YOU WANT TO LIVE LIKE COMMON PEOPLE; YOU WANT TO SEE WHATEVER COMMON PEOPLE SEE; YOU WANT TO SLEEP WITH COMMON PEOPLE; YOU WANT TO SLEEP WITH COMMON PEOPLE LIKE ME; BUT SHE DIDN'T UNDERSTAND; SHE JUST SMILED AND HELD MY HAND; RENT A FLAT ABOVE A SHOP, CUT YOUR HAIR AND GET A JOB; SMOKE SOME FAGS AND PLAY SOME POOL, PRETEND YOU NEVER WENT TO SCHOOL

ART SCHOOL

Eve Kosofsky Sedgwick
Touching Feeling: Affect, Pedagogy, Performativity//2003

[...] The photograph on the frontispiece of *Touching Feeling* is one of many taken by the Californian photographer Leon A. Borensztein of Judith Scott (b. 1943), with her work.

The sculpture in this picture is fairly characteristic of Scott's work in its construction: a core assembled from large, heterogeneous materials has been hidden under many wrapped or darned layers of multicoloured yarn, cord, ribbon, rope and other fibre, producing a durable three-dimensional shape, usually oriented along a single axis of length, whose curves and planes are biomorphically resonant and whose scale bears comparison to Scott's own body. The formal achievements that are consistent in her art include her inventive techniques for securing the giant bundles, her subtle building and modulation of complex three-dimensional lines and curves, and her startlingly original use of colour, whether bright or muted, which can stretch across a place, simmer deeply through the multilayered wrapping, or drizzle graphically along an emphatic suture.

All of Scott's work that I've seen on its own has an intense presence, but the subject of this photograph also includes her relation to the completed work, and presumptively also the viewer's relation to the sight of that dyad. For me, to experience a subject-object distance from this image is no more plausible than to envision such a relation between Scott and her work. She and her creation here present themselves to one another with equally expansive welcome. Through their closeness, the sense of sight is seen to dissolve in favour of that of touch; not only are the artist's hands and bare forearms but also her face is busy with the transaction of texture. Parents and babies, twins (Scott is a twin) or lovers might commune through such haptic absorption. There is no single way to understand the 'besideness' of these two forms, even though one of them was made by the other. The affect that saturates the photo is mysterious, or at least multiple, in quality: besides the obvious tenderness with which Scott embraces the sculpture, her relaxed musculature and bowed head suggest sadness, for example, as perhaps does the abandon with which she allows her features to be squashed against it. The height and breadth of her embrace could suggest either that she is consoling herself or seeks consolation from the sculpture, which is slightly cantilevered towards her while she stands upright on her own feet; the loose-jointed breadth of her embrace can also be read as a sign of her Downs syndrome. Yet the jaunty top and bottom points of the rounded shape are only the most visible of the suggestions that this soberly toned black and white photograph is at the same time ablaze with triumph, satisfaction and relief.

Inevitably, both before and since her recent recognition within the framework of 'outsider' art, Scott has been repeatedly diagnozed in terms of lack. Her deafness, one deficit that went undiagnosed until middle age, led to extreme exaggerations of the severity of her retardation; classed as 'ineducable' in childhood, she was warehoused in a crushingly negligent Ohio asylum system for over thirty-five years.[1] Even after she emerged as an artist with the support of California's Creative Growth Art Centre, her most encouraging and excited teacher, the fibre artist Sylvia Seventy, inexplicably decided she was colour-blind[2] and unable to decide for herself when a piece was finsished.[3] And John MacGregor, the psychoanalytic critic of Art Brut who was been her strongest proponent, is nonetheless compulsive in applying to her the language of emphatic negation: 'There is not the slightest possibility that Judith envisions the eventual outcome, the final form, of her work';[4] 'Judith was certainly not engaged in the production of works of art';[5] 'Judith is completely unaware of the existence of sculpture';[6] 'The notion of abstract, non-representational form is a complex idea totally out of Judith's ability to conceptualize'.[7] MacGregor also seems to consider that all of Scott's artistic activity – maybe all her activity, in fact – must be categorized as 'unconscious', perhaps because she does not use language.[8] [...]

1 John M. MacGregor, *Metamorphosis: The Fiber Art of Judith Scott. The Outsider Artist and the Experience of Down's Syndrome* (Oakland, California: Creative Growth Art Center, 1999) 49–51.

2 Ibid., 69.

3 Ibid., 72.

4 Ibid., 33.

5 Ibid., 72.

6 Ibid., 92.

7 Ibid., 109.

8 Ibid., 106; 111.

Eve Kosofsky Sedgwick, extract from *Touching Feeling: Affect, Pedagogy, Performativity* (Durham, North Carolina: Duke University Press, 2003) 22–3.

Irit Rogoff
Academy as Potentiality//2006

[...] Tensions have increased between different tendencies surrounding the field of educating 'creativity': old-fashioned notions of inspiration without articulation, and slightly less old-fashioned notions of the importance of analytical and critical proficiency all vie with contemporary pedagogies of actualization, embodiment and criticality as the lived out consequences of knowing. All these jostle around in the same institutional stew, occasionally producing head-on collisions but most of the time co-existing in the kind of liberal indifference in which the contradictions and contentions of 'difference' are ignored for the sake of some ill-conceived harmony, in which all the bases are covered.

I would argue that these factions produce a false set of conflicts and engagements; that the questions in education in general, and in art education in particular, the questions that we have not yet begun to deal with, are not those of specifying what we need to know and how we need to know it, of who determines this and who benefits from it. Instead it is a question of how we might know what we don't yet know how to know. And it is here, in the aim of accessing this complex aspiration, that we need to change our vocabulary – to swap knowledge transfer and knowledge assessment, professionalization, quantifiable outcomes and marketability, for another set of terms and another set of aspirations.

[...] What I would like to pursue here is a set of alternate emergent terms that operate in the name of this 'not-yet-known-knowledge'. Terms such as potentiality, actualization, access and contemporaeinity, which for me are the building blocks and navigational vectors for a current pedagogy, a pedagogy at peace with its partiality, a pedagogy not preoccupied with succeeding but with trying. [...]

Potentiality

First then to potentiality. Potentiality, following an old Aristotelian argument, is the opposite of actuality, so that it inhabits the realm of the possible without prescribing it as a plan. Giorgio Agamben says he might characterize his subject as an attempt to understand the meaning of the verb 'can':

> What do I mean when I say 'I can, I cannot'? ... In an exergue to a collection of poems she called 'Requiem', Anna Akhmatova recounts how her poems were born. It was in the 1930s, and for months she joined the line outside the prison of Leningrad, trying to get news of her son who had been arrested on political grounds.

> There were dozens of other women in line with her. One day one of these women recognized her and turning to her, addressed her with the following question: 'Can you speak of this?'. Akhmatova was silent for a moment and then, without knowing how or why, found an answer to the question: 'Yes', she said, 'I can.' Did she perhaps mean by these words that she was such a gifted poet that she knew how to handle language skilfully enough to describe the atrocious things of which it is so difficult to write? I do not think so, this is not what she meant to say ... For everyone a moment comes in which he or she must utter this 'I can' which does not refer to any certainty or specific capacity; to be able to write, or paint, or forecast the weather, but is nevertheless absolutely demanding. Beyond all faculties, this 'I can' does not mean anything – yet it marks what is, for each of us, perhaps the hardest and bitterest experience possible: the experience of potentiality.[1]

There are, says Agamben, again following Aristotle, two kinds of potentiality. There is generic potentiality, and this is the one that is meant when we say, for example, that a child has the potential to know, or that he or she can potentially become the head of state. And there is another sense of potentiality that belongs to someone who has knowledge or an ability. In this sense we say of the architect that he or she has the *potential* to build, of the poet that he or she has the *potential* to write poems. One of the most interesting aspects of potentiality is that it is as much the potential for *not* doing as it is for doing, and radical evil is not this or that bad deed but the potentiality for darkness which is at the very same time the potentiality for light. 'To be potential', says Agamben, 'means to be one's own lack, to be in relation to one's own incapacity. Beings that exist in the mode of potentiality are capable of their own impotentiality; and only in this way do they become potential. They can be because they are in relation to their own non-being. In potentiality, sensation is in relation to anaesthesia, knowledge to ignorance, vision to darkness'.

So thinking 'academy' as 'potentiality' is to think the possibilities of *not doing, not making, not bringing into being* at the very centre of acts of thinking, making and doing. It means dismissing much of the instrumentalizing that seems to go hand in hand with education, much of the managerialism that is associated with a notion of 'training' for this or that profession or market. Letting go of many of the understandings of 'academy' as a training ground whose only permitted outcomes are a set of concrete objects or practices. It allows for the inclusions of notions of both fallibility and actualization into a practice of teaching and learning. [...]

1 Giorgio Agamben, *Potentialities: Collected Essays* (Stanford: Stanford, University Press, 1999) 178.

Irit Rogoff, extract from 'Academy as Potentiality', in *A.C.A.D.E.M.Y.*, ed Angelika Nollen, et al. (Frankfurt am Main: Revolver, 2006) 14–15.

WEB

Consciousness-Raising Rules//1972

1 Select a topic
2 Go around the room, each woman speaking in turn. Don't interrupt, let each woman speak up to 15 minutes and then ask questions only for clarification.
3 Don't give advice, don't chastize, don't be critical.
4 Draw generalizations after everyone has spoken, or, before that, go around the room and talk again.
5 Draw political conclusions – if you can.
6 Keep the group below 10 women.
7 In order to develop trust and confidence, don't repeat what has been said in the meeting or talk about members outside of the group.
8 This is not a therapy, encounter or sensitivity group situation.

Topics

How do you feel about other women? Why did you become an artist? How do you feel about yourself as a woman artist? How do you feel about being a mother? How do you feel about your own mother? Father? How about passivity? About your body? About growing older? About dividing the housework, if you live with a man? How do you feel about friendship? Therapy? Your difficulties in working? What, if anything, do you need from a man? What about men in power? Do you think of yourself as a woman artist or an artist who happens to be a woman? Do you think that the woman artist has any degree of responsibility to commit her art to the fight against women's oppression? If so, in what way? If not, why not? Does the feminist artist have something to offer that no other artist has? To what degree and in what manner can a successful woman artist use her success as a weapon or resource to improve the status of the woman artist in society? How have you been encouraged to be an artist/creative? Discouraged? By whom? Do you feel you have a responsibility to your audience? Are you a male-oriented woman or a female-oriented woman? What does this mean? What did you used to be? What kind of lifestyles are available to women? How was your education affected by your sex? What kind of work do you do? How do you feel about it? Define female identity and how it has evolved, socially and personally. Are you competitive with women? With men? Why are women's masturbation fantasies often masochistic? Do you feel that masochism or 'being the victim' has been a large part of your life? Why is this? How does male supremacy poison communication between men and women? Women and men? Women and women? Children and adults? What are the problems between married women and single women which make close relationships difficult? Between younger women and older women? Between working women and housewives? Between women of different social classes? Between women of different races? Is there a connection between violence and heterosexual sex? Do you feel that this is true from your own life experience? How much is fear, intimidation or terrorism used to keep women in their place? What are you doing to reduce this in your own life? Why do men rely so heavily on vision for erotic stimulation and how does this enslave women? What is the difference between male and female ego? Why is it so easy to 'put a man down'? Why are we so afraid of doing it? Feminist historians are revealing evidence of early civilizations which were matriarchal and/or women dominated (*The First Sex* – Elizabeth Gould Davis, 1971). Speculate as to how the shift from a feminist to a masculist society took place and why.

WEB (West–East Coast Bag), 'Consciousness-Raising Rules' (Chicago, June 1972); reprinted in *Feminism–Art–Theory*, ed. Hilary Robinson (Oxford: Blackwell, 2001) 85.

Miriam Schapiro
The Education of Women as Artists: Project Womanhouse//1972

The Feminist Art Programme at the California Institute of the Arts has just completed its first quarter of the school year. [...]

Twenty-one young women artists elected to join this exclusively female class. We do not teach by fixed authoritarian rules. Traditionally, the flow of power has moved from teacher to student unilaterally. Our ways are more circular, more womb-like; our primary concern lies with providing a nourishing environment for growth. Classes begin by sitting in a circle; a topic for discussion is selected. We move around the room, each person assuming responsibility for addressing herself to the topic on her highest level of self-perception. In the classical Women's Liberation technique, the personal becomes the political. Privately held feelings imagined to be personally held 'hang-ups' turn out to be everyone's feelings, and it becomes possible to act together in their solution, if there is a solution. Our use of this technique serves a different purpose. We are artists. We search for subject matter. It is often wearying to struggle alone for the courage to bring material to the surface that would be fit for artistic form. In our group we make laws based on mutual aesthetic consent to encourage and support the most profound artistic needs of the group.

Sometimes the struggle for subject matter assumes a different cast. We are able to find material to make art from, but we sense that the material is inappropriate. There are some interesting unwritten laws about what is considered appropriate subject matter for art-making. The content of our first class project Womanhouse reversed these laws. What formerly was considered trivial was heightened to the level of serious art-making: dolls, pillows, cosmetics, sanitary napkins, silk stockings, underwear, children's toys, washbasins, toasters, frying pans, refrigerator door handles, shower caps, quilts, satin bedspreads. [...]

Miriam Schapiro, extracts from 'The Education of Women as Artists: Project Womanhouse', *Art Journal*, vol. 31, no. 3 (Spring 1972); reprinted in *Feminism–Art–Theory*, ed. Hilary Robinson (Oxford: Blackwell, 2001) 125–6.

Paula Harper
The First Feminist Art Programme: A View from the 1980s//1985

[...] In discussing the advantages and disadvantages of the Feminist Art Programme with a number of its former students, I found general agreement on the nature of the advantages. The programme provided a psychological environment that gave them the confidence to trust their own instincts and judgement, even if their judgement was to leave or rebel against it. It released their creativity. It was stimulating, demanding. It created a strong feeling of community and a conviction that the group was engaged in an experiment that was making history. Mira Schor described it as the 'boot camp of feminism', implying an affectionate nostalgia for the hardships of its members' initiation. That feeling is one that bonds former students, no matter how severe their criticisms. Most of them acknowledge that for better or worse the programme changed their lives.

When they assessed the programme's disadvantages, the former students showed more variety in their viewpoints. Some criticisms recurred, particularly that both Miriam Schapiro and Judy Chicago had, in carrying out their ideas, been psychologically manipulative; that Chicago's psychodrama exercises created more emotional disturbance than her training could manage and therefore were potentially dangerous; that the students were encouraged to express anger towards men that not all may have felt; and that Chicago, especially, projected her own goals on the students and tried to dictate the content of their art. On the last point, Robin Mitchell noted, 'The students were not supposed to make abstract art. Making images like mainstream art was a terrible no-no. Judy was so doctrinaire about what art was: it had a hole in the middle. That was okay for her but not for me'.[1] These pressures to conform to the ideology of the community were resisted in varying degrees by many of the students, but Chicago felt them to be necessary: 'Since women have so much trouble bonding, it was very important in the early seventies to build an artificial environment which supported bonding'.[2] A former student's response was, 'It couldn't last too long. It was a forced situation, too artificial. At one time I thought I would throw up if I saw another drawing of a split pear'.[3]

The most troublesome aspect of the programme, the one that generated the most serious and searching criticism from those involved, was its separatism. The students acknowledged that the sense of community was strongest when as a totally female group they were working on Womanhouse in close, daily association away from the Cal Arts building. When the separatism was most complete, the programme was most successful. But a number of the former students are now bitter over what they see as the programme's hostility to men. Students who were in relationships with men were often criticized; some were encouraged to repudiate their boyfriends or husbands. The emphasis was on the building of careers and the development of a professional life. They now question the sacrifices that were made for the goals of the feminist community and accept the goal themselves only as they can be modified as part of a larger social framework that includes men.

Was the separatism of the programme worth the difficulties it caused? Faith Wilding's response is, 'That's a hard question ... I guess I'd have to say it was worth it, but it cost a lot. I'm only now beginning to realize how much it cost. But we wouldn't have made the gains without that drastic, radical dislocation of the status quo. Once you've done that you can't go back. You can go somewhere else but you can't go back.'[4]

1 Robin Mitchell, interview with author, Los Angeles, California, July 1982.

2 Interview with Judy Chicago.

3 Mira Shor, telephone conversation with author, June 1982.

4 Interview with Faith Wilding.

Paula Harper, extracts from 'The First Feminist Art Programme: A View from the 1980s', *Signs*, vol. 10, no. 4 (1985); reprinted in *Feminism–Art–Theory*, ed. Hilary Robinson (Oxford: Blackwell, 2001) 126–7; 129.

Elma Askham and Harry Thubron
The Case for Polytechnics//1967

We have for a long time striven for a closer relationship between art and other disciplines, and only by such a leavening can we see the emergence of a more complete art school, educationally and otherwise. [...]

Over the last ten years art schools have been requiring machinery for wider usage, together with attendant skills, and have given more thought and care to what is called 'liberal studies' and means of communication: in this sense they have sought knowledge and practice in wider and richer terms. So art schools themselves have moved towards what can only be a pre-polytechnic or pre-university situation. The proposed polytechnic plan is but a step in the logical and evolutionary development of the art schools. [...]

Present fears for a Polytechnic are coloured by the unhappy histories of art schools in technical colleges – little autonomy, prescribed policies, whittled finances and wide philosophical cleavage. It was a mess in the 1930s, when the art school lacked both the teeth and the guts to hold any realistic position.

Certainly the art school could be vulnerable in a game of catch-as-catch-can against the stoicism of the technical colleges grown fat – fat on the 'bread and butter' certainty given them by their real and imagined relationship with commercial and industrial life [...] [or] they might become second- and third-rate 'universities'. This can only be so if the art school/technical situation emerges without clear educational aims and planned objectives.

Francis T. Villemain, an American professor, has written:

> If one sees art and science as interdependent and continuous spheres rather than enemies, then the problem has shifted. It becomes one of infusing all types of education and society with adequate art experience, whilst at the same time making use of the assistance that only science and technology can give. The problem is not to curtail the obvious resource of science and technology but to enlarge and redirect their problems so that it may more effectively provide the conditions necessary for widespread art experience.[1]

Essentially we see the university and the polytechnic with very different concerns. Certainly we do not see one as either superior or inferior to the other. Certainly they are different, and both are necessary. We believe that the art schools have provided the best general education in the country in the post-war period, a fact not sufficiently recognized.

Since the real capital of the future is knowledge and understanding, the creative in education has a key role to play where its form is audio-visual and based on the well defined principle that progress can take place only where 'being' and 'doing' keep pace with knowledge.

Educationally the polytechnic idea is inescapable for the art school, but it is also educationally the right step. [...]

1 F. T. Villemain, 'Democracy, Education and Art', *Educational Theory*, vol. XIV, no. 1 (January 1964).

Elma Askham and Harry Thubron, extracts from 'The Case for Polytechnics', *Studio International*, vol. 174, no. 892 (September 1967) 83; 86.

Patrick Heron
Murder of the Art Schools//1971

A disaster of massive proportions is going unnoticed; namely, the government-decreed, and therefore forcible, absorption of nearly all the country's biggest and most important colleges of art by the new polytechnics. [...]

About ten years ago British art students suddenly became conspicuous on the pavements of our cities in a way they had never been before: it wasn't just hair, or clothes, or style of walking – but a mixture of all three – and all three were revolutionary. Take clothes: what was really startling was the utterly personal way in which each student put together 'unfashionable' and unlikely bits and pieces with a sense of complete personal authority: suddenly there seemed no need to conform to any accepted canon, still less to look over one's shoulder at Paris or even New York. [...] By 1963 all the office girls in the land were indistinguishable from the art students; while now, in 1971, young city directors go out for the evening or the weekend looking like passable imitations of the chaps at the Slade. Yet the Government is worried about the cost of the art schools. If they added up the export earnings of the Beatles and the rest, not to mention those of the rag trade, whose famous designers cream off scores of ideas all the time from the endlessly varying gear of the art students, they might begin to see an economic justification for the 'art school scene', not in spite of, but because of, its notorious freedoms and excesses. [...]

Freedom of intention and direction and of method and means has evolved to such proportions that it is impossible to go now into almost any art school in the country without finding that no two students overlap in terms of the idioms in which they are working. It is not an exaggeration to say that in a school where there are 70 students of fine art one will probably find almost as many wholly distinct idioms being explored in as many media. And such profusion is the normal condition which one expects to find in any major college of art, and even in many minor ones, and is even more likely in a provincial than a London school. [...]

If one compares the scene I've just described with the pattern that prevailed before the war, where all 70 students would have been pretending to arrive at almost identical visual results as the outcome of a single exercise in a single acceptable idiom, the measure of the present revolution begins to be apparent. What is indisputable is that this enormously prolific and fertile educational method has evolved in an atmosphere of almost unlimited freedom and liberalism. Teachers are mere catalysts in this situation: innovation springs from below, from the students themselves: and one often feels the teachers' open indebtedness to the students as a source of ideas. One thing is quite certain: the organizational pattern which makes these freedoms possible is not imposed from above. [...]

[T]he Government chose to ignore and override the urgent and considered advice of its two most distinguished advisers in art education – the two men whose names identify the bodies which have been responsible for administering art education in this country, the Coldstream Committee and the Summerson Council. The complex but liberal constitution under which the British art schools have flourished in the way that I've been describing was the work of these men [William Coldstream, John Summerson], to whom great credit is due.

Anyone can see what was behind governmental and civil service thinking. [...] Was it not a truism that from, say, 10,000 art students only a tiny handful would emerge as successful artists? And that, among the rest, the majority would simply be fed back into that circular, self-perpetuating stream of teachers of teachers of art? Would it not be much better to streamline the whole system in such a way that the vast majority of art students were sidetracked from the beginning into a host of useful, economically justifiable, skills and disciplines and indeed trades – in a word – were discouraged from the madness of pursuing the uselessness of fine art, which is always an end in itself, and were encouraged instead to think from the start of the relevance of the *applied* arts to society? [...]

Although it is fashionable to imagine that art and technology are drawing closer all the time, and as justification of this view to point to creative artistic involvement with scientific and pseudo-scientific processes and techniques, the truth is that art and science remain wholly distinct and separate areas. Still more is it certain that mere technology and art remain apart and different from one another. [...]

However you express it, the art schools are simply being dismembered and swallowed piecemeal. It is just possible that one might be persuaded that this was not so if, for instance, there was a single case of a painter or sculptor being appointed director of a polytechnic. But I know of no such case. The nation's artists are being expected truthfully to relinquish control of art education, leaving it in the hands of scientists. What would the country's chemists and physicists think of a plan which placed scientific education administratively under the control of painters and sculptors? [...]

Patrick Heron, extracts from 'Murder of the Art Schools', *The Guardian* (12 October 1971); reprinted in Patrick Heron, *Art and Education* (Wakefield, Yorkshire: Bretton Hall, 1996) 30–35.

Lisa Tickner
Hornsey 1968: The Art School Revolution//2008

[...] [The new 'A' Course at St Martin's School of Art] devised by Peter Kardia aimed to open the sculptural field to influences from other disciplines, including linguistics, phenomenology, cybernetics, psychology and cultural theory.

Kardia believed that habit was the greatest threat to creativity, and from the first day of the autumn term in 1969 the new students were locked in a white studio, for eight hours a day, for the rest of the term. They were provided with a particular material for an unspecified time – a bag of plaster, a roll of paper, a block of polystyrene – but given no instructions, no advice and no response. They were not allowed to leave, and they were not allowed to speak. Kardia's aim was deliberately to disorientate the students, 'to put them in an experiential situation where they couldn't grasp what they were doing'.[1] This was either one of the most radically inventive moves in art education, or what one of the students called 'an obtuse behavioural experiment', or some combination of the two: the sculptor Richard Deacon found it liberating and the filmmaker Tony Hill, authoritarian and oppressive.[2] As pedagogy it bridged two models in Thierry de Duve's schema [creativity–medium–invention; attitude–practice–deconstruction; see page 64], merging a modernist exploration of medium with an emerging stress on process over the fine adjustment of the sculptural object.

At Coventry College of Art, the 'Art Theory' course was introduced by Terry Atkinson, Michael Baldwin and David Bainbridge, members of the Art & Language group, in October 1969. It drew on emerging critiques of mainstream modernism developed by conceptual artists on both sides of the Atlantic and 'lived critically and thus precariously within the institutional framework of the Dip.AD'.[3] It was not part of the 'complementary studies' required by the Coldstream Report as an adjunct to studio work for the Diploma in Art and Design, but neither was it 'studio activity' in the usual sense of the term. The course offered a deconstructive critique of the assumptions which, in its view, fatally compromised studio practice, including a belief in the primacy of the art-object, the importance of formal experiment in the medium, and the creative autonomy of artists and students.[4] This was a source of friction with other staff and administrators irritated by its influence and sceptical of its claims.[5] Baldwin and Bainbridge were dismissed, and the course dismantled, in 1971, after the Summerson Council confirmed that only 'studio work' in 'its commonly accepted meaning, that is to say the production of tangible, visual art objects' was acceptable for assessment.[6]

It seems reasonable to suppose that despite the radicality of these courses – and perhaps because of its vehemence – neither was in a position to escape what Paul Wood calls a 'faultline of endemic sexism' across art-college culture in general.[7] [...]

As the sculptor Reg Butler put it, bluntly, to the Slade students in 1961, the question was whether 'a woman [can] become a vital creative artist without ceasing to be a woman except for purposes of census?' Robert Strand, from the perspective of the Summerson Council, admittedly unsympathetic, claimed that at Coventry many students were 'virtually brainwashed and disoriented' by a theoretical programme beyond their reach.[9] Trudi Gurling, at St Martin's in 1966–9, recalled that women sculpture students 'received little support and encouragement' and had to 'survive the course (literally) by negotiating a way between those overbearing male egos'.[10]

In Britain in 1968, fine art students made up 42 per cent of the final-year Diploma in Art and Design cohort and in 1969 just under 40 per cent of these were women. In some respects they had been better served by the tail-end of the academic tradition or by the Bauhaus model. The academies began by excluding them, at least from the life-room, but once they gained a foothold a sense of métier and structured discipline sustained them (think of Gwen John at the Slade).[11] The Bauhaus or modernist model, too, could prove productive, extending to women the idea of a basic training in visual grammar and experiment with the medium (think of Lee Krasner with Hans Hofmann).[12] The 'attitude–practice–deconstruction' model was more of a challenge, at least at first. To put it schematically, in terms of how women were perceived by themselves and their peers, in the academic model the principal sticking point was talent (did they have it?); in the Bauhaus model, invention (could they do it?); and in the post-Bauhaus model, attitude (were they up to it?).

In their sociological study of Coventry College of Art, Charles Madge and Barbara Weinberger noted the observations of a colleague on the pre-diploma students enrolled in 1968–69. They fell into 'three main categories of roughly equal size': 'firstly, those whose self-confidence was severely shaken; secondly, those who though confused were not so worried by this; and thirdly, those who had positively gained in confidence and understanding ... In the first group were a majority of girls, in the last a large majority of boys.'[13] Like other writers, Madge and Weinberger stress the central place accorded to the 'crit': the more or less combative event in which students are required to articulate and defend the direction of their work. The art student is in their view 'driven to behave as though he [sic] had access to a charisma which may not be his to command; and he has to justify this, to himself and to his peers and teachers, in intellectualized terms and under conditions of almost unbearable ambiguity.'[14] The goal was no longer manual competence but the possession of certain kinds of knowledge and the ability to occupy a particular position.[15] The additional ambiguity for female students was that 'attitude' – requiring the forceful assertion of one's work and identity as an artist – was at odds with the commonplace assumption that girls were essentially decorative and compliant. Lacking in vitality and invention, their destiny was to marry artists, take teacher-training courses, or find some other way to square the circle until they could face the contradictions down.[16]

There is a considerable psychological literature on the distribution of supposedly 'masculine' and 'feminine' traits in the art and art-school population. One study, funded by the Calouste Gulbenkian Foundation and published shortly before the sit-in [at Hornsey College of Art in 1968], acknowledged that 'although an *interest* in art is a feminine trait in our culture ... young women quickly learn at art college that *practical, professional* art is a male preserve.'[17] In 1985 Griselda Pollock concluded that women had trouble in art schools because they were the 'bastion of reactionary ideas about art, teaching, self-expression and above all individualism', and that the 'positions sustained by these ideas are difficult if not impossible for women to adopt without some severe distortion or negation of aspects of their particularity as persons'.[18] Madge and Weinberger noted at Coventry that 'an emphasis on the freedom of the individual was regarded somewhat cynically by some students who were subjected to quite persistent bullying by some staff'. Women's names do not emerge in accounts of the short-lived Art Theory course which helped initiate conceptual art as a pedagogic project.[19] But conceptualism, a moment of 'radical fissure' around 1968, proved fertile for women.[20] Attitude, practice and deconstruction came together: deconstruction, as a tool tuned to the analysis of cultural meanings and effects (especially around gender and sexuality); practice as a new political aesthetic (often combining images and texts); and attitude as a confident staking out of the grounds (supported by a shared conversational community).[21] That art schools are not what they were is an achievement as well as a source of regret.

1 [footnote 58 in source. Regrettably, for space reasons the footnotes are here abbreviated to published references only; please consult the original text for the detailed discussion and documentation.] Kardia (originally Atkins) quoted in Hester Westley, 'The Year of the Locked Room', *TATE etc.*, no. 9 (Spring 2007).

2 [59] Ibid.

3 [60] Charles Harrison and Fred Orton, *A Provisional History of Art & Language* (Paris: Éditions Eric Fabre, 1982) 26.

4 [61] See Charles Harrison, *Essays on Art & Language* (Cambridge, Massachusetts: The MIT Press, 2001) 269.

5 [62] See Philip Pilkington, Kevin Lole, David Rushton, 'Some Concerns in Fine Art Education', *Studio International*, vol. 183 (October 1971) 120–22; Terry Atkinson, Michael Baldwin, 'Art Teaching', *Art-Language*, vol. 1, no. 4 (November 1971) 25–50.

6 [63] The internal politics were complex and disputed. See Charles Harrison, *Essays on Art & Language*, op. cit, 70; Harrison and Orton, op. cit., 26–7; Pilkington, Lole, Rushton, op. cit., and 'Some Concerns in Fine Art Education II', *Studio International*, vol. 183 (November 1971) 168–70; 'Four Midland Polytechnic Fine Art Departments' and 'Remarks on Art Education' *Studio International*, vol. 184 (November 1972) 176–9; 179–81.

7 [64] See Paul Wood, 'Between God and the Saucepan', in Chris Stephens, ed., *A History of British Art: 1870 to Now* (London: Tate Publishing, 2008) 162–87 (178).

8 [65] Reg Butler, *Creative Development: Five Lectures to Art Students* (London: Routledge & Kegan Paul, 1962) 21. [...] These lectures were delivered in June 1961, i.e. after the Coldstream Report but before its implementation.

9 [66] Robert Strand, *A Good Deal of Freedom: Art and Design in the Public Sector of Higher Education, 1960–1982* (UK: Council for National Academic Awards, 1987) 98.

10 [67] Trudi Gurling, email response to BBC website on Vanessa Engle's documentaries on *Art & the 1960s*. http://www.bbc.co.uk/bbcfour/documentaries/features/ask-vanessa-engle (accessed 3 May 2007).

11 [73] See Sue Row, *Gwen John: A Life* (London: Chatto & Windus, 2001); Lisa Tickner, '"Augustus' Sister": Gwen John: Wholeness, Harmony and Radiance', in *Gwen John and Augustus John* (London: Tate Publishing, 2004) 29–45.

12 [74] See in particular Anne Wagner, *Three Artists Three Women: Modernism in the Art of Hesse, Krasner and O'Keeffe* (Berkeley and Los Angeles: University of California Press, 1996).

13 [75] Charles Madge and Barbara Weinberger, *Art Students Observed* (London: Faber & Faber, 1973) 35.

14 [76] [For further discussion of the problems encountered with both combative and supportive models of the 'crit' see] Charles Harrison, 'Educating Artists', *Studio International*, vol. 183 (May 1972) 222–4.

15 [77] Howard Singerman, *Art Subjects: Making Art in the American University* (Berkeley and Los Angeles: University of California Press, 1999) 173.

16 [78] See ibid., 144–5.

17 [79] Peter Stringer, 'Masculinity-Femininity as a Possible Factor Underlying the Personality Responses of Male and Female Art Students', *British Journal of Social and Clinical Psychology*, vol. 6 (1967) 186–94.

18 [80] Griselda Pollock, 'Art, Art School, Culture: Individualism and the Death of the Artist', *Block*, no. 14 (Winter 1985–6) 50–67 (63).

19 [81] Lynn Lemaster contributed to Art & Language in the mid 1970s.

20 [82] See Pollock, op. cit., 63.

21 [83] Ibid., 50–1.

Lisa Tickner, extracts from *Hornsey 1968: The Art School Revolution* (London: Frances Lincoln, 2008) 95–6; 97–9.

Dr Annette Gomperts
Thin Air: The Psycho-Vocalic Discoveries of Alan Smithson//2009

[...] In 1971, whilst studying Three-Dimensional Design at Leeds Polytechnic, Alan Smithson encountered a book on the 'new acquisitions' shelf in the Art and Design library. The book was *Breakthrough*, Latvian experimental psychologist Konstantin Raudive's study of the new Electronic Voice Phenomena research. In *Breakthrough*, Raudive describes the strange voice phenomena that had been recorded by himself and others from radio or TV broadcasts, or which had been discovered through the process of simply recording empty space. The voices, uttering enigmatic phrases in undefinable accents and with strange stresses and tones, seemed to be coming from a world other than our own. Smithson was instantly fascinated by these new discoveries and rapidly became the foremost EVP enthusiast in the UK.

Another crucial event for Smithson at this time was his attendance, in 1972, at a lecture given to the Leeds polytechnic Landscape Architecture Department by artists Rose McGuire and Jeff Nuttall. The latter was also a tutor in the Leeds polytechnic Fine Art department. The lecture was about an 'old friend' of Nuttall's whose loss of identity led him to be able to merge himself experientially with any space, be it a building or landscape, enabling him to sense the traces of any significant events that had happened in that location. One phrase from the lecture struck Smithson as perfectly capturing the sonic potential of space, a potential that he was just beginning to explore: 'I know that emptiness is not a zero but a significant absence of what has been or will be. Thus no place is static but partakes continuously of its own change by recalling its past and projecting its future.' [...]

Smithson had stayed in Leeds to study largely because of the reputation of Leeds College of Art, most of which had been absorbed into the new Leeds Polytechnic, and into the new H building, both of which opened in January 1970. In order fully to understand Smithson's research and findings it is necessary to be aware of the history of this context.

In the mid 1950s Harry Thubron had turned Leeds College of Art into one of the most revolutionary art schools in the world, basing his famous Leeds 'basic research' course on the principles of the Bauhaus. Students were taught to articulate their own ideas rather than to specialize in specific skills or particular media, and were even dissuaded from making 'art' as such: process being more important than result. 'In many ways we were walking into the unknown', Thubron wrote, '[but] I think this is a vital and necessary element'. This revolutionary approach was continued into the sixties and seventies. Students were also given instruction in current ideas in a wide spectrum of areas such as technology, poetry, psychology and music, as well as having access to a programme of visiting lecturers that included artists, composers, literary critics, playwrights and historians. A *Studio International* article on Leeds in 1969 compared it to the nomadic Living Theatre; the democratic musical environments created by Cornelius Cardew (who was a regular visitor); and the Esalen Institute in California. Patrick Heron, writing in *The Guardian* at the time, described Leeds College of Art as 'the most influential in Europe since the Bauhaus'. In 1972 the ICA, London, gave the entire college a show in its galleries: 'Leeds in London', an unprecedented event for any art school, regional or not. Fluxus members Robin Page, Robert Filliou and George Brecht often taught at Leeds, Brecht providing a link right back to Black Mountain College and John Cage. Brecht and Filliou were a major influence on the young Alan Smithson, who – perhaps because of the subtlety of his own design ideas, or the fleeting and barely audible nature of his sound recording process – was fascinated by their self-effacing artworks, by the idea that art or design could almost disappear, that any artistic or designed statement could be on the edge of not being said at all. Brecht and Filliou's ideas inevitably extended to teaching and learning. One of their collaborations involved the creation of the Non-School of Villefranche, which, perhaps appropriately, never got further than a letterhead. The motto, translated from the French, stated:

> Carefree Exchange of Information and Experience.
> No students. No teachers.
> Perfect freedom,
> At times to listen,
> At times to talk.

Is this the ideal that Leeds was heading for? [...]

Smithson, as I have said, had been attracted to studying at Leeds because of its reputation for radicalism, but he now also became convinced that the disruption of educational norms that was being initiated in the H block had somehow contributed to the building's anamnetic uniqueness. The building had hosted so much freedom of thought and action that the resulting electromagnetic storm, so to speak, had left its mark on H building permanently.

Happenings, then performance art, became the means for the most radical practices in the Leeds Fine Art department in the seventies. During these years the performances that occurred in the H block Fine Art studios became more and more cathartic and provocative, often involving physical harm to the artists or their audience. This prevalence of violence seemed to be another factor in increasing the H Block's susceptibility to Smithson's sonic experimentation: 'For the electromagnetic wave forms within the rooms to be distorted to the right degree', Smithson wrote, 'a building requires a substantial magnitude of disturbance, sustained over a period of time, as this seems to be a contributing factor in transforming it into a depository of spatially recorded thought.'

The Fine Art lecturers provided the initial source of disturbance at Leeds. Robin Page, according to Smithson's journal, tried to scream a plant to death in one performance. Fellow tutor Jeff Nuttall campaigned for human body parts to be allowed in art performances, and in a local newspaper press cutting found pasted in Smithson's journal, Nuttall claimed: 'So far as student violence is concerned I am warmly in support of it ... There are no plans for violence, it is a spontaneous thing, an action, to precipitate fracture.' Interviews to get onto the Fine Art course were famously tough, in order to weed out those not up to the demands or to coping with the hostility of the wider public to confrontational work. 'I think I heard some tale', wrote Smithson, 'about an interview where the applicant was asked whether he thought his work was "precious". When he replied "no" one of the interviewers threw his portfolio out of the window.' The Fine Art prospectus, appropriately, had a picture of a mousetrap on the front of it.

Over these years Smithson noted some of the more charged student performance art events at Leeds in his journal. Claire Watson dissected a parrot in a local pub, and made Molotov cocktails out of oil-cans (Watson, incidentally, also lived in an upturned boat from one menstrual cycle to the next, a performance to which I refer in my 1996 essay 'Maternal Space'). Ron Crowcroft invited people to a performance, then proceeded to hammer the entrances of the space shut with timber, trapping the audience inside (with hammering by Claire Watson). Ian MacKay performed with a guillotine and a latex-cast penis. Mari Hobbs used her own blood to make prints (attracting the attention of the media in the process). Rob Elliot did a performance which involved walking on broken glass.

Kevin Atherton was told to 'finish his glass' in the Fenton – the main Fine Art pub, where most of the teaching also took place – so he ate it, and excreted blood for a week. Another two students beat people up as art. [...]

A neighbour of his at this time, Rita Dowd, told me that he was always very friendly, though not exactly outgoing. She said that 'he seemed to become more and more melancholy whenever his sleepwalking increased, which was often accompanied at this time by loud bangs and yells.' She told me:

> Around springtime that year [April 1986] Alan showed me some newspaper articles about all the trouble in the Fine Art department at the Poly, he was really distraught about it. Desperate he was. He kept mentioning 'H' in connection with it all, he was very concerned for her. I presumed this was a friend of his who was still studying there. The *Yorkshire Evening Post* had said that some women students had alleged that Art degrees were being given in return for sexual favours. The staff were saying that this was a smear campaign by students unhappy with their degree marks. The tutors claimed that the Fine Art course was suffering because staff numbers had declined, resources had been cut and more was to come – the Thatcher government were going to cut all fine art courses by at least 20 per cent. Education would soon have to compete in the marketplace like everything else. Meanwhile the National Advisory Board had recommended closing the Leeds course. Students had given evidence about lack of teaching, that the sound studio had run into disrepair and had been closed down, that performance work, which Leeds had been famed for, had been marginalized or not supported, even that the Poly building itself was falling apart – the glass roof in the Fine Art area was covered in polythene sheets to keep the rain out. [...]

Paul Rooney (in the persona of Dr Annette Gomperts, scholar of 'marginalized architectural histories'), extracts from *Thin Air: The Psycho-Vocalic Discoveries of Alan Smithson* (London: Sound & Music, 2009) 3–6; 10–11; 24–5 [footnotes not included].

Griselda Pollock
Art, Art School, Culture//1987

[...] Consider the organizing principles of many schools. The basic pedagogical plan is that the privileged independent spirits selected for the course at interview are given the opportunity to sink or swim. Space is provided, materials, a few technical resources. The student is expected to develop a programme of work, 'my work', that precious phrase, a project about which, from time to time, a conversation is held in unequal, ill-defined and educationally lamentable conditions. Assessments, when recorded, tend towards personal comment and register from the staff point of view the kind of contact (was the student aggressive, resistant to advice, willing to take up suggestions, etc.?). Undoubtedly many students thrive in this hostile and unsupportive environment, especially where their own sense of identity is implicitly reinforced by the hidden agenda of macho self-reliance and aggression, the son's battle with the father. (Maybe Norman Bryson's 1984 book *Tradition and Desire* does have a place somewhere after all?) The hidden agenda is institutional sexism. Let there be no flippant underestimation of what this intimidating and bizarre parody of an education means to women. Some have literally died of the experience.

One response to such a critique would come from educationalists. Many professional teachers not involved with fine art traditions find the typical art school scenario quite horrifying in the licence it potentially gives to those in full-time paid employment at an educational institution. Better teaching methods, more pastoral care cannot, however, be the answer, though they might be an improvement in the worst cases. What is overlooked in such a response is the structural contradiction which is at the root the collision of two professions – artist and teacher; the collision of two ideologies – individualism and socialization.

Education has been named as one of the major ideological state apparatuses, that is, not just a place of learning but an institution where we are taught our places within a hierarchical system of class, gender and race relations. [...]

Professionals of course deny their implication in state strategies, by proclaiming the high ideals of critical education. Art schools are a particularly contradictory site. They are a location for the perpetual production of key ideologies. But in practice art schools deliver very little education. Indeed art students are put at a scandalous disadvantage (and ironically glory in it) vis-à-vis other students in higher and further education. The absence, however, of systematic induction into an (ortho)doxy leaves open unexpected possibilities for counter courses, women's workshops, etc. The rationale of the art school is to train rather than educate artists to become professionals who must compete with each other and other professionals in a difficult market for jobs and sales. Yet their training leaves them totally unequipped to grasp their place in the competitive world of business, professionalism or, no longer so inevitable, education. The school sustains a powerful sense of the being of an artist in total mystification of what working as one entails.

Art schools are not immune from the social strategies of the present government and the political culture which supports it. All sectors of education are being asked to be more productive, i.e. to produce something quantifiable, both in terms of marketable goods and saleable personnel.

Against this radicalism, traditional ideologies of art schools offer the weakest of defences, the ideals of High Culture:

> We certainly need to remain open to public needs and opportunities in the field of public art, but we must remain firmly established in the traditional role that art has held in society in the past. Art schools should be there to preserve and keep alive the higher values of art. As educationalists teaching in art schools we have a role to play in society. We need to remain firmly entrenched in values that society in its quest for economic survival tends to ignore. The values that artists hold inevitably have their source in a spiritual, rather than a mental or material one. [Phillip King][1]

Art is thus the realm apart from the utilitarian demands of economic survival, which as in the early nineteenth century must be protected for fear the higher values it alone secures will wither. Few ever dare to question what these values are, whom they serve or how justified is this division of spiritual versus utilitarian. History does not bear out the defence of higher values or the spirit in art.

There would seem, however, to be a contradiction between what has been suggested above about the compatibility between Thatcherite conservatism's cult of the self-made individual and its ideologies of art, and what is now being said about the incompatibility between the Thatcherite demand for productivity and the defence of pure art. [...]

I have argued in an earlier article that the notion of the artist formed by the culture of the British bourgeoisie articulated contradictions within the norms constructed around masculinity, satisfying fantasies of freedom from social constraint within a world of strict regulation of sexualities, behaviours, gestures and common senses, while art itself was elevated to a repository of values which were desirable in terms of social prestige but were expendable in the logic of capitalism. Historically, therefore, the middle-class ideologies of art and artist demonstrate a series of fissures which have permitted the accommodation and appropriation of notions of the role and purposes of culture and its sacred individualism which are, if not necessary to, sometimes even in conflict with, economic ideologies. [...]

It is however possible that the relation between the support of High Culture and the apparently antagonistic demand for a more economistic view of its use and productivity may in fact relate within the ideological formation characteristic of multinational capitalism, which can crudely be said to have dispensed with the forms of social hegemony required in the nineteenth and early twentieth centuries with still localized and highly visible power struggles between fractions of the ruling bloc. Such an argument leads towards the position advanced in Fredric Jameson's article 'The Cultural Logic of Late Capitalism' (1984) in which the following propositions are made: We are currently witnessing a major cultural rupture ushering in a new era, the postmodern, a moment which is in turn explicable in relation to the latest, multinational phase of capitalism. This world of multinational capitalism has become for its inhabitants 'illegible' and incomprehensible. We have been shifted from a world experienced in terms of historical time to one experienced in terms of space, a kind of postmodern hyperspace which transcends the capacities of the individual human body and consciousness to locate itself and to organize its immediate surroundings perceptually and cognitively. The disjunction between the body and the environment, both social and economic, points to the inability of our minds to map the global, multinational and decentred communicational networks in which we are caught. In a world so bewilderingly vast – or sublime – forms of social control such as the nineteenth-century bourgeoisie desired, which still depended on visible displays of authority and 'cultivation', leadership and personalized mastery, become redundant. [...]

The insistence on artistic practices as products of a socially produced discursive category sustained by a community of specialist users – makers, consumers, managers and related professionals – is often coupled with more elaborated theories about the social production of the individual. Indeed, in several influential trends in twentieth-century theories, the individual is completely dissolved as an ideological category into the notion of a split, fragmented and mobile subject, held only in the place of illusory unity by the structures of language and society of which being a subject is but an effect. The most extreme statement of this position derives from the structuralist Marxist theories of ideology and the interpellated subject associated with Althusserian writings. Related but distinct is the psychoanalytical intervention, also based on a structuralist premise about the split subject – conscious/unconscious – produced as an effect of entering into the social/symbolic system of language. Feminist theory has explored the implications of both these resources and articulated specific theories about the production of the gendered subject, that is our sexuality is not natural, pre-given, innate, but the product of multiple determinations at the psychic and social levels. Many of these have been deployed in the specific area of cultural analysis to argue for the so-called 'death of the author'.

A great deal of traditional literary and artistic criticism concerns itself with discovering in the works analysed the presence of the originating subject, the author. The meaning thus found is often no more than what is claimed as the artist's intention. In art history in particular, supporting evidence is often directly biographical. In contrast it can be argued that the reader is in fact the author of the meanings of the work read or viewed. Yet to be able to make a reading of a work the reader/viewer must possess a modicum of social knowledge about the practice (what is a novel, a painting, a photograph?), what kinds of behaviour are appropriate, what kinds of readings will be recognized as art consumption and so forth. The reader/viewer therefore herself becomes a site for social exchanges which displace meanings from being a something put there or taken out to being a process of productive activity predicated again upon a social community. The death of the author, or the artist, as privileged individual speaking herself through the medium of work to a sensitized receiver is displaced by an awareness of the calculations and ventures of producers working within, for, or against the community of knowledges and expectations which constitute the social practice of which she is but one active participant. Where this knowledge is mobilized by feminist producers, the challenge to the orthodoxies of art, art school and culture begins to appear in its true proportions. Feminist practices in art schools therefore do more than irritate the established staff at the level of personal affronts to their masculine privilege as Fathers and Sons of Culture. They threaten the dominant modernist paradigms of art and artist. Modernism is traditionally posed as radical, anti-establishment. This is of course a myth. [...]

1 Phillip King, speaking at a debate on art schools and art education at the Royal College of Art, London, where he was Professor of Sculpture, on 14 June 1985.

Griselda Pollock, extracts from 'Art, Art School, Culture: Individualism after the Death of the Artist', *Block*, no. 11 (Winter 1985/86); reprinted in *The Block Reader* (London: Routledge, 1996) 53–9.

Dinah Dossor
To Claim an Education//1982

[...] Women who wish to use the expressive and communicative potential of needlework, fabric, clay or textiles in 'fine art' work may still find such materials unacceptable to fine art staff, and be denied access to the considerable technical expertise of staff in design departments. Students may have to take preliminary steps to enforce the acceptability of such media either from the considerable body of published material which supports cross-departmental and interface work by arranging visits to colleges where such work flourishes – Goldsmiths or Bradford for example – or by pressurizing for qualified and sympathetic external assessors. Students can co-opt additional accessors onto their examination boards and these could be from other departments, art history, complementary studies or applied arts staff. Conversely, women who wish to learn traditionally 'male' techniques – casting, welding or joinery – may not get the additional technical help they need. [...] Restrictions on media then become restrictions on visual language, on what may be expressed and to whom art may speak. The forms that many women choose, traditional 'craft' forms, accessible media such as postcards, posters, film and video, all have this power to stretch the frames of reference of an art school training out from the ingrown 'isms' of the art world and into the shared concerns of a non-art-world audience in the community outside the institution. Liverpool's fine art course has developed a number of changes in emphasis [...]. I am an art historian/theorist but also a full member of the fine art staff with timetabled commitments to studio teaching and studio seminars. This level of integration is important, for it is difficult for art historians to effect the CNAA [Council for National Academic Awards] policy recommendations towards the studio relevance of theoretical and academic studies without a close working knowledge of the aims and methods of studio practice. I am therefore able to shape my curriculum partly in response to changing student needs and interests as these appear in studio work, to participate in studio assessment, to help shape fine art future policy [...]. The fine art course has a strong subjective basis in the first year of studies and I can already see some changes in the work – interestingly most clearly in the work of men who are required to explore their self image and motivation and to question the social and community uses of art. [...]

In colleges where women are isolated, or unable to shape their own curricula, work may be achieved outside the formal study programmes, particularly in the women students' art groups which are proliferating in colleges. These groups can be funded by the students' union and can function not only as pressure and support groups but also as an effective alternative educational sector within the college. The Liverpool women's group shows women's films, organizes visits to women's shows, discusses student work and employs visiting lecturers. The group also has links with the women's art community outside the college.[1] [...]

1 [For example, the Women's Art Library in London, which was founded in 1978 by a group of artists and art historians as an alternative public space to experience and study women's art. The library (initially called the Women Artist's Slide Library until 1992) also became the catalyst for an arts organization that published catalogues, books and the magazine *MAKE* (1983–2002). The library is now housed in Goldsmiths College, London. http://www.gold.ac.uk/make/]

Dinah Dossor, extracts from 'To Claim an Education', *FAN* (Feminist Art News), no. 10 (1982) 7–8.

Monica Ross
Something Old, Something New, Something Else//2001

[...] The first difference in the structure of change that occurred in 1990 was in the pattern of the traditional incorporation of the new. This was no longer a matter of recharging established currencies, but a demand, through the insertion of new educational components, that tradition be rethought *per se*. A cultural reversal, within and beyond the institution, was taking place. Traditions of all kinds were becoming relativized by the new, rather than the other way round.

Specifically, in the creation of Critical Fine Art Practice, the [Central Saint Martins] school's established fine art tradition had to countenance the reality of other, parallel and incipient art practices on equal terms, a development which, when seen from a modernist standpoint, threatened to supercede or erase it. The necessity of having to meet salient change by the creation of a parallel subject of equal status, which was differently premised in every aspect of its aims, content and structure, was not only the insertion into the curriculum of an alternative choice of study but also a critique of the modernist ethic which continued to underpin the established positions and methodologies in the school.

A second significant difference was that Critical Fine Art Practice was led by a team of women artists and, in common with the film and video subjects, which also had a substantial number of women staff, one which included artists and theorists from other so-called minority groups who had historically been excluded from the modernist frame of art education.

The actual and directive presence of the formerly excluded and their cultural and social agendas of difference tended not to be perceived as a cohort of the avant-garde but as an invasive force of opposition.

But the third difference was perhaps the most crucial, and underpinned the conflicted scenario within which the radicalization of higher education in Britain as corporate business was now situated. The introduction of any new element into the curriculum, whether it was a department or new media equipment, was, literally, only to be gained at the expense of the old. [...]

[A]ll the specialist subjects were summarily written out of the course and replaced by a general programme which was directed from the centre and from the top downwards. In a typically corporate line-management structure, an overarching singularity swept aside the remnants of academic autonomy, whether of tradition or the multiplicity of difference. It was a classic modernist move in the pattern of the sudden and absolute break: a non-negotiable overthrow of what had gone before. This supercession, which depended on the denial of existing academic expertise and the erasure of prior and continuing academic achievements, also positioned Critical Fine Art Practice, the contemporaneously different, as having become an anachronism. It was argued that, since the innovative aspects of its curriculum could now become incorporated into the single, general programme, it was, like the FACS [Fine Art and Critical Studies] course before it, no longer required. [...]

In one significant respect, the new model was what it claimed to be: entirely new. A specific attribute of the postwar British art school, although widely and differently interpreted, was a consensus that education is delivered, debated and developed through the sustained trajectory of a given curriculum. Whatever the differences between the specialist subjects, all had prided themselves on providing an accordingly structured and taught curriculum. This was the structure which had facilitated the productive terrain for an interactive discourse between practice and theory, integrated curriculum development and a sustained and shared academic forum which supported student development.

The architects of the new model claimed to have changed nothing about the course except the modes in which it was delivered. This was the new and crucial change. The new model reversed the provision of a multiplicity of educational and artistic positions and methodologies, the hallmark of the school's contemporary reputation, into a structure premised on consumer choice rather than on curriculum diversity. Although students now had the possibility to work more freely across what had become, through economic pressures, territorialized academic boundaries, the quality of diversity on offer had been reduced, as in film for example, to almost the level of a media resource where previously study of a specialist media had been within a contextual curriculum. [...]

Already, the managers of Central Saint Martins are having to rethink the structure of a fine art programme whose architects seem to have mistaken the short-term demands of the marketplace for the considered reflectivity of an educational curriculum 'at the cutting edge'. [...]

Monica Ross, extracts from 'Something Old, Something New, Something Else' in *Education, Information, Entertainment*, ed. Ute Meta Bauer (Vienna: Institut für Gegenwartskunst, 2001) 66–8; 73.

Griselda Pollock
Opened, Closed and Opening: Reflections on Feminist Pedagogy//2010

[...] Given that difference in society enters into the ethics and politics of the classroom, Elsa Barkley Brown, reflecting on her experience of teaching African-American history in the US academy, argues that the challenge for critical pedagogy is both to centre oneself in the experience of the lives of those about whom we are teaching and to challenge the power of normative thinking for which those lives are 'other', different, non-normative. She draws on Bettina Aptheker's concept of 'pivoting the centre'. No one has to imagine they can understand the experience of another; but they can learn to 'validate it, judge it by its own standards without need of comparison or the need to adopt the framework as their own.' Thus Elsa Barkley Brown is not talking about decentring, but pivoting the centres, allowing there to be many centres of experience, creating a patchwork of realities rather than hierarchies and norms.

Thus learning from the real pain and conflict that emerged in the first year of the [Master's Programme in Feminism and the Visual Arts],[1] because I had not fully attended to class vulnerabilities and power, I realized that in introducing feminism into the curriculum, I would have to engage the students fully in the nature of the challenge that feminism, when informed by an extended understanding of how race, class and sexuality constantly inflected any instance of gender, posed at the level of the embodied and subjective process of entering the institution and learning together.

To this end, I worked towards the idea of creating a safe space to learn. Engaging with the kinds of issues feminism poses both theoretically and existentially required responsibility on my part because of the reality of what feminism itself asks us to address in both ourselves and the world. Thus following the classic feminist recognition of 'speaking' for oneself, and learning through attention to the everyday, the lived and the hitherto unspoken, I asked the students each year to begin with a story: how had each person arrived here and now? Inspired by *Historia*, part III of Mary Kelly's installation *Interim* (1990), which traces the entry of women into feminism since 1968 through individual stories that reveal its many points of access and changing priorities, I asked them: How did they learn about feminism? What brought them to this moment? Some responded with ease, writing stories or making artworks, doing performances or bringing in objects, relaxed by being able to make their stories available to others in their own terms. Others found the very concept tasteless and soppy. They had come to engage with tough theory and felt that this request exhibited the worst kind of feminist sentimentality. A few, never having been asked to integrate intellectual and personal elements of their lives were simply rendered silent, unable to speak other than in the combative ways learned as the articulate feminist challenger in the patriarchal classroom. The hesitant tended to be middle-class, successful already in the existing models of education and modes of patriarchal ventriloquism. But in time, participating in the process revealed something else: that the feminist questioning of the hierarchies of knowledge, the divisions between public and private spheres, the asymmetrical valuing of formal and informal knowledges was fundamental, necessary and ultimately emancipatory. It enabled the union of theory and practice. Furthermore, this initiating story process made palpable, sometimes in blushing stutters, in constricted throats, in embarrassed participation in uncomfortably novel procedures, the otherwise theoretically formulated propositions about women being silenced, othered in discourse and exiled from language. Since much of the subsequent study was going to explore, practically, theoretically or art-historically, the questions of women and (self) representation, the voice and the feminine, this starting point of women students being asked to experience how difficult it is to tell their own stories, to write, to speak, to represent in the first person, a situated, classed, gendered, ethnically specific, sexually oriented first person, was already an experiment that made vivid the otherwise abstracted and theoretically distanced analysis of the disjunctures or creative possibilities of women speaking as women of things patriarchal cultures disowned, erased, ignored, devalued or simply failed to know. By the time the students came to the second module on feminism, art and history, or the third module on contemporary art, their understanding of texts by Hélène Cixous or Luce Irigaray, or the artists themselves, was 'real'.

Thus introducing feminism into a curriculum implies a much deeper confrontation with the very structures, protocols and habits of the academy. If these are not questioned, feminism ceases to have feminist effects on either the institution or its participating subjects. It cannot simply be a new academic topic assimilated to existing models of learning or teaching. The creation of a safe space for learning does not domesticate the seminar space; it does not reproduce a kind of mothering. It is undertaken precisely as a political recognition of how power operates at a capillary level, at work endlessly in our exchanges, destroying the very possibility for the kinds of rigorous intellectual or artistic transformations ambitious students rightly seek. [...]

1 [Founded by Pollock at the University of Leeds in 1992, closed by the university in 2003.]

Griselda Pollock, extracts from 'Opened, Closed and Opening: Reflections on Feminist Pedagogy in a UK University', *n-paradoxa*, vol. 26 (2010) 20–24.

Stuart Bailey
(Only an Attitude of Orientation)//2010

[This text] aims to provoke a discussion around how a contemporary art/design school might reasonably reconfigure itself in light of recent and projected changes in how institutions and disciplines actually operate in the early 21st century.

> Here's an opportunity freely to imagine what should be done, unhindered by administrative worries about what can't possibly be done. (Frances Stark)

Towards a Critical Faculty [a reader produced for students and faculty at Parson's School of Design, The New School, New York, 2006–7] was an attempt to grasp what my colleagues meant by 'design thinking'. Though I initially considered this term a tautology, it was seemingly regarded by my colleagues as a major aim of contemporary art/design education. So I tried to perform what I presumed it meant, a kind of loose, cross-disciplinary problem-solving, by collecting past and present fragments of insight that could inform a future mandate. Where the majority of these excerpts were directly concerned with pedagogy, from seminal Arts & Crafts and Bauhaus statements onwards, this follow-up looks further afield, seeking tangential reinforcement and extension of the same line of thinking. Its sources reside in the more pop end of sociology, philosophy and literature. [...]

Other Schools

In his book *The Shape of Time* the art historian George Kubler proposed a model which broke apart and reconstituted the prevailing compartmentalization of the arts. In his new system, architecture and packaging – both essentially containers – were conflated under the rubric 'envelopes': all small solids and containers under 'sculpture' and all work on a flat plane under 'painting'. These reclassifications already fell within Kubler's broader call to supplant the regular distinctions of useless (= art) and useful (= design) with those of desirable (= objects that last) and non-desirable (= objects that don't last). His new system emphasized objects that stood the test of time, regardless of whether they fulfilled a more quantifiable purpose (a hammer) or a less quantifiable one (a painting). Alternatively, in *What is a Designer*, the self-described cabinet-maker Norman Potter distinguished between 'things', 'places' and 'messages'. As far as I know, neither system was pursued beyond these two books, but they remain useful places to begin the productive destabilization of prevailing classification.

One contemporary model that appears to operate on this principle is Cittadellarte, established in the 1990s by the artist Michelangelo Pistoletto in Biella, Italy. The name is a contraction of the Italian words for 'city' and 'citadel', which amounts to a semantic paradox and an example of Michel Foucault's term 'heterotopia'. A heterotopia is an actual place (as opposed to a utopia) which is simultaneously open and shut off (his prime example is a cruise ship), comprised of apparently contradictory facets and therefore outside the norm by definition. Citadellarte's aim is explicit and without irony: directly to question and effect the contemporary role of art in society, operating as a 'mediator' between all arts disciplines and other broad social categories, such as economy, politics, science and education. It is organized into 'uffizi', offices with irregular titles like Nourishment, Spirituality and Work, alongside Fashion and Architecture. Participants pass through for varying amounts of time to engage in projects instigated through contact with local businessmen, politicians, economists and so on, and the whole enterprise is couched in global ambition, typified by the many one-liner slogans which Pistoletto employs as catch-all common denominators between insular industries: 'Art at the centre of a socially responsible transformation', 'Italian enterprise is a cultural mission', or 'The artist as the sponsor of thought.' [...]

Solitude

In *Abecedaire*, a testimonial interview intended for posthumous screening on French TV, the philosopher Gilles Deleuze discusses his experiences as a teacher. In the first of three distinct moments of unscripted insight, he describes the enormous amount of preparation involved in 'getting something into one's head' just enough – to a teetering degree of comprehension – to be able to convey it with the inspiration of live realization in front of a class. The preparation, then, amounts to a kind of rehearsal for a performance, at best a form of planned improvisation. If the speaker doesn't find what he's saying of interest, no one else will, and so there must be an element of mutual education in which he (the teacher) is stimulated by learning something at the same time as conveying it. Deleuze insists this shouldn't be mistaken for vanity: it's not a case of finding oneself passionate and interesting, only the subject matter.

Later, Deleuze makes a distinction between schools and movements. A school is a negative force, he suggests, because it is heavy, fixed and exclusive. It implies rules, leaders, administration, hierarchy and bureaucracy. A movement by comparison is light, flexible and open. Less easily defined, it is characterized more by intentions, attitudes, diversions and the passage of ideas. He gives an example from art history: Surrealism as an example of a 'school', with Breton its headmaster imposing rules, excluding personnel and settling scores, as opposed to Dada as a 'movement', a flow of ideas involving many people, places and forms without apparent hierarchy.

The final example is aligned with [a particular notion of] solitude. Deleuze relates how, in his experience, immature students operate primarily as a consequence of being alone. Lacking the sophistication to think otherwise, 'education' is foremost an opportunity to communicate, to share – and those interested in participating are naturally drawn to a 'school' which traditionally represents this opportunity. His job, he says, is to work towards reconciling these students with their solitude, to teach them the benefit of it – and to this end, he attempted to introduce notions or concepts that would circulate in a course. Not to establish these ideas, not so they become something as definite and ordinary as a 'school', but in order that they were and are perpetually manipulated by others, according to a series of unique interests and talents, continuing to circulate – as 'movement'.

Trial and Error

Established in Arnhem in 1998, the postgraduate Werkplaats Typografie (Typography Workshop) is an example of an institution founded on apparently ideal conditions. It is officially affiliated to the local art school and so sufficiently state-funded, but remains physically and spiritually autonomous. In theory at least, it seems set up to foster conditions as close to those of Deleuze's idea of 'movement' and unlike those of his 'school' as I can imagine. As one of its initial clutch of students, and having maintained irregular contact with its teachers and subsequent participants since, I've been able to consider it first and second hand with the detachment of a case study. In fact, I've been asked to write about it for one context or another in handy five year gaps, each an excuse to note my changing ideas about the place, about what has actually happened from its conception to its current incarnation from the inside out.

In 1998, 'Incubation of a Workshop' was written from the vantage of an idealistic student in his first year spent in an institution under construction. It's a kind of prose home movie, walking around, documenting the essential openness of the place in progress, emphasizing its quirky, homegrown nature, lack of hierarchy and supposed 'two-way teaching' between not-quite-teachers and not-quite-students. The founding idea is an art/design school based on 'real' (= commissioned) work rather than fictional projects or complete self-direction, because only this connection with the outside provides the 'correct sense of requiredness' for substantial, meaningful work.

In 2003, 'Some False Starts' was written as the introduction to a book accompanying what its by now mildly jaded author thought was a dubiously young 'retrospective' of work at the Stedelijk Museum in Amsterdam. It begins by denouncing the 'relentless sugary pitch' and 'wide-eyed positivity and woolly moralism' of the former piece, then tries to recount what had actually happened despite those good intentions. Almost hidden in the middle is a tenuous criticism of the establishment's increasing obsession with its image, its 'suppression of mistakes' which the writer thinks fundamental to any real art/design school. A few arguments and trips are recounted, with each negative offset by a positive. 'It was all human enough in the end', he writes. The idealism has shifted to accommodation.

Finally, in 2008, an 'Errata' for the school's tenth anniversary book was essentially a reconsideration of such self-aggrandizing which now, it seemed to me, had become a large part of the whole point of the place. In other words, this relentless reflection seemed to have become its defining characteristic: it was now a school about school, about its inner principles rather than outside work. This is manifest not only by their making the book in the first place, but also by the work shown in it, which 'runs a small gamut from the very local to the very personal'. I used to think this was disappointingly narcissistic or solipsistic, but now I consider it more affirmatively symptomatic of a discipline (or a few blurred disciplines) between states, a little lost, trying to work out what it has been, is, and might become. In lieu of any acceptable work – meaning, I guess, seemingly worthwhile work – from the wider world, the overwhelming locality of all the self-initiated books, posters for guest lectures and flyers for film screenings that pack the book's pages suggest its main purpose is simple community building – in search of Deleuze's reconciliation with solitude. This, then, is an example of a school currently experiencing a reflexive reconsideration of its founding discipline. I'm not sure how much the school realizes this itself, or needs to, really, but that's not to say the process mightn't be reasonably recognized and utilized elsewhere.

Stuart Bailey, extracts from *(Only an Attitude of Orientation)* (Oslo: Office for Contemporary Art Norway, Winter 2009–10) 1–5.

Tom Holert
Art in the Knowledge-Based Polis//2009

Lately, the concept of 'knowledge production' has drawn new attention and prompted strong criticism within art discourse. One reason for the current conflictual status of this concept is the way it can be linked to the ideologies and practices of neoliberal educational policies. [...]

I am particularly interested in how issues concerning the actual situations and meanings of art, artistic practice and art production relate to questions touching on the particular kind of *knowledge* that can be produced within the artistic realm (or the artistic *field*, as Bourdieu prefers it) by the practitioners or actors who operate in its various places and spaces. The multifarious combinations of artists, teachers, students, critics, curators, editors, educators, funders, policymakers, technicians, historians, dealers, auctioneers, caterers, gallery assistants, and so on, embody specific skills and competences, unique ways and styles of knowing and operating in the flexibilized, networked sphere of production and consumption. This variety and diversity has to be taken into account for these epistemes to be *recognized* as such and to obtain at least a slim notion of what is at stake when one speaks of *knowledge* in relation to art – an idea that is, in the best of cases, more nuanced and differentiated than the usual accounts of this relation. [...]

The consequences of the intersecting developments within the rebelling body of students and staff at Hornsey College of Art (and elsewhere) in 1968, as well as the general changes within society and culture, had to become manifest in the very conceptual framework not only of art education, but of art discourse as such.

> Hence, there was a widespread recognition that in future all higher education in art and design should incorporate a permanent debate within itself. 'Research', in this sense, came to appear an indispensable element in education. We regard it as absolutely basic that research should be an organic part of art and design education. No system devoted to the fostering of creativity can function properly

> unless original work and thought are constantly going on within it, unless it remains on an opening frontier of development. As well as being on general problems of art and design (techniques, aesthetics, history, etc.) such research activity must also deal with the *educational process itself* ... It must be the critical self-consciousness of the system, continuing permanently the work started here in the last weeks [June and July 1968]. Nothing condemns the old regime more radically than the minor, precarious part research played in it. It is intolerable that research should be seen as a luxury, or a rare privilege.[1]

Though this emphatic plea for 'research' was written in a historical situation apparently much different from our own, it nonetheless helps us to apprehend our present situation. Many of the terms and categories have become increasingly prominent in the current debates on artistic research, albeit with widely differing intentions and agendas. It seems to be of the utmost importance to understand the genealogy of conflicts and commitments that have led to contemporary debates on art, knowledge and science. [...]

Becoming institutionalized as an academic discipline at the interface of artistic and scientific practices at increasing numbers of art universities throughout Europe, artistic research (sometimes synonymous with notions such as 'practice-led research', 'practice-based research', or 'practice-as-research') has various histories, some rather short, others spanning centuries. The reasons for establishing programmes and departments fostering the practice-research nexus are certainly manifold, and differ from one institutional setting to the next. When art schools are explicitly displaced into the university system to become sites of research, the demands and expectations of the scientific community and institutional sponsorship vis-à-vis research outcomes of art schools change accordingly. [...]

Making the decision that something is practice as research imposes on the practitioner-researcher a set of protocols that fall into: 1) the point that the practitioner-researcher must necessarily have a set of separable, demonstrable, research findings that are abstractable, not simply locked into the experience of performing it; and 2) it has to be such an abstract, which is supplied with the piece of practice, which would set out the originality of the piece, set it in an appropriate context, and make it useful to the wider research community. [...]

When articulated in terms of such a regime of academic supervision, evaluation and control (as it increasingly operates in the Euroscapes of art education), the reciprocal inflection of the terms 'practice' and 'research' appears rather obvious, though they are seldom explicated. The urge among institutions of art and design education to rush the process of laying down validating and legitimating criteria to purportedly render intelligible the quality of art and design's 'new knowledge' results in sometimes bizarre and ahistorical variations on the semantics of practice and research, knowledge and knowledge production.

For applications and project proposals to be steered through university research committees, they have to be upgraded and shaped in such a way that their claims to the originality of knowledge (and thus their academic legitimacy) become transparent, accountable and justified. However, to 'establish a workable consensus about the value and limits of practice as research both within and beyond the community of those directly involved' seems to be an almost irresolvable task. At the least, it *ought* to be a task that continues to be open-ended and inevitably unresolved. [...]

The implications of this proposal [a research project titled 'Art in the Knowledge-based Polis'] are manifold, and they are certainly open to contestation. What, for instance, is the qualifier enabling it neatly to distinguish between artistic and non-artistic modes of knowledge production? Most likely, there isn't one. From (neo-) avant-garde claims of bridging the gap between art and life (or those modernist claims which insist on the very maintenance of this gap) to issues of academic discipline in the age of the Bologna process[2] and outcome-based education, it seems that the problem of the art/non-art dichotomy has been displaced. Today, this dichotomy seems largely to have devolved into a question of how to establish a discursive field capable of rendering an epistemological and ontological realm of artistic/studio practice as a scientifically valid research endeavour. [...]

However useless the deployment of terms such as 'research' and 'knowledge' may seem, such uselessness is bound to a reading and deployment of the terms in a way that remains detached from the particular modes of discourse formation in art discourse itself. The moment one enters the archives of writing, criticism, interviews, syllabi and other discursive articulations produced and distributed within the artistic field, the use of terms such as 'research' and discussion about the politics and production of 'knowledge' are revealed as fundamental to twentieth-century art – particularly since the inception of conceptual art in the late 1960s. After all, the modernists, neo- and post-avant-gardists aimed repeatedly at forms and protocols relating to academic and intellectual work – of research and publication, the iconography of the laboratory, scientific research or think tanks.

Administrative, information or service aesthetics, introduced at various moments of modernist and post-modernist art, emulated, mimicked, caricaturized and endorsed the aesthetics and rhetoric of scientific communities. They created representations and methodologies for intellectual labour on and off-display, and founded migrating and flexible archives that aimed to transform the knowledge spaces of galleries and museums according to what were often feminist agendas. [...]

Since the neo-avant-gardes of the 1960s (at the latest), knowledge generation within the visual arts has expanded through the constitutive dissolution (or suspension) of its subjects and media. Meanwhile, however, its specific aesthetic dimension has continued to be marked by elusiveness and unavailability – by doing things, 'of which we don't know what they are' (Adorno). A guiding hypothesis of the 'Art in the Knowledge-based Polis' conceit is that this peculiar relationship between the availability and unavailability of artistic knowledge production assigns a central task to contemporary cultural theory, as such. This not only concerns issues of aesthetics and epistemology, but also its relation to other (allegedly non-artistic) spaces of knowledge production.

To advance this line of reasoning, the various reconfigurations of knowledge, its social function and its distribution (reflected within late modernist and post-modernist epistemological discourse) have to be considered. From the invocation of the post-industrial information society to the critique of modernist 'meta-narratives' and the theorization of new epistemological paradigms such as reflexivity, transdisciplinarity and heterogeneity, the structure, status and shape of knowledge has changed significantly. Amongst other consequences, this has given rise to a number of specific innovative policies concerning knowledge (and its production) on national and transnational levels.

A point of tension that can become productive here is the traditional claim that artists almost constitutively work on the hind side of rationalist, explicated knowledge – in the realms of non-knowledge (or emergent knowledge). As a response to the prohibition and marginalization of certain other knowledges by the powers that be, the apparent incompatibility of non-knowledge with values and maxims of knowledge-based economies (efficiency, innovation and transferability) may provide strategies for escaping such dominant regimes.

Michel Foucault's epistemology offers a hardly noticed reasoning on artistic knowledge that appears to contradict this emphasis on non-knowledge, while simultaneously providing a methodological answer to the conundrum. In his 1969 *L'Archéologie du savoir* (*The Archaeology of Knowledge*), Foucault argues that the technical, material, formal and conceptual decisions in painting are traversed by a 'positivity of knowledge' which could be 'named, uttered and conceptualized' in a 'discursive practice'.[3] This very 'positivity of knowledge' (of the individual artwork, a specific artistic practice, or a mode of publication, communication and display) should not be confused with a rationalist transparency of knowledge. This 'discursive practice' might even refuse any such discursivity. Nonetheless, the works and practices do show a 'positivity of knowledge' – the signature of a specific (and probably secret) knowledge.

At the heart of 'Art in the Knowledge-based Polis' would be a recognition, description and analysis of such 'positivity' – as much as an exploration of the epistemological conditions in which such positivity appears. Just as the forms and discourses through which artists inform, equip, frame and communicate their production have become manifold and dispersed, so has a new and continuously expanding field of research opened up as a result. [...]

The pertinent notion of 'immaterial labour' that originated in the vocabulary of post-Operaismo (where it is supposed to embrace the entire field of 'knowledge, information, communications, relations or even affects')[4] has become one of the most important sources of social and economic value production. Hence it is crucial for the visual arts and their various (producing, communicating, educating, etc.) actors to fit themselves into this reality, or oppose the very logic and constraints of its 'cognitive capitalism'.

Amongst such approaches is an informal, ephemeral and implicit 'practical wisdom' that informs individual and collective habits, attitudes and dialects. Moreover, the influence of feminist, queer, subaltern or postcolonial epistemologies and 'situated knowledges' is of great importance in relation to the visual arts. Thus, for the purposes of enquiring into 'Art in the Knowledge-based Polis', the array of artistic articulations (both discursive and those deemed non-discursive) will be conceived as reaching far beyond common art/science and theory/practice dichotomies, while a careful analysis of the marks left on artistic epistemologies will be pursued throughout. [...]

1 [footnote 13 in source] 'Notes Towards the Definition of Anti-Culture', in *The Hornsey Affair*, ed. students and staff of Hornsey College of Art (Harmondsworth, London: Penguin, 1969) [Document 46] 128–9.

2 [The 'Bologna Process' is defined and discussed further in the text by Dieter Lesage below.]

3 [31] Michel Foucault, *L'Archéologie du savoir* (Paris: Gallimard, 1969).

4 [33] Antonio Negri and Michael Hardt, *Multitude: War and Democracy in the Age of Empire* (New York: Penguin, 2004) 126.

Tom Holert, extracts from 'Art in the Knowledge-based Polis', *e-flux journal*, no. 3 (February 2009), 1–9.

Dieter Lesage
The Academy is Back//2009

[...] With the 1999 Bologna Declaration, the then 29 participating countries committed themselves, but were not formally obliged to the

- Adoption of a system of *easily readable and comparable degrees* ... in order to promote European citizens' employability and the international competitiveness of the European higher education system;
- Adoption of a system essentially based on *two main cycles*, undergraduate and graduate. Access to the second cycle shall require successful completion of first cycle studies, lasting a minimum of three years. The degree awarded after the first cycle shall also be relevant to the European labour market as an appropriate level of qualification. The second cycle should lead to the master and/or doctorate degree as in many European countries;
- Establishment of a *system of credits* – such as in the ECTS system – as a proper means of promoting the most widespread student mobility;
- Promotion of *mobility* by overcoming obstacles to the effective exercise of free movement;
- Promotion of *European co-operation in quality assurance* with a view to developing comparable criteria and methodologies;
- Promotion of the *necessary European dimensions in higher education*, particularly with regards to curricular development, inter-institutional cooperation, mobility schemes and integrated programmes of study, training and research. [...]

The standard anti-Bologna rhetoric of expanded academia is to say that the Bologna Process leads to the homogenization of European education. [...] So far, the Bologna Process has proved more successful at showing all the differences between educational systems in its expanded version of Europe (which includes 46 European countries, not only the 27 member states of the EU) than at homogenizing them. [...]

The argument for autonomy is splendidly made by those academies in Europe that have been able to maintain or even augment their autonomy, such as the impressive Academy of Fine Arts in Vienna. At art academies of this scale, there is enough critical mass to allow them to stand confidently next to their big sister the university, rather than becoming a department within it. Even more, they've become universities themselves. [...]

It is my bet that the art academy is going to be *the* defining innovative institution within the art field in the next twenty years, much more so than museums, galleries, biennials [...]

Dieter Lesage, extracts from 'The Academy is Back: On Education, the Bologna Process and the Doctorate in the Arts', *e-flux journal*, no. 4 (March 2009) 1–7.

Andrea Phillips
Education Aesthetics//2010

[...] The very languages of resistance asserted by alternative pedagogical schema (free schools, night schools, open academies, caucuses, etc.) would seem to be contradicted by the assertion of practice-as-research, an institutionally serviceable and assessable construct. Such a knot demands careful attention, not least in order to commit, as I would like to, to the possibility of gallery sites and education sites being equally, and occasionally collaboratively, capable of developing projects that relocate the politics of terms such as 'practice-based' and 'participatory' to a more rigorous realm of enquiry.

From Work to Practice

Providing the background noise to this situation are questions of immateriality and affectivity, brought about by shifting relations of work and production in the world at large. The by now widely understood evolution from material to immaterial concepts of labour (literally, the production of services that 'result in no material and durable good')[1] ushers in terms such as practice-based. 'Practice' is radically different from 'work' in its temporal and spatial, operational and aesthetic organization. To be practice-based is to be more flexible; more embedded in the immanence of operations; more responsive to material and conceptual change; more reflexive. In art and education, this has widely been recognized as a useful reshaping of what constitutes work and/or research; in terms of labour, more generally, a division occurs between those who regard immaterial or affective labour as a new form of social collectivization and those who strongly oppose it on the grounds of exploitation. Many post-Marxist thinkers determine that this shift produces major problems with regard to the development of new forms of poverty; the deskilling of traditions; social exclusions; the eradication of traditional structures of democracy in the workplace (unionism, bargaining power, etc.), which results in lowering wages;

deregulation of state structures such as welfare, housing and medical provision; and the increase in privatisation linked to developing forms of capital. Of great influence, however, and particularly within art and higher education, is the view that such critiques delimit workers as reactive rather than active authors of new forms of production. Chief theorists of immaterial labour emerging from and influenced by, the Italian Operaismo ('Workerist') movement, Michael Hardt and Antonio Negri, suggest that, through the understanding that labour 'produces an immaterial good, such as a service, a cultural product, knowledge, or communication',[2] there comes 'a new kind of intelligence, a collective intelligence, a swarm intelligence'. This new 'collective intelligence' is based on what occurs when workers are released from the ties of productivist or Fordist forms of labour relations and instead turn to autonomous and self-defining modes of practice.[3] Meanwhile, Maurizio Lazzarato understands immaterial or affective labour as a new form of hyper-exploitative 'totalitarianism' – which uses the precariousness and mobility of a widely defined 'working class' – and as a labour system within which 'it becomes increasingly difficult to distinguish between leisure time and work time' and '[l]ife becomes inseparable from work'.[4] Like Hardt and Negri, Lazzarato also believes that:

> An analysis of immaterial labour and a description of its organization [...] can lead us to define, at a territorial level, a space for a radical autonomy of the productive synergies of immaterial labour [...] a polymorphous self-employed autonomous worker has emerged as the dominant form, a kind of 'intellectual worker' who is him or herself an entrepreneur, inserted within a market that is constantly shifting and within networks that are changeable in time and space.[5]

Furthermore, immaterial labour 'constitutes itself in immediately collective forms that exist as networks and flows', opening up 'antagonisms and contradictions' to capitalism via this immanent socialization, making both production and consumption 'a creative act' within the newly available milieu of practice.[6]

Richard Sennett, writing in opposition to immaterialist conceptions of labour, mourns the processes of deskilling that accompany the development of contemporary forms of work practice. Arguing that 'inequality has become the Achilles' heel of the modern economy', he suggests that contemporary, 'creative' 'cutting-edge' forms of work organization exacerbate a 'divorce between power and authority',[7] resulting in a weakening of institutional knowledge and a widening gap between power and authority: 'the social has been diminished; capitalism remains. Inequality increasingly becomes tied to isolation. It is this peculiar transformation that has been seized upon by politicians as the model for the "reform" of the public realm'.[8]

For Sennett, the term practice is necessarily more closely aligned with the repetition of actions in order to perfect skill or, in his recent terms, crafting. Practice is here modified towards rehearsing, a process through which the worker/practitioner is subservient to the task of perfect production. Arguing, after Ruskin and in a manner similar to de Certeau, for a return to the traditions of workshop learning, in which masters teach apprentices craft skills which are then rehearsed endlessly until perfect (the artistic-educative model would here be the conservatoire), Sennett proposes that 'one element has irretrievably gone missing' in the loss of master-apprentice culture; '[t]his is the absorption into tacit knowledge, unspoken and uncodified in words, that occurred there and became a matter of habit, the thousand little everyday moves that add up in sum to a practice'.[9] Here, the artist/craftsman gradually gains autonomy but on politically different ground to the immaterial labourer. Most evident here is the difference in understanding with regard to resistance. For Lazzarato *et al.*, the concept of immaterial, affective or 'illegible' labour allows for the possibility of collective and autonomous organization – resistance – in the face of, and in utilization of, new forms of capital. Whereas, for Sennett, whether he is describing violin-making or software production, resistance is subservient to material conditions and limitations: 'The skills of working well with resistance are, in sum, those of reconfiguring the problem into other terms, readjusting one's behaviour if the problem lasts longer than expected, and identifying with the problem's most forgiving element.'[10]

The argument between immaterial and material labour, between practice as a form of deregulation and practice as a form of rehearsal, might be characterized as this: if when we *work*, we expect remuneration and discrete satisfaction for our part in the production of an object, an event or an outcome; when we *practice*, we do not have such discrete expectations – rather, we understand that we participate in a flow of process that is both immanent and interdisciplinary, through which we develop an event-based and ongoing, improvisatory state of productivity. We also repeat ourselves, in the sense that we work at this productivity every day, every week, to get better at it (we can always work harder to get better but there is never a final state of achievement). If we are artists, we produce objects that do not summarize this process but rather embody states in the level of flow. This practice, then, asserts a different way of being in the world, one that modifies the concept of work, and thus has a different relation to the politics of production. Pedagogy slips between these definitions. It is at once involved in the production and promotion of skills-based training (however ambiguous) and in the production and promotion of immaterial conceptions of practice-based knowledge; this situation is perhaps most exacerbated by arts education itself.[11]

Angela McRobbie sees this contradiction in the relationship between the influx of young women into higher education institutions – resulting from the expansion of universities and colleges to broader capacities of inclusion at entry level – and the precarious and often self-exploitative patterns of work in the cultural sector within which those same women aspire to work on graduation. Working in fashion, art and design industries, educated to a high degree to recognize the cultural politics and modes of distinction of these industries, paid poorly or not at all and existing on a portfolio of occupations in order to maintain contact with work which is – wrongly in McRobbie's view – considered 'privileged or even [...] elitist', these women 'emerge as the archetypal subject of work-without end', performing 'women (in movement) as the multitude, and the non-elitist university as a site for a new politics of immanence'. What happens, McRobbie asks, when a whole diversity of occupations, all variously and loosely defined as creative, get 'absorbed under the couplet of immaterial and affective labour?'[12] She goes on to enquire:

> What is at stake in contemporary radical democratic politics is then this boundaryless field of life itself, Do we allow ourselves to belong wholly to the world which is shaped and defined by capitalism, or can we join forces to invent other worlds?[13]

McRobbie points to Lazzarato's declaration of the necessity to 'co-invent values which resist the market and the forces which harness and pollute our minds', reminding us that feminism has long been involved in the networked and micro-political establishment of such ideals on a practical basis (e.g. crèches, women's refuges, support structures of many sorts).[14] It is interesting to note that both these sets of terms, McRobbie's reminders of what women have done and continue to do and Lazzarato's call for market resistance through autonomous social invention, are utilized by artists and curators who seek to use pedagogy as a critical tool and aesthetic format for their work. In a manner similar to the paradox that McRobbie reveals, artistic pedagogy and art-as-pedagogy present the two faces of practice – one an opening to social aesthetic invention, the other a potentially compliant formatting of creative entrepreneurship: 'As is the case with all of these potentials there is only ever a thin line between what can be grasped onto and retained for the common good as critique, and what finds itself given over to improve the functioning of the new capitalism.'[15] [...]

1 [footnote 3 in source] Michael Hardt and Antonio Negri, *Empire* (Cambridge, Massachusetts: Harvard University Press. 2000) 290.

2 [4] Ibid.

3 [5] Hardt and Negri, *Multitude: War and Democracy in the Age of Empire* (Harmondsworth: Penguin, 2004) 93–5.

4 [6] Maurizio Lazzarato, 'Immaterial Labour', in Paolo Virno and Michael Hardt, eds, *Radical Thought in Italy: A Potential Politics* (Minneapolis: University of Minnesota Press. 1996) 137.

5 [7] Ibid., 40.

6 [8] Ibid., 145.

7 [9] Richard Sennett, *The Culture of New Capitalism* (New Haven and London: Yale University Press, 2006) 62.

8 [10] Ibid., 145.

9 [11] Richard Sennett, *The Craftsman* (London: Allen Lane, 2008) 77.

10 [12] Ibid., 222.

11 [13] Recent debates in the art department at Goldsmiths [University of London] demonstrate this paradox: in 2007, the department chose to re-brand its well-known Masters in Fine Art as 'MFA Art Practice', in the acknowledgement of the shift away from the discrete nomenclatures that artists themselves took up ('sculptor', 'painter', 'printmaker', etc.) and in recognition that the historically important MA in Textiles had been subsumed into a general MFA, resulting in a need to reflect the diversity of practices students might take up (and the diversity of practical options open for training via departmental technical workshops). At the time of writing, a reversion to the old programme title, MFA Fine Art, is tabled, signalling, amid other market-led arguments, a discomfort amongst many staff in having their (often very material) practice labelled as 'practice' as such.

12 [14] Angela McRobbie, 'Women as Multitude? Notes on Feminism and Immaterial Labour', unpublished text for forthcoming book: *Be Creative: Precarious Labour in Art and Cultural Worlds.*

13 [15] Ibid.

14 [16] Ibid.

15 [17] Ibid.

Andrea Phillips, extract from 'Education Aesthetics', in *Curating and the Educational Turn*, ed Paul O'Neill and Mick Wilson (London: Open Editions/Amsterdam: De Appel, 2010) 85–90.

Radical Philosophy Collective
The University and the Plan//2010

[...] At the current stage of capitalist socialization in Western countries, there remain only a few areas of life where individuals can become aware of their common political interests with others – that is to say, of their political and economic interests. Interest groups of the kind commonly recognized by the state, such as employees' organizations, student unions, trade unions and reform-oriented parties, rarely prove to be the initiators of social struggles, not least because their own bureaucratic structures are designed to balance corporate interests. When struggles do arise, they generally do so outside of them. This is partly because economic competition, consumer individualism and the reorganization of industrial production have helped create a situation where people either no longer go through, or are no longer aware of, the classic collective experiences of politicization. But there is another reason as well: as fields of production and work become increasingly immaterial, demand has risen for workers with uniquely individual abilities – indeed, with carefully cultivated idiosyncrasies, stylish quirks and personal (physical) attractiveness. The self is no longer a place of retreat but a productive force, obliged to operate on deregulated markets, deploying as many unique selling points as possible. The result is an encroachment of the working day into traditional leisure activities: going to parties, concerts, exhibitions and the cinema or engaging in the never-ending (in)voluntary rounds of networking become mere opportunities for honing this constructed self further. These processes of individualization and compulsory Bohemianization gradually take hold of the entire individual, affecting ever more areas of his or her life. Those subject to them must maintain a good mood in order to appear creative and original – survival depends on it. As semi-self-employed small entrepreneurs running their own businesses, or as precariously employed workers, they represent the new proletariat of deregulation and neoliberalism. The situation in the universities, by contrast, looks very different. Here it is not deregulation that is the problem, but increasing regulation; the trend is not towards compulsory self-invention and self-management, but external controls, bureaucracy and the dumbing-down of courses. [...]

Radical Philosophy Collective, extract from 'The University and the Plan: Reflections from Vienna', *Radical Philosophy*, no. 162 (July/August 2010) 1.

Andrea Fraser
From the Critique of Institutions to an Institution of Critique//2005

[...] [A]nyone familiar with his work should recognize that, far from trying to tear down the museum, Hans Haacke's project has been an attempt to defend the institution of art from instrumentalization by political and economic interests.

That the art world, now a global multibillion-dollar industry, is not part of the 'real world' is one of the most absurd fictions of art discourse. [...]

And the art market is not the only art-world site where the growing economic disparities of our society are reproduced. They can also be seen in what are now only nominally 'nonprofit' organizations like universities – where MFA programmes rely on cheap adjunct labour – and museums, where anti-union policies have produced compensation ratios between the highest- and lowest-paid employees that now surpass 40 to one.

Representations of the 'art world' as distinct from the 'real world', like representations of the 'institution' as discrete and separate from 'us', serve specific functions in art discourse. They maintain an imaginary distance between the social and economic interests we invest in through our activities and the euphemized artistic, intellectual and even political 'interests' (or disinterests) that provide those activities with content and justify their existence. And with these representations, we also reproduce the mythologies of volunteerist freedom and creative omnipotence that have made art and artists such attractive emblems for neoliberalism's entrepreneurial, 'ownership-society' optimism. That such optimism has found perfect artistic expression in neo-Fluxus practices like relational aesthetics, which are now in perpetual vogue, demonstrates the degree to which what Peter Bürger called the avant-garde's aim to integrate 'art into life praxis' has evolved into a highly ideological form of escapism. But this is not just about ideology. We are not only symbols of the rewards of the current regime: in this art market we are its direct material beneficiaries. Every time we speak of the 'institution' as other than 'us', we disavow our role in the creation and perpetuation of its conditions. [...]

Andrea Fraser, extracts from 'From the Critique of Institutions to an Institution of Critique', *Artforum* (September 2005) 132; 133.

Bruce Ferguson
Art Education//2009

[...] [Skills have been] the elephant in the room of art education since mid last century. The tired pingpong between 'skills' and 'theory', and the seemingly infinite number of linguistic formations of the concept of 'deskilling' have thankfully had at least one fruitful consequence. In good schools, they have led to and contributed to the formation of 'need-to-know' curricula in studio programmes. This means that rather than a body of knowledge to be handed down by gatekeepers, in the conservative tradition of academia, advanced schools teach students in relation to the individual student's needs. These schools see art as a 'methodological field' rather than a 'body of knowledge'. [...]

There is a set of necessary professional skills, many of them social, that is more of a priority than ever before: networking, writing and speaking skills, fiscal planning, the mastery of intellectual property rules, and most importantly, research, to name just a few. These combine with the heavily practical skills associated with conceptualizing and mounting exhibitions, developing a student's capacity to turn ideas for isolated objects into an encompassing exhibition experience, and an awareness of the role that the audiences play in the reception of work. [...] Simply put, as the arts have become professionalized, the need and demand for more professional skills have emerged.

The growth of professionalization that I mentioned is being driven by an ever-expanding globalization of art. Think of the sheer numbers of biennials, art fairs and galleries. Personally, I welcome the fact that MFA programmes are now more directly connected to markets and dealers and curators and critics and collectors. Students enrolling in graduate programmes have generally been out of school for a while and are committed and urgent about their professions, evidenced by their coming back into the educational system. They are likely to take on great financial loads by the time they have completed their studies. They are not naïve or monastic, and the schools are as much involved in the 'real' world as they are. [...]

In touring European schools, I found that the obvious difference between our studies and theirs is that the European approach is entirely based on charismatic figures and the myth of 'free' education. What they mean by this, of course, is education underwritten by government funding. It is not only *not* 'free' but, as a result, European educators and administrators don't have any idea what it actually costs to educate a student. [...] With the European Union's demand for unit education, the Continent's art schools are likely to see the introduction of transnational criteria based on curricula and performance-based budgeting, ending a very long reign of romantic pedagogy. [...]

In viewing art schools as professional environments aligned to a professionalized art world and obligated to prepare their students for financially and critically successful careers, the hippy vision of art school as a 'safe' environment or monastery, where students are encouraged to fail, experiment and explore, is outdated and dangerous. Schools now should be seen for what they are – professional entrées into a professional world with a responsibility to guide young artists through the dilemma of how simultaneously to take advantage of both a critical history and a new set of career possibilities. Business schools change their curricula in relation to the way in which business is done, and art schools must be flexible enough to do the same. Indeed as amusingly related by the Harvard Business Review in 2004, the MFA is the new MBA.

But this does not mean that the market is the only determining factor. Attention and comprehension of the theoretical climate surrounding the fine arts continues to be a critical component of graduate education. [...]

Bruce Ferguson, extract from 'Art Education', in *Educação para a arte, Arte para a educação*, ed. Gabriel Pérez-Barreiro and Luis Camnitzer (Porto Alegre: Fundação Bienal de Artes Visuais do Mercosul, 2009) 300.

Ernesto Pujol
On the Ground//2010

[...] At the dawn of the twenty-first century, American middle-class students now enter art school with eight evolving tools including: (1) cable, satellite and web-accessible televisions; (2) laptop computers; (3) cell phones, and particularly smart phones; (4) DVDs and game players, portable and stationary; (5) MP3 devices and iPods; (6) credit cards and ATM cards; (7) digital cameras, integrated and stand-alones; and (8) scanners. All generate instant information, communication and currency to goods and several include image capture. A pivotal historical perceptual change is taking place among us, making the abyss between past and present modes of perception greater than ever before in terms of attention, translation, forms, aesthetics and production. The future of art education will be based on the notion of universal immediate access. [...]

So what does this all mean for foundation curriculum development? It means that art schools stand at the threshold of multidisciplinary art research and intradisciplinary art production – not as one more theoretical seminar or 'multimedia' studio among stubbornly traditional course offerings, or one more state-of-the-arts degree, but as the next wave of cultural production. The artists of the twenty-first century may become in some sense renaissance folk, deploying a panoply of disciplines and mediums for their work. But we must seek to understand these new patterns of creativity fully in order to ensure our nation of historical memory and true experimentation beyond Internet shopping for global materials and fabrication technicians.

Industrialism triggered the end of craft and divided makers from thinkers. Photography relieved painting and sculpture from the burden of documenting reality. And modernism allowed art decades of important psychological self-regard that affirmed the individual but unfortunately created a hermeticism that disconnected art from middle America, making it suspect and irrelevant. Conceptualism brought in a class system that turned artists into producers who hired shop technicians. We dismissed middle America as cattle and their artists as nostalgic artisans of the landscape. In turn, they responded by electing politicians who dismantled our nation's cultural life, and worse. The art world retrenched, thinking itself superior and believing it could survive through the benefaction of the private sector. Yet our recurring incestuousness, evidencing the decadence of empire and globalism, has finally crumbled our walls.

Contemporary art is evolving not only beyond traditional tools and techniques (the paint-stained academic studio, the macho foundry shop and the cave-like photo laboratory) but also beyond the upper-middle-class, white-encoded traits of modernism's Puritan roots, as all art is generated by a specific people in a specific place; as whiteness is a colour. [...]

What does this mean for foundation programmes in our art schools, which are increasingly outdated and are the refuge of surviving but isolated and frustrated American modernists? It does not mean substituting Photoshop and crappy recycling for painting and sculpture. Historic means of production can be informed by conceptual and multidisciplinary methods that can save them from becoming the stuff of hobbyists, a visual macramé. Students should receive training in the basic tools of conceptualism, such as scholarly research and literary writing, as applied to traditional painting, sculpture, printrnaking, glass, ceramics and photographic processes, making muscled and poetic gestures more conscious and articulate and balancing craft with thought, while also gazing selectively at other disciplines.

Students should have to develop fully thought-out written proposals before, during and after painting and sculpting. I don't mean that they should do this simply to defend an image or object during individual and group critiques, as students have always done, but to learn how to justify that creation intellectually, beyond the subjective, in our visually dense and materially cluttered world. If they don't want to do this, they have no business being professional contemporary artists. They should be doctors and lawyers who paint on Sunday, or they should be the fine two-dimensional technicians who paint for Jeff Koons. We are all creative; creativity is part of the human condition. However, not everyone is a cultural producer. Our art schools' counselling departments should be sharper in vocational counselling. [...]

Ernesto Pujol, extract from 'On the Ground: Practical Observations for Regenerating Art Education', in *Art School (Propositions for the 21st Century)*, ed. Steven Henry Madoff (Cambridge, Massachusetts: The MIT Press, 2010) 3–5.

Caroline Tisdall
The Free University//1975

[...] [A] group was founded in Düsseldorf to investigate the possibilities of establishing an alternative model of education.

In 1972 this founding group, which included prominent cultural figures among whom were the sculptor and educationist Prof. Joseph Beuys and the writer and Nobel prize winner Heinrich Böll, both of whom are involved with the Dublin Project, published the manifesto from which the following are excerpts:

> Creativity is not limited to people practising one of the traditional forms of art, and even in the case of artists creativity is not confined to the exercise of their art. Each one of us has a creative potential which is hidden by competitiveness and the aggressive pursuit of success. To recognize, explore and develop this potential is the task of this school.
>
> Creation involves not merely talent, intuition, powers of the imagination and application, but also the ability to shape material which could be extended to other socially relevant spheres.
>
> Conversely, when we examine the ability to organize material that is expected of a worker, a housewife, a farmer, doctor, philosopher, judge or works manager, we find by no means that their work exhausts the full range of their creative abilities.
>
> Creative democracy is increasingly discouraged by growth of bureaucracy,

coupled with aggressive proliferation of standardized mass-culture. Political creativity is reduced to the mere delegation of decision-making and power. The imposition of an international cultured and economic dictatorship by the constantly expanding media-combines leads to a poverty of articulation, learning and the quality of verbal expression.

In the consumer society, when democratic creativity, imagination and intelligence are not articulated and their expression prevented, they can become harmful and damaging, and find outlets in corrupted criminal creativity. Criminality can arise from boredom and repressed inarticulated creativity. To be reduced to consumer values, and to see democratic potential reduced to occasional elections can also be regarded as a rejection or dismissal of democratic creativity.

Environmental pollution advances with the pollution of the individual. Hope is rejected as utopian or illusionary, and discarded hope breeds violence. In the school we shall research into the numerous forms of violence, which are by no means confined to the use of weapons or physical force.

As a forum for the confrontation of political or social opponents, the school can set up a permanent seminar on social behaviour and its articulate expression.

The specialist's insulated point of view places the arts and other kinds of work in sharp opposition, whereas it is crucial that structural, formal and thematic problems of the various work processes should be constantly compared with one another.

The school does not discount the specialist, nor does it adapt an anti-technological stance. It does however reject the notion of experts and technicians being the sole arbiters in their respective fields. In a spirit of democratic creativity, without regressing to mechanical defensive or aggressive clichés, we shall discover the inherent reason in things. [...]

Since the school's concern is with the values of social life, we shall stress the consciousness of solidarity. The school is based on the principle of interaction, whereby no institutional distinction is drawn between teachers and learners. The school's activity will be accessible to the public, and it will conduct its work in the public eye. Its open and international character will be constantly reinforced by events. [...]

Caroline Tisdall, extract from 'Report to the European Community on the Feasibility of Founding a Free International University for Creativity and Interdisciplinary Research in Dublin' (September 1975) (Free University Press, January 1976) n.p.

AHA!

NICE IDEA!

GOOD POINT!

SEEMS LIKE A WINNER!

THAT'S A GREAT IDEA. THANKS!

WE'RE GETTING SOMEWHERE WITH THIS.

HMM, LOOKS LIKE WE COULD PUSH THAT IDEA FURTHER

LET'S TAKE THAT SAME CONCEPT AND USE IT OVER HERE

YOU KNOW, THIS COULD BE BETTER THAN WHAT WE'RE CURRENTLY DOING

ET'S STAY WITH THAT IDEA LONGER AND SEE WHAT MILEAGE WE CAN REALLY GET FROM IT

PEDAGOGY AS MEDIUM

Alex Farquharson
The Avant-Garde, Again//2002

[...] Carey Young, dressed in a smart business suit, paces back and forth in a slick office space. The wall behind her is made entirely of glass. It looks out onto the vast central atrium of a sparkling postmodern office complex. Beyond the atrium are similar offices to the one she's in, where executives in shirt-sleeves sit before computer monitors. Young is alone in the room with a tall middle-aged man, also smartly dressed, who is in the process of offering her instruction – coaxing her, giving praise and supporting her efforts with constructive advice. 'I am a revolutionary', Young exclaims for the nth time, weary but determined to better her delivery. Again, but with different emphasis: 'I ... am a revolutionary.' She doesn't sound quite certain, and knows she needs to believe what's she's saying herself if she is to convince the prospective audience. Alisdair Chisholm of Marcus Bohn Associates, a company that specializes in business skills training, sketches out a scenario and, improvising, alludes to passages of the speech we haven't heard that are supposed to have preceded this declaration. He encourages her to step a couple of paces towards her audience on reaching the tricky phrase; towards us, in fact, since, when the work is projected, the room appears lifesize, and we seem to occupy the other half of the office space that the screen seems to bisect.

Carey Young's *I am a Revolutionary* is on one level a delirious postmodern reading of Keith Arnatt's Wittgensteinian *Trouser Word Piece* (1972) – a photo of the artist holding a sign that reads 'I AM A REAL ARTIST'. Young's video performance includes Arnatt's original tautologies while overlaying them with contemporary corporate versions of each term: artist/businesswoman rehearses artistic statement/corporate speech about herself in an art video/corporate training video for a small art audience/imaginary business audience. As well as Arnatt's work, the substitution of 'revolutionary' for 'artist' evokes Joseph Beuys, implying that today's corporate guru is the progeny of Beuys' now antiquated radical shaman routine, his legendary persuasive powers and inexhaustible ego now redirected from participatory democracy to profit. But why are these four words causing her so much trouble? Is it, as artist, because she can't quite bring herself to believe in either the avant-garde or political utopia, if that is her message? Or, as executive, does she doubt that she is indeed a radical leader, a visionary? Or, can't she bring herself to accept the co-option of the rhetoric of radical politics by modern-day business, and the redundancy of opposition that this seems to imply?

Joseph Beuys' own take on the art/life dichotomy was that the active reshaping of society by the people themselves was itself a form of art – an art he termed 'social sculpture'. His primary medium for propagating this idea was a didactic form of performance in which the use of language and speech was instrumental – 'to be a teacher is my greatest work of art', he said. For the entire duration of Documenta 5 (1972), he put himself in the position of the artwork in what he called an 'office', rather than 'gallery', where people could meet him at all times for social and political debate (the 'Information Office of the Organization for Direct Democracy through Referendum'). Carey Young's recent 'corporate works' relocate Beuys' notion of social sculpture within the modern business environment; its 'soft' yet didactic techniques of training, brainstorming and skills workshops displacing Beuys' charismatic proselytizing and with it, by implication, his utopian vision for society. In an act of double irony, Beuys' parodic 'office' becomes, quite simply, an office. Another work by Young, *Social Sculpture* (2001), performs a similar manoeuvre, whereby Beuys' famous rolls of felt – which in his symbolic world signified the preservation of human life – are substituted by a roll of its visual equivalent in the modern workplace: beige contract carpeting.

In *Everything You've Heard is Wrong* (1999), Young herself assumes the role of the instructor, this time at Speakers' Corner in Hyde Park (a piece that *I am a Revolutionary*, in many ways, mirrors and reverses). Speakers' Corner is itself a kind of cacophonic mini-Beuysian participatory democracy, where anyone, no matter what their status, can get up on a 'soapbox' – actually, a step ladder – and promote his or her world view to whoever happens to be assembled. Providing a forum for the amateur orator, the fanatic, the oddball or the disenfranchised, it is inevitably a site for leftfield or idiosyncratic opinion. In the video of the performance Young is shown giving a sober 'skills workshop' on corporate presentation, again dressed impeccably in a businesswoman's suit. On an obvious level the humour derives from the disparity between the methodologies Young advocates and the calmness of her delivery, compared to the style and content (religious, political, other) of her neighbours' more feverish oratory. Though the corporate persona Young adopts believes her act to be a helpful one, and that her audience shares her aspirations, the dark lining of the humour resides in the unwelcome proposition that even this carnival of free thought might be absorbed by the corporate world some time in the not-so-distant future. The title *Everything You've Heard is Wrong*, which is borrowed from the title of a business book, suggests further paradoxes and ambivalences: does it mean to say that it is the 'presentation skills' of her fellow speakers that are at fault (i.e. on the level of the signifier), or that their messages are 'wrong' too (the signified)? More generally, is it suggesting that all the knowledge we've each acquired throughout our lives is now corrupted? Or self-reflexively, is it saying that it's what the piece itself appears to represent – i.e. the corporate absorption of free debate – that's 'wrong'? Characteristically, Young presents us with continuum rather than closure. [...]

Alex Farquharson, extracts from 'The Avant Garde, Again', in *Carey Young Incorporated*, ed. Steven Bode (London: Film & Video Umbrella/Southampton: John Hansard Gallery, 2002) 17–21.

Frances Stark
Professional Me//1999

I just read a book about art schools. Then I read a book about the media. In between, I read a book that was sort of about suicide. The first one is dense with information and I cannot possibly summarize. The second one is itself a summary, delivered in a medium demanding nothing more. The third is a biography of a woman made famous by America's nascent magazine culture, who in the end only wanted to be taken 'seriously' as an artist. The first book elucidates the evolution of 'seriousness' as regards the pursuit of life as an artist. The second describes a mediated world in which there is not enough time for serious seriousness. The third suggests that a world lacking seriousness, from the point of view of the serious-minded, is a place one might only be brave enough to badmouth before threatening to bow out of it entirely.

The first book is Howard Singerman's *Art Subjects: Making Artists in the American University* (1999). Its personal aspect is foregrounded in the preface and on the jacket commentary, as well as in the pre-prefatory acknowledgements. The book, however, rigorously defies the personal, by way of an extensive referencing of administrators who have penned the constant flow of ideologically ambitious copy for their art departments' various institutional apologia. The author (now with a Ph.D in art history) has an MFA degree in sculpture, but does not possess any 'traditional' sculpture skills. He asks bluntly 'what constitutes training as an artist now, and what has determined its shape?' This is a fairly direct question, and Singerman's research answers it. But that, of course, is not the personal part.

Here is where it starts to get personal, for me and for him. Before finishing art school, I had the opportunity to co-edit a critical journal out of the graduate studies programme, in which we published an article by Singerman called 'Professing Postmodernism: The Visiting Artist and the Model'. This six-year-old contribution, now chapter six of *Art Subjects*, cites an essay he wrote directly out of graduate school which was the seed of the entire endeavour. In it, he coined the phrase 'the journeyman' artist – one who travels, installs, lectures, visits, all with the aim of discussing and promoting himself. Me, I was accepted into a Fine Arts Graduate programme without having obtained an undergraduate art degree. When talking to a room full of students I confess this when showing my first slide, often of a 1992 work titled 'self-portrait/ autobiography' – a carbon tracing of my transcripts from a state university. It lists things like Fundamentals of Oral Communication, Thought and Image II, Nietzsche and Postmodernism, Architecture and the American Life, Comparative Form and Culture. The grade column starts off as hopeful, then turns into a relentless stream of 'Unauthorized Withdrawals' and 'Incompletes' which eventually reappear in their own conspicuously indented columns as F's. In a review that referenced this work, the editor of this very publication [*art/text*] introduced me to the word *Bildungsroman*. For six years I never saw the word again, until I read it described by Singerman as 'the story of education by trial and error; where each individual fashions and is fashioned by his wrong turns and false starts.' Today my presence in the classroom says 'success', and emphasizes that despite (or because of) my failure, I am a professional, a professional me. [...]

'"The will to art" has been called the private attribute of the individual artist and the opposite of skill', Singerman says. Volition replaces ability, and 'from Cézanne on, that volition rests, or rather ferments – in the artist himself. This desire gives the artist's life the character of the *Bildungsroman*.' It is interesting to note that he got on the topic of Cézanne by way of Clyfford Still's master's thesis. Given the slew of magazine and newspaper articles launching rants against theory-loving academies instigating the production of boring, visually wan works of art, this book provides perspective. The 'visual power' of Diego Rivera recently convinced one columnist to assert that '"teacher-artists" who scratch white surfaces with faint traces of graphite and fill the heads of their students with the drivel of Derrida and Foucault are slouching towards the insignificance they so richly deserve.' It's worth it to consider the history of teacher-artists and their 'faint traces of graphite'. The chapter 'Innocence and Form' links drawing exercises used in Kindergartens (resulting from nineteenth-century educational reform) to Josef Albers' curriculum at the Bauhaus, to their uncanny manifestation in the works of Sol LeWitt and Agnes Martin. But what's to stop Singerman's research from being turned into pap? The *New York Times Magazine* recently ran an article 'How to Succeed In Art' (19 June 1999) with a sub-heading that read 'Applications to art schools are at a record high. Which might explain why art these days looks a lot like homework.' A couple of days later I ran into a radio journalist soliciting responses to the article. I immediately launched my complaints. 'I suspect the writer to have lifted her only interesting propositions and statements straight out of this new book about art school.' [...]

Frances Stark, extracts from 'Professional Me', *art/text* (Winter 1999–2000); reprinted in Frances Stark, *Collected Writing 1993–2003*, ed. Lisa Panting (London: Book Works, 2003) 52–3.

David Elliott
Darcy Lange: *Work Studies in Schools* (1976–77)//2008

Darcy Lange's *Work Studies in Schools* was one of the first shows I programmed as Director of the Museum of Modern Art, Oxford, and it was designed to kill three birds with one stone: the first was to commission an important piece using the still relatively new medium of video by one of the leading artists working in that field in the UK; the second was to build up links with the community around Oxford – not one renowned for its love of or interest in contemporary art; the third was to provide a reflection, and through this a critique, of divergent attitudes in both art education and society in the public and private sectors. Made during the twilight years of the previous Labour Government, this latter aspect of the work has since acquired a poignancy that we could have hardly anticipated at the time – our notions of what constitutes 'public' and 'private' have now been completely turned on their heads. Who better to create such a materially modest, yet spiritually ambitious work as this than Darcy Lange. His energy, openness and ability to communicate gave this work its unique attraction. This was 'real life' – cinema verité if you like – but through a prism of innocent enthusiasm that completely negated the reflexive poststructuralist approach of so many video artists of the time, as well as the potential boredom of its grisaille medium. Darcy's work transcended the specificity of each school to give a portrait of adolescence and control to which we could all relate. [...]

David Elliott, extract from recollection of Darcy Lange's *Work Studies in Schools* (Oxford: Museum of Modern Art, 1977), in *Darcy Lange: Study of an Artist at Work*, ed. Mercedes Vicente (New Zealand: Govett-Brewster Art Gallery/Birmingham: Ikon Gallery, 2008) 92.

Darcy Lange
Work Studies in Schools//1976–77

[...] Studies have been made of four schools in Oxfordshire and a consistent methodology has been used for each.

The guidelines I have used in undertaking this work are broadly as follows:

1 to investigate teaching as work.
2 to illustrate the skills of the teacher through vocal and gestural communication with the class and the class's response to this.
3 to illustrate the process of teaching and learning in the classroom.
4 to illustrate the social breakdown within each class.
5 I am particularly concerned to prevent what I make, whether it be a photograph or video, from becoming an end in itself – not dissimilar to the loved art object.

There is no word for art in the Polynesian language, and the Polynesians attempt to do everything as creatively as they can. Creativity in schools is not necessarily confined just to the art class. The choice of recording history, art and science classes in schools shows this.

Art is important because of its observation of material life. Creativity when applied though music, poetry, art, to life and work could become a protection against object worship, beyond functionalism. It might help to recreate involvement and creativity within manual work or build non-object recreational expression.

In some of the discussions I have recorded, art itself seems difficult to define. It appears as research into both the unknown and the known. History, in contrast to this, has an evidently valuable role in assessing and researching the past, the known. It is, however, interpreted according to society's needs.

The logicality, in itself, of many of the science subjects appears to inspire confidence in people, yet its methods of teaching do have some correspondence with those of history and art, as they entail research into and observation of a given fact.

The process of education seems to me to be subtly but totally political. It is concerned with the establishment of values and parameters of behaviour; its criteria of success are mostly oriented towards middle-class academic aspirations. [...]

Darcy Lange, extract from *Work Studies in Schools* (Oxford: Museum of Modern Art, 1977) 18.

Lawrence McDonald
Exacting Reproduction//2008

Darcy Lange's *Work Studies in Schools* (1976–77), is fundamentally concerned with patterns of reproduction, the manner in which society maintains and renews itself inter-generationally, focusing on the education system as a site where class differences are reinforced or contested. And given that one of the major outcomes of societal reproduction is the maintenance of socio-economic inequality, it isn't surprising that Lange's exclusive concentration on working-class and peasant labour in his earlier work expands to include middle-class subjects in the school studies. [...]

Lange conducted his *Work Studies in Schools* in two UK locations, Birmingham (1976) and Oxfordshire (1977), and at several schools in these areas. The three Birmingham schools studied were: Leabank Junior School (i.e. a primary school); Ladywood Comprehensive School; and King Edward's School.[1] The four Oxfordshire schools studies were: Cheney Upper School (comprehensive); St Mary's School (public school, i.e. private); Banbury School (comprehensive); and Radley College (public school, i.e. private).[2] The lessons videotaped in the three Birmingham Schools varied from school to school: they were devoted to social studies and music (Leabank), English literature, biology, geology and physics (King Edward's) and geometry, history, physics and shorthand (Ladywood). However, in the Oxfordshire project, Lange settled on recording lessons in art, history and science (chemistry or biology) across all the schools, with classes ranging from forms three to seven. The mix of public (i.e. private) and state schools (grammar, comprehensive and primary) that makes up Lange's 'sample' of the English education system demonstrates his interest in mapping and correlating class-based differences in educational provision in the 1970s.[3] [...]

Perhaps the most influential of the 1970s UK-based studies that employed ethnography as its principal methodology is Paul Willis' *Learning to Labour: How Working Class Kids Get Working Class Jobs* (1977).[4] When he carried out the research and wrote up the results for this study, Willis was a member of the Centre for Contemporary Cultural Studies at the University of Birmingham. However, even though theories of ethnography were an important component of the Centre's general intellectual orientation, particularly in relation to the study of subcultural identities and resistance, *Learning to Labour* is the only large-scale and sustained use of ethnography in the Centre's canon. Furthermore, Willis' work stands somewhat apart from the more abstracted neo-Gramscian approach of the Centre in its emphasis on sensuous, lived relations embodied in socio-symbolic practices.[5]

Learning to Labour provides an in-depth case study of Hammertown Boys, a fictional name for a (then) boys-only secondary modern school in the Midlands. Willis focuses on a core group of 12 non-academic students at a school whose entire intake was working class. These 12 boys form a group of 'lads', which constitutes itself as a 'counter-school culture' in opposition to the conformist 'ear'oles' who please teachers by striving for academic success. Willis' research explores the lads' attitudes, responses and resistance towards schooling and how their 'counter-school culture' steers them directly towards their preferred post-school destination of 'shop floor culture'.[6] Thus he demonstrates how their rituals simultaneously resist the educational priorities of the school and serve to secure their (self) reproduction as another generation of working-class labourers. [...]

By contrast, Lange's videotapes are both research data (document) and finished study (documentary) at once. There is no moment of separation between data collection and interpretive processing, as there is in Willis' shaping of his field materials for education and cultural studies readerships. And given the sheer scale of Lange's project, the only means of delivery to a non-specialist audience is via curatorial intervention in the form of rigorous selection and editing. [...]

At the beginning of his book *The Ethnographic Imagination* Willis asks a key question: 'What are the consequences of viewing everyday relations as if they contained a creativity of the same order as that held to be self-evidently part of what we call the arts?' And, shortly after, he asserts that 'meaning-making is not an internal quest ... Meaning-making can be considered a work process involving its own kind of labour and expressive outcomes issuing into some kind of intersubjective space.'[7]

The first chapter of Willis' book, entitled 'Life as Art', begins with an epigraphic quotation from the appendix to *Learning to Labour*, a comment from 'Joey' about his and the other lads' 'own sort of artform'. Willis glosses Joey's comment as follows: 'Joey offers no finished poems. His poems are situated, performative and embodied in and through his whole social life and activity at school.'[8] In light of this claim, we might ask what forms of creativity do Lange's school videotapes reveal? In all instances, the classroom sequences are to a large degree teacher-centred, not by virtue of the visuals, which, as Guy Brett notes, are delivered from 'no special vantage point' and are ruminative,[9] but by means of the soundtrack, which directs viewer attention through the teachers' continuous monologues. [...]

1 David MacDougal, 'Beyond Observational Cinema' in Paul Hockings, ed., *Principles of Visual Anthropology* (The Hague/Paris: Mouton, 1975) 119–20.

2 *Studies of Teaching in Four Oxfordshire Schools* (UK, 1977).

3 'In 1969, 26.2% of all secondary pupils were in comprehensive schools. In 1974 this had risen to 62%, and in 1978 the figure was 83%'. Stephen Ball, *Education* (London and New York: Longman, 1986) 21. Comprehensive schools were founded on what Ball refers to as the 'integrative view', which assumes that 'by providing one school for all, with social classes mixed together, greater tolerance and social harmony will result and class tensions will abate'. (Ibid.) 24.

4 Paul Willis, *Learning to Labour: How Working Class Kids Get Working Class Jobs* (1977) (Aldershot, Hampshire: Gower, 1980) 81; 83.

5 The Centre for Contemporary Cultural Studies' major publication on education is the Education Group's multi-authored historical and theoretical study *Unpopular Education: Schooling and Social Democracy in England since 1944* (London: Hutchinson, 1981).

6 Willis discusses 'shop floor culture' in 'Human Experience and Material Production: The Culture of the Shop Floor', *Working Papers in Cultural Studies*, no. 9 (Spring 1976) 154–61. This article is an extract from a lecture related to work completed for a project with the title: 'The Transition from School to Work'.

7 Paul Willis, *The Ethnographic Imagination* (Cambridge: Polity Press, 2000) xiv.

8 Ibid., 3–4.

9 Guy Brett, introduction, *Darcy Lange: Work Studies in Schools* (Oxford: Museum of Modern Art, 1977) 4. Lange's camera frequently wanders away from the teacher and class to take in details of the classroom setting. A particularly striking instance of this practice can be found in the study of Tony Morgan's art class at Banbury School, Oxfordshire. Here I would note an affinity with the camera style of Andy Warhol, of whose films Wayne Kostenbaum has written: 'the stationary camera is his trademark. (In his other films, when the camera budges, it erratically disregards the action, it digresses, ignores the star...)'. *Andy Warhol* (London: Phoenix, 2001) 62.

Lawrence McDonald, extracts from 'Exacting Reproduction: Darcy Lange's *Work Studies in Schools*' in *Darcy Lange: Study of an Artist at Work*, ed. Mercedes Vicente (New Zealand: Govett-Brewster Art Gallery/Birmingham: Ikon Gallery, 2008) 116–25.

Janna Graham
Between a Pedagogical Turn and a Hard Place//2010

[...] One of the often-cited mechanisms through which 'alternative' pedagogies produced in the spaces of art are rendered 'disinterested' is the extremely short-term, spectacular mode of presentation that arts institutions habitually employ. This often prevents transformative processes of education from occurring. For this and other reasons, many artists and curators have turned to the longer time periods and more experimental possibilities offered by the formulation of radical or experimental projects as 'research'. Rather than merely situating this notion of research in relation to artistic processes or to notions of study that can be known and shaped in advance, I have for some time been guided by the idea of the 'possible study', the study that is not yet constituted and emerges only through relations formed between artists and transversal constituents. Such a study situates itself within the context of relations across the divisions of the creative class and its others, decentring the artist researcher as author and propellant.[1]

In this, strategies described within contemporary social movements as 'militant research' have become important to my understanding of the potential that research might lend to projects attempting to engage in socially consequential and politically meaningful artistic work. As described by the Argentinean collective Colectivo Situaciones, 'Militant research works neither from its own set of knowledges about the world nor from how things ought to be.' Rather, it is carried out in 'theoretical and practical work oriented to co-produce the knowledges and modes of an alternative sociability, beginning with the power of ... subaltern knowledges'.[2]

Among these traditions, two genealogies of research practice have become particularly instructive. The first is a movement in which sociological researchers turned away from their field of specialization and repositioned their work in relation to concrete social and political struggles under the name 'Participatory Action Research' (PAR). The second is a development in which transversal relations were actively cultivated within institutions and between institutional actors and outsiders under the names 'Institutional Pedagogy' and 'Institutional Analysis'.[3] Together, these genealogies promote a twofold practice. This includes the production of honest accounts of, and interventions into, the conditions which shape us as educators, students, curators and artists vis à vis relations of power, hierarchy, sensibility and desire. It also entails the intersection of these accounts with the struggles and desires of 'others' – with those that find themselves semiotized as outside of our specialized milieu of 'expertise' or competency.

Looking first to the histories of Participatory Action Research [initiated by university-based intellectuals, primarily sociologists in the 1960s, many of them based in the global South], we might find a path that privileges neither the knowledge paradigm of the university nor that of the vanguardist or autonomous intellectual/artist. [...]

1 The idea of the possible study has recently been launched by transversal groups of artists, residents, shop owners, students, teachers and other workers in the neighbourhood of Edgware Road in London, the base for which is 'The Centre for Possible Studies'. This work is sponsored by the Serpentine Gallery and grows out of the gallery's long term work on Edgware Road.

2 Colectivo Situaciones, 'On the Researcher-Militant', trans. Sebastian Touza (2004). (www.situaciones.org)

3 While I encountered PAR and Institutional Analysis through research undertaken with young people while working at the Art Gallery of Ontario in Toronto between 1999 and 2004, a useful overview of these processes and their links to other forms of Militant Research, including those used by feminist collectives and workers' groups, can be read in Marta Malo de Molina's *Common Notions*, part 1: Workers-Inquiry, Co-research, Consciousness-raising, and part 2: Institutional Analysis, Participatory Action-Research, Militant Research (2004) (http://transform.eipcp.net/transversal/0707/malo/en)

Janna Graham, extracts from 'Between a Pedagogical Turn and a Hard Place: Thinking with Conditions', in *Curating and the Educational Turn*, ed Paul O'Neill and Mick Wilson (London: Open Editions/Amsterdam: De Appel, 2010) 125; 129–30.

Emily Pethick
Resisting Institutionalization//2008

[...] One of the described intentions of the *Nought to Sixty* programme is to focus on practices that are rarely represented in the institution, usually because they are 'conversational' and more closely linked to self-organized activity. This notion of conversation is closely related to some of the projects realized at Casco – Office for Art, Design and Theory, in Utrecht, during the time I worked there; these projects functioned as a way of thinking through different models of interaction, participation and collaboration.

Conversation generates forms of exchange that are not fixed or static but rather sustain ongoing processes of engagement, responsiveness and change. As Brazilian artist Ricardo Basbaum (who realized the project *Re-projecting (Utrecht)* with Casco in April 2008) describes this:

> 'Conversations' are a way of thinking, where the self opens to the outside, producing a special social space where no single language of truth is prevalent. It enables the transformation of the voice of the other ... 'Conversations' are a sort of dialogue that have their own dynamics, always surprising the participants ... 'Conversations' succeed as a play-like situation, and involve a certain practice of how to keep yourself in a permanent state of awareness and change (flexibility). There's nothing specific to be achieved in a conversation, except that when the participants feel they are out of it – that is, when they finish a particular dialogue – they just cannot go back to the same places they left before (some transformation might have happened). Therefore, 'conversation' is a modality of movement.[1]

On the international cultural landscape there are a number of small to medium-scale contemporary art institutions whose emphasis lies in discourse and exchange rather than presentation. Artist-led organizations such as Sarai in New Delhi,[2] the recently closed Copenhagen Free University[3] and 16 Beaver Street in New York,[4] are all examples of progressive models for small organizations. These spaces are sites for sustained critical inquiry where the activities of artists, writers, researchers and other cultural practitioners can intersect, where discourse may build up over time and where new reflexive practices, methods and ideas can be developed in order to address the contemporary condition and to think about (or sometimes even enact) the possibilities for change, if only on a micro-level. Perhaps the main qualities that distinguish these spaces – and other artist-led or grassroots organizations and small institutions – from more mainstream institutions is their commitment, sustainability and flexibility. These are also qualities that are fundamental to the make-up of Casco, both as I inherited it and continued to run it.

Nina Möntmann has written about these types of organization in relation to opacity, where the institution is a site of research and analysis that does not have to be immediately visible but is continuously at work in the background. As an attempt to work between engagement and autonomy, we tried at Casco to combine this kind of opacity with forms of openness by realizing projects with artists that had multiple points of entry and layers of resonance. A number of projects had very public moments, or direct forms of activity that were often embedded in the city, or were formed through collective processes that mixed publics. These sometimes began with a theoretical proposal or led to critical reflection, creating forms of feedback between practice and theory.

Copenhagen Free University described its activities as working with 'forms of knowledge that are fleeting, fluid, schizophrenic, uncompromising, subjective, uneconomic, acapitalist, produced in the kitchen, produced when asleep or arisen on a social excursion – collectively'. This approach is close to that of a number of Casco's projects that employed experimental or collective research processes and produced what might be described as unstable forms of knowledge. In particular, works produced through the involvement of many voices or forms of input – as opposed to the singular voice of the artist – were open to conflict, forms of disagreement and uncertainty, wherein conversation becomes a way of preventing a fixed representation

Wendelien van Oldenborgh's *Maurits Script* (2006), produced by Casco, examined Dutch colonial history in North East Brazil and the often contradictory stories that surround the period. Van Oldenborgh's script comprises conflicting historical accounts of Maurits' governorship, and the film was shot in the renowned Dutch museum Mauritshuis, the house of Johann Maurits, Governor of North East Brazil in the early 1600s. The actors, who each had a different relationship to the history of colonization, read their scripted roles. However, during the screening of the film, which also occurred in Mauritshuis, these same actors appeared on the other side of the room, engaging in a live conversation about their own relationships to the legacies of colonial history. Participation in this discussion was open to the museum's public, and during this second staging a new script was written. With the input of multiple voices, this second script was at times a contradictory reflection on the personal experiences of a multicultural society – it did not produce one single truth or perspective. In some respects this project performed what Irit Rogoff describes as 'smuggling – an embodied criticality',[5] where critical practice shifts away from a distanced, analytic mode and moves towards an inhabitation of a problem that is open to participation – in this case entering into the museum and destabilizing its official narrative from within through conversation. [...]

Dave Hullfish Bailey's project *What's Left to its own Devices (On Reclamation)* (2007), produced by Casco, also attempted to unravel conventional patterns in the way we read spaces and places. Bailey researched the manner in which public spaces are formed and the relations between the public and private spheres. The project drew comparisons between the highly structured city centre of Utrecht and Slab City, an ad hoc squatters' camp in the California desert. Bailey's experimental geography initially examined the role of hydrological processes in creating specific spaces of sociability and private retreat. This approach led him to find similarities between the narratives of individual freedom and communal living associated with Slab City, and the historical development of Utrecht, a city that arose from the collective task of managing a system of canals, and which has also been cited as an early model of democratic political organization.

In Utrecht, Bailey discovered instances of people creating individual ways of inhabiting or occupying space. He discovered that an old man had been living in a van and a boat around the corner from Casco for over thirty years. Earlier, in the 1920s, Gerrit Rietveld's famous de Stijl building the Schröder House had been built on the outskirts of the city centre. The product of a collaboration between Rietveld and his client Truus Schröder-Schrader, the ground floor was structured according to planning regulations but she and Rietveld designated the second floor as an 'attic', thus giving themselves the freedom to experiment with utopian ideas of living.

Bailey focused on such micro-sites in both Utrecht and Slab City, drawing them together using non-linear heuristic methods to forge links across a range of subjects, both social and geographical, that were as varied as forms of sedimentation and accumulation, water diversion structures, barricades as tools of spatial control, DIY culture and the social functions of books and libraries. The project highlighted the way in which things collect or gravitate towards one another, be they people, detritus or books, as well as ways in which people realize their individual freedoms within existing structures. Bailey's findings were tested in *Manual Intuition and Makeshift Fashion*, a group workshop that experimented with constructing devices that altered existing relations between public and private space, and examined what other ambiguous or unstable positions might be opened up. Not only did this challenge how the structure of public space is understood, it initiated a collective, speculative thinking-by-doing. As a consequence the project formed an activity-driven process, generating alternative ways of conducting research in opposition to purely cerebral, analytical or planned approaches.

These projects have each negotiated institutional structures – whether those of the museum, an official history, the school or public space – rethinking existing relations and acknowledging that nothing is stable or fixed. Bailey describes his practice as an approach in which he disorganizes and reorganizes information in order to find new connection points. This activity of creating non-standard links between art and other fields is common in art practice, yet many art institutions have remained relatively isolated. Simon Sheikh describes the art institution as the 'in-between, the mediator, interlocutor, translator and meeting place between art production and the conception of its "public"'.[6] Sheikh continues:

> I would suggest that we take our point of departure in precisely the unhinging of stable categories and subject positions, in the interdisciplinary and intermediary, in the conflictual and dividing, in the fragmented and permissive – in different spaces of experience, as it were. We should begin to think of this contradictory and non-unitary notion of a public sphere, and of the art institution as the embodiment of this sphere.[7] [...]

1 Ricardo Basbaum, *Re-projecting(Utrecht)* (Utrecht: Casco, 2008).
2 Sarai: 'a space for research, practice and conversation about the contemporary media and urban constellations'.
3 The Copenhagen Free University opened in May 2001 at the apartment of Jakob Jakobsen and Henriette Heise in Copenhagen. It was an artist-run institution dedicated to the production of critical consciousness and poetic language.
4 16 Beaver Street: a network of artists, curators, writers, thinkers and activists who converge on a regular basis at a space in Lower Manhattan to discuss issues, exchange ideas and raise questions.
5 Irit Rogoff, 'Smuggling – An Embodied Criticality' (2006) (www.eipcp.net)
6 Simon Sheikh, 'Public Spheres and Functions of Progressive Art Institutions' (2004) (www.republicart.net)
7 Ibid.

Emily Pethick, extract from transcript of 'Resisting Institutionalization', presentation at the Institute of Contemporary Arts, London (2008).

Claire Bishop
The New Masters of Liberal Arts: Artists Rewrite the Rules of Pedagogy//2007

How can you bring a classroom to life as though it were an artwork?
– Félix Guattari, *Chaosmosis*, 1992

Nestled in the Schlossgarten meadow in Münster, Germany, between George Brecht's *Three VOID Stones* (1987) and Herman de Vries' circular brick *Sanctuarium* (1997), now covered in graffiti, is a temporary settlement of tents surrounded by trees with coloured mobiles hanging from their branches. Produced by Amsterdam-based artist Maria Pask for the latest instalment of Skulptur. Projekte in Münster (which occurs every ten years), *Beautiful City* is maintained and populated by a different group of students each week. It also features a notice board announcing the latest events, a vegetable plot, and a makeshift shower; in the middle of these is a large white tent housing a library of books on various religious persuasions (including tomes on witchcraft and the theological musings of Derrida), some colourful rugs printed with the artist's drawings, and a dodgy woven wall hanging of the world religious leaders conference in 2000. Inside the tent are lectures on Sundays at 2 p.m., when a wide variety of speakers address the coexistence of different forms of faith in a modern age.

I managed to visit *Beautiful City* on a Sunday afternoon and found a Protestant Filipino lawyer in discussion with a Dutch Ph.D student (also a Protestant) on the role of religion in civic life. The debate was informal (meanderingly bad towards the end) and lasted for almost two hours, during which time the audience dwindled from about forty to fewer than ten. The lecture didn't quite come to grips with the privatization of religion in civil society, which had been its billing, but it did have the inadvertent effect of making me aware of how little I knew about the history of world religion. Theology has a vocabulary as specific as that of contemporary art.

Pask's project contains many of the features that can be associated with a pedagogic turn in contemporary art: a library-*cum*-reading-room, a lecture programme, the artist as producer. It perhaps comes as no surprise to find that Pask teaches at two art schools in the Netherlands (in The Hague and Den Dosch), since *Beautiful City* seems inseparable from the history of alternative education. But with such a pedagogically oriented project presented as a work of art, it's hard to know what exactly we're judging: is it the quality of the lectures, the curatorial selection of speakers, the books in the library, the social space, or all of this together? It's precisely this openness and undecidability that Pask finds appealing, as visitors will never be able to see the work in its totality. Whatever my reservations about its homespun New Age-ness, *Beautiful City* is led by questions rather than answers; as such, its scholastic attitude stands in contrast to more didactic works in Münster, like *Trickle Down* (2007), Andreas Siekmann's diagrammatic critique of global capitalism.

Pask's project is typical of a rising field of art that engages with collective learning at the level of adult or higher education, in contrast to children's workshops that form the mainstay of so many museum education programmes. But why is this happening so conspicuously today? Art-historically, we could argue that it represents a development of the relational practices of the 1990s: giving content to conviviality, while aiming to produce a concrete intervention in the social field. This tendency also dovetails with the present decade's mania for discussion in art, whereby no exhibition is complete without a symposium, conference or webcast interview. This increasingly discursive and intellectual approach to exhibition-making was set in motion by Catherine David's Documenta X (1997), and now seems to have migrated into the work of art itself. But outside the art world, we might equally see the the pedagogic as a reaction to the neoliberalization of higher education, in which the continual withdrawal of public money has led universities and colleges to operate within a business framework. It is unlikely that artists such as Pask would regard themselves as consciously reacting to this ideological shift, but it seems difficult to view the two trends as unrelated.

Another artist who has frequently employed an educational framework is Thomas Hirschhorn. In autumn 2004, Hirschhorn organized *24h Foucault* at the Palais de Tokyo in Paris, a project that included an auditorium, library-documentation centre, sound library, video library, bar, souvenir shop, newspaper and archive. The conceptual core of this installation was a 24-hour programme of lectures over one weekend in October. Rather than producing a 'straight' academic conference, after which one would be equipped to discuss the French philosopher's ideas, Hirschhorn took an approach that was chaotic and multidisciplinary. Twenty-four philosophers, art historians, poets, artists and musicians each performed for one hour within a specially constructed auditorium bearing the hallmarks of Hirschhorn's sculpture in provisional materials: cardboard, photocopies, slogans, brown tape, and so on. Significantly, Hirschhorn operates from a position of amateur enthusiast, rather than informed professional. 'Concerning Foucault, I do not understand his philosophy, and I think that I don't have to understand philosophy in general', he said in an interview with *Flash Art* in 2004. 'I am not a connoisseur. I am not a specialist. I am not a theoretician ... I want to work as a fan.'

Both Hirschhorn and Pask represent an approach that differs distinctly from typical contemporary university pedagogy. Professional teaching is steered towards the production and measurement of successful results. Speak to any academic, and you will be swiftly inundated with groans concerning the administrative burden of today's university education learning outcomes and assessment criteria, which have become more important than imaginative content and delivery. These changes have been instigated by neoliberal economics: over the past decade, fees have been introduced in universities and colleges in Europe, and the ethos of education has changed accordingly – from freedom, discovery and exploration to a financial investment (or crippling debt, especially for those studying the humanities). With students perceived as consumers, experimental teaching has been phased out and teachers have become accountable providers of knowledge. Whatever we think of the success of Pask's and Hirschhorn's projects as art, their freedom of operation represents an unthinkable autonomy and an unencumbered passion for knowledge.

Outside Europe, other artists have adopted a less event-based mode of educational engagement, often to compensate for the failures of art schools operating in their regions. Here the resistance is to traditional or outmoded ways of teaching, and promotes an integrated access to international debates. In August 2002, Cuban performance artist Tania Bruguera established an experimental art school in Havana called Arte de Conducta, or Behaviour Art. (Bruguera's school is notably hosted by an accredited art academy, the Institutio Superior de Arte.) The course began in January 2003, and the programme is planned to last five years. Students come from a variety of disciplines, as do visiting lecturers. 'We had workshops from a former prisoner, a mathematician, sociologists, architects, DJs, philosophers, writers, activists, political figures, historians, lawyers, and of course art critics/historians and practising artists', explains Bruguera. Workshops have taken place in a park, an office, a museum, a science lab, a conference centre, private homes, and on city streets, reflecting the school's philosophy of bringing art into engagement with society. It's hard to understand Arte de Conducta from a distance, not least because there is no representation of it currently available. The only way to 'see' the school – in terms of conventional art spectatorship – is to participate. Bruguera is adamant that the project be perceived as a work of art, but what differentiates it from works by Pask and Hirschhorn is her desire for art to be consciously 'useful'. The aim is to effect long-lasting changes in the artists' production of Cuba, compensating for the shortcomings of official education provision and offering firsthand (rather than mediated) exposure to international artists and their work. By contrast, the works of Pask and Hirschhorn are less urgently connected to the provision of education and stand more symbolically for the creation of community through the energy of shared ideas.

A project comparable to Arte de Conducta might be Lia Perjovschi's Centre for Art Analysis (CAA), based out of her studio in Bucharest. Perjovschi describes the CAA as a 'museum in files': the hundreds of boxes that line the walls of her studio, containing articles, photocopies, images and so on. Unlike an institutional archive, the boxes are organized around an idiosyncratic array of themes and issues that have contributed to Perjovschi's own artistic formulation. Prior to the 1989 revolution, Romania had no access to such information. For Perjovschi, the ability to have a dialogue and explain art in her context depends on having a shared body of knowledge, and this starts with sharing a technical vocabulary of specific words (such as performance, institution, installation). For all its idiosyncrasy, the CAA is an important alternative resource to the Universitatea Nationala de Arta (located in the same neighbourhood), which still adheres to traditional – rather than conceptual – approaches to art. Perjovschi's studio provides an informal haven and alternative pedagogic playground for renegade students seeking a more open frame of discussion.

There are important precursors to these efforts. Perhaps the most towering educator in recent art history is Joseph Beuys, whose legacy provides direct inspiration for Hirschhorn, Bruguera and many others. Significantly, however, he kept his commitment to free education at one remove from his sculptural practice. Arguably more relevant (and recent) precedents can be traced to the late 1980s, when Martha Rosler and Group Material produced groundbreaking exhibitions at the Dia Center for the Arts in New York that reconfigured the space into a social forum for critical thinking on homelessness and democracy, respectively. Their approaches anticipated what has been dubbed New Institutionalism in Europe: an attempt to broaden the remit of a gallery from an exhibition space to a centre for the production of publications, archives, symposia and residencies. Unlike Beuys, whose pedagogic performances invariably resulted in objects or installations, these contemporary efforts demote the art object to just one component of an integrated research project.

Other approaches may be as much about the artists' collective research as they are about their learning. Polish artist Pawel Althamer, for example, realized *Einstein Class* in 2005 after being commissioned to make a work celebrating Einstein's centenary. Althamer developed a six-month project in Warsaw to teach physics to a small group of juvenile delinquents, led by a rogue science teacher who had recently been laid off. For another project, this time in Paris (*Au Centre Pompidou*, 2006), Althamer himself became a teacher, taking ten students from different art schools to a secluded wood in Poland. The experience during the workshops on this trip became a basis for a collectively produced puppet show in Espace 315 at the Centre Pompidou.

More interesting than the final product of *Au Centre Pompidou* was Althamer's professed desire to 'study amongst students': to explore, communicate and continue the way of learning that he experienced in classes taught by Professor Grzegorz Kowalski in the late 1980s. The so-called Kowalski Studio at the Warsaw Academy of Fine Arts rejected the traditional model of serving as 'master' to student 'apprentice'. Instead Kowalski taught through 'visual games', open-ended tasks that also functioned as a form of collective analysis, both critical and therapeutic. Many of today's leading generation of Polish artists were taught by Kowalski, including Artur Zmijewski, whose video *Them* (2007), at Documenta 12, epitomizes this task-based way of working. In 2005, Zmijewski and Althamer revisited Kowalski's approach in 'Choices.pl.', an exhibition organized as a group studio for all former pupils of Kowalski. Constantly mutating, process-based and chaotic, this exhibition-as-studio-laboratory spread throughout several galleries of the Centre for Contemporary Art in Warsaw. It was critically panned as incomprehensible, and even Kowalski sought to distance himself from what was being done in his honour.

Like many of the projects I have discussed, 'Choices.pl.' may not mean much to viewers anticipating a cohesive and completed exhibition. It's more significant as an attempt to present a pedagogic process self-reflexively rather than by illustration. Althamer described the project to me as 'therapy for artists' – in other words, as a liberation from the pressure of producing a packaged show for easy consumption. One has to admire the CAA Warsaw for allowing this experiment to take place, even while its communicability is less amenable to a general audience than the lectures organized by Pask and Hirschhorn. But what links all these projects, despite their disparate ideological contexts, is a commitment to experimental thinking about the relationship between art and society, and a desire to preserve a collective space of non-bureaucratized investigation. Their significance derives not from the issue of what it means to reimagine the work of art as education (because this would play into the hands of those who wish to instrumentalize art to socially useful ends), but to rethink the possibility of non-alienated learning through the lessons of artistic sensibility. This is what I understand to be the import of the rhetorical question, posed by Félix Guattari, that serves as the epigram of this essay. The straitjacket of efficiency and conformity that accompanies authoritarian models of education seems to beg for playful, interrogative, and autonomous opposition. Art is just one way to release this grip.

Claire Bishop, 'The New Masters of Liberal Arts: Artists Rewrite the Rules of Pedagogy', *Modern Painters* (September 2007) 87–9.

Michael Hardt and Antonio Negri
Multitude//2004

[...] In the final decades of the twentieth century, industrial labour has lost its hegemony and in its stead emerged 'immaterial labour', that is, labour that creates immaterial products, such as knowledge, information, communication, a relationship, or an emotional response. Conventional terms such as service work, intellectual labour and cognitive labour all refer to aspects of immaterial labour, but none of them captures its generality. As an initial approach, one can conceive immaterial labour in two principle forms. The first form refers to labour that is primarily intellectual or linguistic, such as problem-solving, symbolic and analytical tasks, and linguistic expressions. This kind of immaterial labour produces ideas, symbols, codes, texts, linguistic figures, images and other such products. We call the other principal form of immaterial labour 'affective labour'. [...]

In general, the hegemony of immaterial labour tends to transform the organization of production from the linear relationships of the assembly line to the innumerable and indeterminate relationships of distributed networks. Information, communication and cooperation become the norms of production, and the network becomes its dominant form or organization. The technical systems of production therefore correspond closely to its social composition: on one side the technological networks and on the other the cooperation of social subjects put to work. [...]

Privatization is a central component of the neoliberal ideology that determines the strategy of the major powers that rule over the global economy. The 'public' that is privatized by neoliberalism are generally property and business enterprises previously controlled by the state, from railroads and prisons to parklands. We have also discussed the great expansion of private property into realms of life that were previously held in common, through patents, copyright and other legal instruments. At the extreme point of this logic, economists go so far as to claim that every good should be privately owned in order to maximize its productive use. In the social, in other words, the tendency is to make everything public and thus open to government surveillance and control; and in the economic, to make everything private and subject to property rights. [...]

Michael Hardt and Antonio Negri, extracts from *Multitude: War and Democracy in the Age of Empire* (London: Hamish Hamilton, 2004) 108; 113; 203 [footnotes not included].

Lars Bang Larsen
Luca Frei//2006

[...] As Öyvind Fahlström once sloganized, to manipulate the world is to take care of the world. This roughly summarizes the way the Swiss-born, Stockholm-based Luca Frei fuses pedagogical strategy with planetary concern. For him art-making, or creativity, is essentially part of public life. Currently there is a curatorial vogue around educational systems, and if we look a little way back in art history we can see how artists' involvement with education (apart from being a staple of art activism) has ranged from populism to parody – in Joseph Beuys' social sculpture principles of form were applied to democracy in a kind of macro-pedagogic effort – or how education has been the butt of conceptual disingenuousness, as in Art & Language's *School* project from the mid 1970s, a spanner in the works of any edifying ideology.

Frei's approach in terms of mediating knowledge and the potential for social change is to create space, to open up means and ends. In *Space Jockeys* (2002) the line between artwork, toy and motivational strategy becomes blurred in a situation with many authors and no beginning or end. The installation is simply an overhead projector placed on a table filled with coloured, transparent plastic pieces and various tactile and formal objects. It is a situation or a stage waiting for the audience to interact with it, to create and project new backdrops to their actions. *Space Jockeys* has that particular lightness that occurs when form and sensation are reduced and separated in order to meet again through surprising postulates or new syntaxes. In this way Frei's works are host bodies that invite parasitic activities, albeit in the form of modest proposals. They convey the suspicion that learning, above all, is the desire to energize social space through an emptying out of some of the stuff that culture habitually accumulates: a process that requires not larger syllabuses and tougher questions but a kind of holistic reconstruction.

The real promise held out by learning, then, is that of revitalization: that the transformation of knowledge into action can be synched into the very groove of life. In Frei this rhythm is sought in narrative environments, such as *Tobacco Warehouse* (2005), created for the 9th Istanbul Biennial. A collaboration with the art group Oda Projesi, based on their book *Neighbourhood, Room, Neighbour, Guest?* (2005), the installation consisted of an arrangement of walls combining domestic and urban architecture, put at the disposal of local stencil and graffiti artists. A number of triangular tables in recycled iron with mirror tops allowed Oda Projesi's book 'to explode in three dimensions into the architecture of the space', in Frei's words. In 2004, in another attempt to focus and disseminate collective energies, Frei founded Gruppo Parole e Immagini, a kind of public reading group whose mission is the free appropriation, elaboration and distribution of textual and visual materials. Accordingly, on one of the group's posters, superimposed on a shadowy image from a Laurie Anderson performance, is a quote from Pier Paolo Pasolini: *Non c'e altra poesia che l'azione reale* (There is no other poetry than real agency).

The terrain between unlearning and re-imagining is one in which modernism sits squarely, with all the ideological optimism of its marooned adventures. 'Everything was to be done. All the adventures are still there', goes the emancipatory swing of a quote from Kodwo Eshun, appropriated in a work consisting of a giant blackboard and magnetic white letters that can be manipulated from a step ladder. Nodding to the built spaces and grand societal imaginaries of the twentieth century, Frei also used the Eshun quote to full ambivalent effect by having it accompany a poster made from a photo of the Beaubourg plateau in Paris before the construction of the Centre Pompidou. The poster shows the plateau as an unsuspecting car park, to our eyes the image of a great absence laden with potentiality. (Sometimes one wishes there were policies against filling up urban space, rather than policies for building things, as both people and culture thrive quite well in the in-between.) The poster also refers to the Swiss sociologist Albert Meister's novel *La soi-disant utopie du Centre Beaubourg* (1976), a science-fiction scenario about a subterranean space for alternative cultural activities more than 70 floors below the foundations of the then newly opened Centre Pompidou.

In the slide piece *Balancing Acts* (2004) the outside of the Centre Pompidou is again the setting. In front of its transparent mega-tubes full of art-goers a juggler is seen rehearsing his routine with balls whose colours match the external mechanical systems of the centre: yellow for power, blue for air, green for water and red for the lifts. The juggler – an outsider removed from any kind of modernity but omnipresent in urban space – embodies an idea of itinerant creativity that for today's networked classes comes across as naked and naïve. But in the slides Frei's street performer simply passes us by as an autonomous figure, inviting neither alms nor attention from people around him. Where urban planners such as Le Corbusier juggled whole cities, this guy simply produces a grammar of keeping the ball in the air, of perpetual motion and improvisation. The juggler's movements oppose the static and the finished in a play that is a kind of pure agency; according to Frei, a 'becoming that is no longer a secondary characteristic but an operating mode'.

Lars Bang Larsen, 'Luca Frei: Making Room for Learning and Un-learning: Jugglers and Public Space', *frieze*, no. 101 (September 2006) 164. www.frieze.com

Felicity Allen
Border Crossing//2009

[...] *Nahnou–Together* translates from the Arabic as 'we together', and in this context implies mutual learning. It is a partnership between Tate Britain, the British Council, the Adham Ismail Centre of Plastic Arts in Damascus, and Darat-al-Funun and the Jordan National Gallery of Fine Art in Amman, with support from the Jordan Ministry of Education. [...]

Conventionally, museum curators identify with the 'self' of the artist, while gallery educators are situated as identifying with the 'other' of the visitor. Artists themselves frequently play with this construction, challenging their own authority as well as that of the museum and the visitor. In the work my colleagues and I are engaged in at Tate Britain, we regularly involve people – 'visitors' – to take on the role of artist or curator so that they, too, can play around, challenge and take authority. In this way we 'deterritorialize' and 'destratify', facilitating a composite meaning-making that springs from the idea of participatory cultural production.

At the centre of Tate, however, is the collection and its implicit authority-bearing status. Although Tate has recently acquired works by artists from the Levant, to date no acquisitions have been confirmed from modern or contemporary Syrian or Jordanian artists. On the other hand, higher proportions of the most important Syrian archaeological objects in public collections are likely to be in North America or Western Europe, a sensitive issue for a country that emerged from five hundred years of colonization only fifty years ago. Further complications lie with Tate Britain's engagement with national identity, migration and postcolonial culture, while issues of authority – who has the right to be shown, or to be seen, to criticize, to select, or to be collected? – inform a core part of Tate Britain's work with young people. While the professionals involved in *Nahnou–Together* have possibly learned more than the young people, it is work with these young people that legitimized the programme. [...]

As well as the wider political situation, there were the internal politics of the institutions involved that influenced the programme's development. [...] Successive governments have introduced models from the private sector to 'improve' public-sector efficiency. [...]

Within an administrative context New Public Management takes the form of a model for project management which proposes aims, objectives and an evaluative framework whose emblem is the Gantt chart [diagrammatically charting progressions in relation to a timeframe]. As a methodology, it impacts on how one thinks or proceeds and, by extension, what one chooses to proceed with or, at least, how one measures one's options. It is a still contested approach, but for younger generations has been completely normalized. [...]

As the project started to take shape, it gradually became clear to me that, as well as Arabic and English, there were different and sometimes conflicting registers of English being spoken: a pragmatic language in which a spade was called a spade, and an institutional language that, for instance, called an artwork an output. The Syrian partner, the Adham Ismail Centre, was represented by practising artist educators, who had been isolated from the conventions of New Public Management, but whose sense of themselves as artists might be described as 'civilizer' and 'border crosser', to use Gaztambide-Fernández's terms.[1] In this context I frequently found myself intellectually and emotionally identifying with my Syrian colleagues who privileged originality, individuality, spontaneity and imagination over organization and team work. [...]

A key objective of the British Council was that everyone in the programme should gain a more nuanced understanding of the two countries involved, but the lack of familiarity with each other's expectations led to difficult, though often stimulating, explorations on the fault lines of misconceptions. Working through these, a deeper commitment and understanding of each other shaped the programme in personal as well as professional ways, transforming it from a managerial model into something uncharted and dynamic.

Ahmad, a twelve-year-old *Nahnou–Together* participant at Adham Ismail Centre, echoed the sense of the uncharted when he wrote in 2005–6, 'When I draw I feel part of the world.' For a Syrian child whose country has been isolated and vilified in some quarters, this has an additional intensity. He reveals the imaginative concentration of power he gains through drawing, which in turn forms a kind of mapping of self. [...]

I have learnt from *Nahnou–Together* that one must focus on process rather than narrowly defined targets, and the process should refer to the knowledge gained about being prepared to fumble in the dark, to doubt and not to know, as well as to keep listening to theory and looking at practice to help reflection. This includes self-reflection. Although I have been engaged in debates about feminism, museums and colonialism all my life, I felt in this project that I had to learn again in a completely different way: the learning now feels embodied, in the body of me as I am now, not as I was ten, twenty or thirty years ago. I have looked again at something that I heard cultural theorist Stuart Hall say years ago and realized it describes where I am now in the museum, through *Nahnou–Together*:

> Museums have to understand their collections and their practices as what I can only call 'temporary stabilizations'. What they are – and they must be specific things or they have no interest – is as much defined by what they are not. Their identities

are determined by their constitutive outside; they are defined by what they lack and by their other. The relation to the other no longer operates as a dialogue of paternalistic apologetic disposition. It has to be aware that it is a narrative, a selection, whose purpose is not just to disturb the viewer but to itself be disturbed by what it cannot be, by its necessary exclusions. It must make its own disturbance evident so that the viewer is not entrapped into the universalized logic of thinking whereby because something has been there for a long period of time and is well funded, it must be 'true' and of value in some aesthetic sense. Its purpose is to destabilize its own stabilities. Of course, it has to risk saying, 'This is what I think is worth seeing and preserving', but it has to turn its criteria of selectivity inside out so that the viewer becomes aware of both the frame and what is framed.[2]

1 Rubén Gaztambide-Fernández, 'The Artist in Society: Understandings, Expectations, and Curriculum Implications', *Curriculum Enquiry*, vol. 3, no. 38 (2008) 255.

2 Stuart Hall, 'Museums of Modern Art and the End of History', in Stuart Hall and Sarat Maharaj, *Modernity and Difference* (London: Institute of International Visual Arts, 2001) 22.

Felicity Allen, extracts from 'Border Crossing', *Tate Papers* (Spring 2009) (www.tate.org.uk/research/tateresearch/tatepapers) and *IJADE* (International Journal of Art and Design Education), vol. 28, no. 3 (2009) 296–308.

Pablo Helguera
Mapping the Republic of Contemporary Art//2007

[...] I had just arrived from Bogotá having covered more than 13,000 miles since setting out from Anchorage, midway to my goal of Tierra del Fuego. This journey was part of a public art project, *The School of Panamerican Unrest*, which consisted of driving across North and South America with a large installation – a schoolhouse – and erecting it in various public plazas, universities, arts institutions and anywhere else possible along the way. A variety of events took place at each stop – panel discussions, civic events and ceremonies, screenings and other impromptu activities. At each gathering various symbols, such as flags and an anthem, praised the fictional country of 'Panamerica'. Local collaborators would write, sign and read public resolutions about their relationship with this fictional nation. A string of resultant debates was videotaped for a documentary intended to function as the reunion of transcontinental voices not normally pitted against each other.

This project emerged out of a word most of us are ambivalent about: Panamericanism – a nineteenth-century idea that was never a reality, and yet the term has taken a controversial turn due to neoliberal economic policy, Chávista neo-socialism and cold war era US policies. These ambiguities, expressed in the fictitious utopian country the project promoted (Panamerica) as well as the kind of institution it purported to be (a school) became a travelling thinktank with the objective of pushing discussion towards defining the tangibility of what connects nationality and culture today. Somehow, however, the SPU ended up existing in flux, between being perceived as art and as an unconventional school, church, political project or missionary enterprise, depending on the places in which it appeared and the audiences it engaged. Discussions often turned into giant group therapy sessions (someone in Argentina nicknamed me the 'Panamerican Therapist') in which people debated topics of their own choosing, usually about their relationship with their own country, local cultural and social conflicts.

Over the course of four months, the *SPU* was officially presented in 30 cities and included three dozen discussions attended by a wide audience, functioning, in many cases, in non-art-related contexts. Captured on video these dialogues, when transcribed, ran to several hundred pages. Responses to the project were so wide-ranging and complex that – along with endless border-crossing adventures and other experiences – one would never be able to describe them all in a single essay.[1] But I do think the engagements that took place amidst different art communities along my route are worth comparing and reflecting upon. [...]

[One] night I logged on at an Internet café and was notified about a post in a widely read Colombian arts blog, *Esferapública*.[2] As in other places in Latin America, blogs are the most effective means of communication among those interested in contemporary art, reaching far beyond newspapers and magazines. Colombian artist Lucas Ospina had posted a piece on my recent passage through Bogotá. The text was a fable-like satire of my project, mixing fact and fiction. Making the points that I was an artist from New York who had worked in a large New York museum and received a US foundation grant to do this project, Ospina's text characterized *SPU* as a flawed attempt at institutional critique, as I was an artist living in the 'centre', endorsed by the centre, operating with like mentality. [...]

The debate went on for weeks, as did my journey. At every remote town when I arrived I logged in and read the latest posting on *Esferapública*. In blogging culture, entries slowly start to feed each other, resulting in an ever-escalating series of misreadings. This debate provoked particular unrest in me, perhaps because it misrepresented the project to thousands of readers throughout Latin America where the smaller but most meaningful face-to-face *SPU* dialogues had taken place. [...]

Meanwhile, in cities with limited financial or critical infrastructure for art production (Anchorage, Asunción, Mexicali, San Salvador, Tegucigalpa), a visitor such as myself was such a novelty that the local art community was entirely well disposed, fully engaged in all the activities and discussion topics that the *SPU* proposed. This context seemed to be where the *SPU* best contributed and where I felt a greater sense of accomplishment and even a small amount of success. For example, through their discussion, the arts community in Mérida recognized the lack of criticism in their area and decided to organize an annual 'criticism month', which was first celebrated last October. In cases like this, discussion of whether the *SPU* was a good or bad art project – or if it was art at all – seemed irrelevant.[3]

It was interesting to me that art communities in places as different as New York and San Salvador generally responded to the project unambiguously. This was due, I think, to the fact that in those places there are no great doubts as to the role of artmaking and as to their place in an international context – New York knowing that they form part of 'the centre' and San Salvador clearly knowing that they exist outside the mainstream. Somehow this allowed us to focus on other subjects. But the discussions became most animated, combative and aesthetically based in cities with strong art activity that are not powerhouses in the international art market. In such cities (e.g., Bogotá, Buenos Aires, Caracas, Guatemala City, Santiago), I received the strongest criticism and scepticism regarding my project, typically, the accusation that I was replicating the institutional structures of the art world, and I was often pressed to define my political and aesthetic positions. [...]

It seemed to me that if we all were quoting Rosalind Krauss – as many were – and invoking Godard, weren't we all coming from the same place anyway? I wrote in *Esferapública*, 'we all are the others and we all are a self, but when it comes down to the art world, we all are New Yorkers.' [Colombian expatriate artist] François Bucher replied, 'To me, to say that we all are New Yorkers is the same as to say that we live in a classless society. It's like in architectural design: the more you use glass in corporate or government buildings to give the impression of transparency, the more intricate the labyrinth of codes security personnel control so that those who don't know the protocol shall not pass.' François' words stayed with me for the rest of the trip. [...]

1 Accounts of some of these events can be read at www.panamericanismo.org.

2 http://esferapublica.org/portal/index.php

3 In fact, the question of whether the project was art or not, ironically, became an issue only when an art-informed audience was present, and not otherwise.

Pablo Helguera, extracts from 'Mapping the Republic of Contemporary Art (Notes from the Panamerican Highway)', *Art Lies*, no. 53 (Spring 2007).

Julie Brook and Johnny Gailey
In Conversation//2010

Julie Brook I feel that drawing and the teaching of drawing is important. It gives children – and adults – skills that currently aren't developed properly in school. By teaching children to draw and involving them in ambitious projects, I offer them a chance to develop their work as an artist might. Although making my own work is very different from teaching, I think the spirit of it is the same: you take time to let something evolve (in this case over two years), to develop something ambitious from straightforward beginnings. I like giving children a sense of ambition and an opportunity to work with artists to realize something on a large scale, and to explore different artistic disciplines. It is all rooted in the idea of observing and drawing your own environment.

Johnny Gaily Is this something you recognize in your own life and work that you wish to pass on to others?

Brook Yes, firstly that feeling that anything is possible. In my own work I've occasionally experienced the feeling that I'm transcending what I had planned or thought I could do. It's a great thing to open a door for someone, but what I love about teaching drawing is that you can't do it for that person, they have to experience this for themselves. What I enjoy about the process is that the children know when they have had a good day, when something has shifted in them and they have learned something new. It's not like conventional learning where you absorb knowledge and then work out a way of using it. With drawing it's about really concentrating, along with a combination of the way you observe something, and the way you use your hands, your head, your heart (and, of course, in children this is very unselfconscious), everything comes together in an expression of what is going on inside you as well as what you are looking at. [...] For some of them it was the first time they had been away from home, so it was a huge personal experience. I think that developing their drawing skills prior to the exchange helped them interpret the experience in their artwork, but it also built their confidence. [...] The effort that the children put into the work was also significant. When I talked to them later, they said it was very important to have worked hard – they wanted it to be an important memory. [...]

In this process of teaching it is not about right or wrong – what I am interested in is who each child is. I just want them to draw like themselves. But you need to work to arrive at that place, it doesn't just happen. Firstly, they need to become more comfortable in themselves, to accept their own language of drawing, because that is where the imagination really lies. Secondly, they become more familiar with the materials – for example they become aware that you can do many different things with charcoal or watercolour. As their ideas grow, their means of expressing those ideas grow as well. They can extend themselves to take on a more complex view, for instance, or can render things spatially without necessarily understanding what they are doing. It just happens for them because they have developed the skills and are not inhibited. I think when you are less confident you tend to be more literal in your thinking, and when you know yourself better, you naturally become more lateral, and your ability to express yourself develops. [...] This is why developing their concentration was incredibly important, particularly considering the dominance of technology today and the fast pace of modern life. To enable children to sit in their environment, whether it is urban or rural, and really look at it for a whole day is an achievement. [...]

Julie Brook and Johnny Gailey, extracts from 'In conversation: Julie Brook & Johnny Gailey' (2010) in *Air Iomlaid*, ed. Fiona Bradley (Edinburgh: Fruitmarket Gallery, 2010) 69–70; 73–4.

Jan Verwoert
The Boss: On the Unresolved Question of Authority in Joseph Beuys' Oeuvre and Public Image//2008

To be certain, art offers answers. Its strength, however, often lies in its unresolved problems. In his statements about his own work, Joseph Beuys absolutely inundated his listeners and readers with answers. As a consequence, the inner tensions and unanswered questions at the heart of his oeuvre are scarcely recognized. An unconditional acceptance of Beuys' interpretive authority over his own practice has caused the discourse surrounding the oeuvre to fail to touch on a central unresolved question within it: *the question of authority itself*. In order to understand the significance of Beuys' work in the context of the artistic and political debates of the 1960s and 1970s, however, it is crucial to grasp the inner conflicts and unresolved contradictions that run through it, as well as the way Beuys publicly performed the role of the artist with regard to this question of authority. On the one hand he incessantly attacked traditional notions of the authority of the work, the artist and the art professor, with his radical, liberating and humorous opening up of the concept of art with regard to what a work, an artist or a teacher could still be and do beyond the functions established by tradition, office and title. On the other hand, however, it seems that in the presentation of his own interpretative discourse, Beuys regularly fell back on the very tradition of staging artistic authority with which he was trying to break. [...]

[I would] argue that the artistic quality and historical significance of Beuys' work are not, as the common view would have it, based upon a realizing of his declared intentions, but rather upon his staging of an unresolved conflict between the urge to demolish authoritarian definitions of what artists are traditionally supposed to be and the need to recoup certain aspects of fascination with the auratic authority of the artistic act and the artist's role. [...]

[D]uring the Festival der Neuen Kunst in the auditorium of the Technische Hochschule Aachen on 20 July 1964, a group of students (whom Caroline Tisdall has described as right-wing) stormed the stage to put a violent end to the Fluxus performance Beuys was engaged in; during the ensuing scuffle Beuys received a bloody nose. His reaction to the violence was to strike a pose in which he provocatively embodied both victim and perpetrator. With a defiant stare and bloody nose, he holds up a small crucifix to the audience in his left hand while he extends his right arm in a Roman salute. It is not necessary, though possible, to see this gesture as a variant on the Nazi salute.

In one sense, Beuys' pose has an accusatory character: he holds a mirror up to the students, interprets their violence as tendentially fascist, and presents himself as their victim. In another sense, however, the pose is also clearly triumphant. In combination with the Roman salute and the defiant gaze, the crucifix in his outstretched arm conveys the message that Christ shall be victorious. In the end, the martyr, here embodied by the bleeding artist, will prevail. Beuys thus intuitively drew on several registers of body language at the same time to produce an impromptu pose of auratic authority, presenting himself as accuser, victor and martyr all at once. The impromptu character of the pose, in turn, shows how Beuys, through free improvisation, managed to orchestrate the chaos that he had himself provoked. The example of the events in Aachen thus demonstrates impressively the extent to which Beuys' artistic practice is based on his intuitive ability to *improvise* freely in unclarified situations, to *absorb* the energies released in the situation, and *manifest* them in strong – if contradictory – gestures. Yet the example also shows that the gestures he uses to manifest the absorbed tensions are taken from a repertoire of postures for the staging of auratic authority. One possible explanation of this may be that, when improvising, Beuys intuitively fell back on familiar gestures of authority that enabled him to control the situation for the moment. If, however, we take into account the observation that Beuys was not just displaying his own emotions but in fact reflecting the tensions inherent in a given situation, this suggests another conclusion: namely, that Beuys channelled the violent energies of collective conflict over the foundation of authority that was in the air at the moment.

The art of provocation lies in forcefully bringing about a debate over the legitimation of authority. Fluxus cultivated this art of provocation as a method. So did the incipient culture of student protest in its successful attempts to expose and dismantle the authoritarian structures on which the National Socialists based their power, and which had not really disappeared from daily life after the collapse of the regime. [...] After the festival had ended, Beuys apparently discussed what had taken place with students until two in the morning. It seems unlikely that they arrived at a conclusion. Nevertheless, a collective experience had been articulated. On the one hand, Beuys' actions therefore need to be seen in the context of the critique of dominant structures of authority that the Fluxus performers gathered at the festival put into practice by destroying the conventions of authoritative (in the sense of being awe-inspiring) musical stage performances. On the other hand, Beuys' martial poses also reflected the desire of the rioting students to see authority restored. They got the Führer-saviour they wanted, if only in the form of a reflexive, inherently contradictory theatrical pose. [...]

In relation to the artistic practices of the 1960s, the relationship between artists' statements about their work and the actual work has generally not been investigated as critically as it probably should be. Beuys is far from being the only artist who intentionally sought to impose a certain meaning on his work. In fact, particularly in the context of early conceptual art, artists aggressively used interpretation as a strategy. The interpretative practice of Art & Language and the artist Joseph Kosuth, who was for a time associated with the group, is symptomatic in this regard. The performative contradiction between the content of their statements and the way they relate them to their work is even more flagrant than it is in Beuys' own practice. Kosuth and Art & Language legitimized their work and imbued it with an awe-inspiring air of authority by citing not myths, but the entire tradition of analytic philosophy (of language), only to declare – in utter contradiction with the complex semantic models that this tradition offers – a one-to-one correspondence between this philosophical content and their art's meaning. They identified critical theory with the literal meaning and the content of conceptual art with the same naïveté that Benjamin Buchloh detects in Beuys' discourse [in 'Beuys: The Twilight of the Idol', 1980].

If anything, the crude Neo-Platonism that Kosuth propagates when he claims in his essay 'intension(s)' that conceptual art can make an artist's intentions immediately transparent can certainly be considered naïve. At the same time, the insistence on the authority of the artist to determine the meaning of his or her work is, for Kosuth, part and parcel of a critical reflection on the power politics of interpreting art. He identifies the practice of artists making statements about their own work as a strategic practice geared towards disputing the interpretive authority of critics and historians and shifting the power balance in the artist's favour. Kosuth writes: 'art historians and critics play an important role in the struggle of the work's "coming to meaning" in the world. But that is the point: they represent the world. That is why a defining part of the creative process depends on the artists to assert their intentions in that struggle. One of the greatest lessons defending the primacy of the intention of the artist, and the increasing importance of writing by artists on their work, is provided by this period of the sixties.'

Motivated by power politics, the main reason for artists to offer their own interpretations would thus be in the interest of eliminating the middleman. In this spirit, Kosuth quotes one of his own statements about the work of Art & Language in the journal *Art-Language* from 1970: 'This art both annexes the function of the critic and makes a middleman unnecessary.' It seems fair to assume that Beuys – perhaps less consciously, but all the more effectively for that reason – realized the historical opportunity which Kosuth articulates to use the propagation of his own interpretations as a means to reinforce his own position of authority vis-à-vis critics and historians. The increasing media interest in (his) art offered him (and not only him) an excellent platform for that.

Against this backdrop, viewing Beuys' practice of interpreting his own work as a strategic gesture can perhaps enable us more accurately to describe its function in relation to his other artistic activities – namely, as a praxis in its own right. As such, it is not situated on some meta-level but on the very same level as the other manifestations of Beuys' work – as a parallel practice. In this context, Beuys' participation in the founding of various political initiatives and utopian institutions, such as the Free International University he co-founded with Heinrich Böll in 1971, for instance, could equally be seen as a gesture that matters in its own right – as an expansion of the concrete possibilities of artistic practice irrespective of any ideological programme. Founding institutions thus becomes one artistic medium among others. Seen in this light, Beuys' practice of speaking publicly should be treated not as a metadiscourse on his art but as an artistic medium *sui generis*. Beuys' statements could therefore be regarded as having the status of material that he produced in parallel with other material. The chalkboards with scribbled lecture notes strewn on a stage constructed of wooden pallets in the installation *Richtkräfte* (Directional forces, 1974–77) offer a graphic example of this. Discourse becomes material, loads of material. And, because of the sheer number of chalkboards and the simple fact that some boards cover others in the pile, the sheer accumulation of material makes it partially illegible. The fascination with the material then could be seen to lie less in its ideological content than in the immanent tension between its legibility and its opacity as material. [...]

The question of why – by virtue of what authority – someone could legitimately hope to act or speak on behalf of others (on behalf of the general public or simply on behalf of an unknown number of people who perhaps have similar feelings) is a question that persistently haunts artistic practice and intellectual discourse – especially since certain catastrophes of modernity called the legitimacy of auratic authority into question. On a constitutive level, the justification for one's own practice and discourse as an artist and intellectual is challenged by this unresolved question.

With particularly pointed humour, Beuys acknowledged the implications of this question in the performance *ÖÖ-Programm* (1967). At an orientation event at the Kunstakademie Düsseldorf, he welcomed the new students by taking a stand at the microphone, an axe in his hand, uttering inarticulate sounds for minutes. On the following day the *Düsseldorfer Express* titled its report on the event 'Professor bellt ins Mikrofon' (Professor Barks into the Microphone). Short and succinct, that describes the situation. By turning the official occasion of an address by the academy staff into an absurd event, Beuys deliberately subjected not only himself but also the office and authoritative speaking position of the professor to mockery. At the same time, however, he also exposed the foundation of this authority: as a professor it was within his power to do such things. By carrying an axe, he intensified this ambiguity even further. If one recognizes the axe as an attribute of power, it is impossible not to see the parallel to the axes wrapped in rods that the lictors (the bodyguards of Roman consuls) carried as a symbol of their authority. The name for these rods – *fasces* – is considered to be one possible origin of the term fascism. If we also take 'barking into the microphone' to be an expression that describes the style of Hitler's public addresses conspicuously well, Beuys' action could indeed also be understood as a caricature of the dictator. Rather than deny the structural authority that accrued in his role as professor (for example, by appearing as an emphatically liberal pedagogue), Beuys exposes this structural authority in a deliberately exaggerated way and demonstrates its complicity with forms of mythical authority. Given the obvious absurdity of the presentation, it seems fair to assume that he did it with the idea of pushing his authority to its limits and thus instigating resistance – for example, by provoking laughter. [...]

Jan Verwoert, extracts from 'The Boss: On the Unresolved Question of Authority in Joseph Beuys' Oeuvre and Public Image', *e-flux journal*, no 1 (December 2008) [footnotes not included]. http://www.e-flux.com/journal/view/12

Jorella Andrews
Critical Materialities//2006

[...] Between December 2005 and January 2006 the installation '*Kiosk: Modes of Multiplication* & *Liam Gillick: Edgar Schmitz*' was on show at the Institute of Contemporary Arts, London. *Kiosk* [initiated by Christoph Keller] is a travelling archive of artists' books, periodicals, alternative magazines, self-publication projects, audio and video work, curated differently and by different individuals in each location of display. *Liam Gillick: Edgar Schmitz* was the title given to the way in which Gillick, with fellow artist and theorist Schmitz, curated the contents of *Kiosk* at the ICA. My interest in this installation is that it provides a rich contemporary context for discussing the pedagogical implications of 'critical materialities'. This is because it enacts and opens up for scrutiny a specific pedagogical challenge that now characterizes a wide variety of communicative contexts.

This challenge is activated by the overlap of two scenarios. One concerns the increasingly democratized, technologized and thus accelerated conditions of information production and circulation, certainly within economically developed regions of the world – the proliferation of 'stuff' that must somehow be navigated. The other is a broadly 'non-representationalist' orientation towards information/communication. This orientation has a fairly long history from a theoretical standpoint,[1] but is becoming ever more recurrent in everyday educational contexts, ranging from the sales promotion to the television documentary, gallery display and university seminar room. A tendency here is to emphasize the 'production' of new meanings through speculative and often uncontextualized explorations of the information/image-world, which is itself conceptualized as an archive of fragmentary phenomena to be sampled, arranged and rearranged. This overall state of affairs leads to pedagogical situations marked by degrees of evasiveness, elusiveness, opacity or muteness. A weakness of this orientation is that the provision of 'background' information is often equated with practices of imposition. But a strength is its openness and the way in which it calls into question the traditional pedagogical value placed on what Merleau-Ponty called the 'schoolmaster's question' – the question that is 'asked of someone who doesn't know by someone who knows'.[2]

In the ICA show, this doubled scenario was enacted though the device of offering (or appearing to offer) its visitors at once 'too much' and 'too little'. 'Too little' was offered because rather than 'examine how publishers and editors, as well as artists, work within the context and constraints of printed and recorded material' as claimed, the show merely presented the uncontextualized outcomes of those activities. [...]

Given the real possibility that some visitors would feel unable to engage with the show beyond the level of the purely superficial, the ICA did in fact proffer a strategy for navigating it. During my visits, it was modelled by the attendant who, regularly, and with apparent casualness, would leave his post and approach the work. He would handle it, move it around, and even sit down on or amongst it, demonstrating that Gillick's surfaces also functioned as seating and that the archive on display was intended for use. In other words, an active and individual route through was authorized, but through *deed* rather than word. Thus, visitors were expected to utilize the space in a variety of ways, as they liked. [...]

Clearly, these personalized and participatory ways of engaging with the (apparently) relatively unregulated display of materials in the exhibition were intended to create an atmosphere of openness and generosity. Certainly, they had the potential to encourage independence of thought and individual agency. [...]

Similarly orientated approaches, combined with practices of analysis and evaluation, characterize my own approach to curriculum design and teaching and that of the department in which I work. Nonetheless, personal and participatory forms of engagement are not sufficient in themselves to enable genuine shifts in understanding. Indeed, in some instances they may actively preclude such learning from taking place.

This is because in reality, and unless carefully nurtured to the contrary, personalized and participatory behaviours may function as just another manifestation of the contemporary drive to consume, with new information and experiences evaluated purely in terms of individual preference and/or merely assimilated into habitual frames of reference. (Indeed, upon reflection, the layout of *Kiosk* evoked the commercial space of a bookshop as much as it did a library or reading room.) This observation leads to another, namely that although various forms of personalization are becoming increasingly strategic within art-making, curatorial and educational contexts, they already have a long and complex history of application in the worlds of commerce and marketing. I am not suggesting that this connection between personalized cultural/pedagogical and personalized commercial practices somehow diminishes the former. Instead, my point is firstly that personalized and participatory practices should not be idealized in and of themselves.[3] Secondly, it is that learning is not fundamentally a matter of consolidating already-embedded patterns of thought but of questioning and possibly departing from them. However, situations characterized by certain kinds of informational or contextual lack, or in which there is inadequate critical provocation, can result in participants being forced to draw solely upon their own, already existent resources. Thus, what may emerge in and through permissive forms of cultural engagement is an unchallenged proliferation of attitudes that, in the final analysis, are autonomous and self-referential as well as 'imperialistic'. [...]

[T]he capacity to take up personalized ways of being in this complex, other(ness)-orientated way is something that must be learned and practised. What are required are environments for learning in which it becomes possible to take a productive detour from autonomy by scrutinizing the divergent ways in which the world operates as world and the self as self, and in which searches for appropriate forms of responsiveness are activated (individual, collective, cultural, political). A vital element here can be the inclusion of that 'background' information, referred to earlier, about the often-conflicting perceptions, even prejudices, experiences, analyses and questions that others have raised in relation to a given issue, or work, or body of knowledge, past and present. But only, I think, as long as this information is not proffered in the form of readymade formulae or facts, but in order to immerse us in difference.

The ICA show actively withheld this kind of information. Therefore, whether it was able to make *this* kind of learning in-and-through-difference possible is an open question. Particularly in question is whether it provided sufficiently concrete, singularized provocations through which to divert its participants (those already well-informed in the histories and theories of contemporary art practices and strategies as much as those less well schooled) from certain well-trodden interpretative paths. [...]

The movement of critical materialities as described here has been a movement in two contradictory but overlapping directions, towards the radically and concretely personal and located, and towards the radically decentred and anonymous. Where both of them end up, however, is immersed in difference. These movements seem important since cumulatively they produce attitudes that run counter to the acquisitiveness that is generally operative in culture and increasingly in the worlds of learning. The question that activates me now concerns how best to enable these flows to be enacted in the specific, contemporary educational contexts with which I am involved. My suspicion is that, as with the ICA show as I have described it, it will probably involve attempting but never managing to balance acts of proffering and withholding. But I write this in a positive spirit because at issue is not finding a foolproof methodology. It is, above all, a question of individual locatedness and singularized questings in the midst of many other, similarly unstable materialized positionings and self-showings, with the aim of provoking thought and interaction. [...]

1 It draws in part on Freudian/psychoanalytic theories of the unconscious and of unconscious drives, and on the Barthian notion of 'the death of the author'. It also draws on calls, derived

mainly from the post-1960s philosophical discourse, to abandon recourse to 'hegemonic' meta-narratives and 'reductive' explanatory or foundational structures in order to make sense of things. More recently, theories of performativity have also had their part to play.

2 Maurice Merleau-Ponty, 'Eye and Mind', *The Primacy of Perception*, ed. James Edie (Evanston, Illinois: Northwestern University Press, 1964) 167.

3 For a perspective on this matter as it relates to relational aesthetics see Claire Bishop's critique of Nicolas Bourriaud in 'Antagonism and Relational Aesthetics', *October*, no. 110 (Fall 2004) 51–79.

Jorella Andrews, extracts from 'Critical Materialities', in *A.C.A.D.E.M.Y.*, ed Angelika Nollert, Irit Rogoff, Bart De Baere, Yilmaz Dziewior, Charles Esche, Kerstin Niemann, Dieter Roelstraete (Frankfurt am Main: Revolver, 2006) 179–82.

Grant H. Kester
Another Turn//2006

I was surprised to learn from Claire Bishop ('The Social Turn: Collaboration and Its Discontents', *Artforum*, February 2006) that 'politically engaged' collaborative art practice constitutes today's avant-garde. [...]

What Bishop seeks is an art practice that will continually reaffirm and flatter her self-perception as an astute critic, 'decoding' or unravelling a given video installation, performance or film, playing at hermeneutic self-discovery like Freud's infant grandson in a game of '*fort* and *da*'. In addition to naturalizing deconstructive interpretation as the only appropriate metric for aesthetic experience, this approach places the artist in a position of ethical oversight, unveiling or revealing the contingency of systems of meaning that the viewer would otherwise submit to without thinking. The viewer, in short, can't be trusted [according to] Bishop's deep suspicion of art practices that surrender some autonomy to collaborators and that involve the artist directly in the (always already compromised) machinations of political struggles. In *Touching Feeling: Affect, Pedagogy, Performativity* (2003), Eve Kosofsky Sedgwick offers a useful interpretation of the rhetoric of exposure in her analysis of the 'paranoid consensus' that has come to dominate contemporary critical theory informed by structuralism, psychoanalysis and Marxism. Based in part on the historical identification of critical theory with the act of revealing the (structural) determinants that pattern our perception of reality, the paranoid approach obsessively repeats the gesture of 'unveiling hidden violence' to a benumbed or disbelieving world. As enabling and necessary as it is to probe beneath the surface or appearance and to identify unacknowledged forms of power, the paranoid approach, in Sedgwick's view, attributes an almost mystical agency to the act of revelation in and of itself. She writes:

> The paranoid trust in exposure seemingly depends ... on an infinite reservoir of naïveté in those who make up the audience for these unveilings. What is the basis for assuming that it will surprise or disturb, never mind motivate, anyone to learn that a given social manifestation is artificial, self-contradictory, imitative, phantasmatic or even violent?

As Sedgwick notes, the normalization of paranoid knowing as a model for creative and intellectual practice has entailed 'a certain disarticulation, disavowal and misrecognition of other ways of knowing, ways less oriented around suspicion'. Sedgwick juxtaposes paranoid knowing (in which 'exposure in and of itself is assigned a crucial operative power') with reparative knowing, which is driven by the desire to ameliorate or give pleasure. As she argues, this reparative attitude is intolerable to the paranoid, who views any attempt to work productively within a given system of meaning as unforgivably naïve and complicit, a belief authorized by the paranoid's 'contemptuous assumption that the one thing lacking for global revolution, explosion of gender roles, or whatever, is people's (that is, other people's) having the painful effects of their oppression, poverty or deludedness, sufficiently exacerbated to make the pain conscious (as if otherwise it would not have been) and intolerable.'

As delightful as it is to hear yet another disquisition on the glories of [Jeremy Deller's] *The Battle of Orgreave* (2001), or [Lars von Trier's] *Dogville* (2003), a more complete account of collaborative art must begin with some measured reflection on the diversity of practices encompassed by that term. And it must include a more substantive analysis precisely of the concepts that Bishop abandons to *ad hominem* cliché: 'activism', 'political engagement' and the aesthetic itself. On one level Bishop's discomfort with activist art is typical of post-cold-war intellectuals embarrassed by work that evokes leftist ideals. At the same time, I think there's something more at stake in her obvious revulsion (the lowest circle of hell in her essay is reserved for 'the community arts tradition'). It would seem, after all, to be relatively uncontroversial to locate the relational projects she embraces (those of Santiago Sierra, Carsten Höller or Jeremy Deller) on a continuum with socially engaged projects that employ processes of collaborative interaction. However, activist work triggers a kind of sacrificial response from Bishop, as if to even acknowledge this work as 'art' somehow threatens the legitimacy of the practices that she does support. A reductive version of engaged or activist art ('free curries for refugees') thus functions as a necessary foil, representing the abject, unsophisticated Other to the complex 'aesthetic' works of which she approves. This isn't to say that there is no reason to interrogate activist-art practices, but only to question the readiness with which critics like Bishop revert to the nuclear option of challenging the ontic status of this work as art qua art. While otherwise quite keen to question the limits of discursive systems of meaning in her criticism, she exhibits an unseemly enthusiasm for policing the boundaries of legitimate art practice. Rather than deploring the fact that some contemporary artists refuse to make the 'right' kinds of work, she might consider the 'uncomfortable' possibility that her own version of the aesthetic is simply one among many.

Grant H. Kester, extract from 'Another Turn', letter, *Artforum*, vol. 44, no. 9 (May 2006) 22.

Claire Bishop
Response to Grant Kester//2006

Thanks to Grant Kester for responding seriously to my article, in a manner consistent with his analysis of socially engaged art in *Conversation Pieces: Community and Communication in Modern Art* (2004). However, he finds in my essay what he wants to read, rather than what I actually say. My attempt to find some aesthetic (i.e. conceptual rather than ethical) criteria for discriminating different socially collaborative practices appears to him as merely 'policing the boundaries' of art and non-art. Kester also thinks I reinforce a distinction between 'aesthetic' and 'activist' works, yet the participatory examples that I cite (from Oda Projesi to Jeremy Deller) clearly occupy a blurred territory between these poles – in a manner that is characteristic of the most interesting European art of the current decade.

Kester's response also bolsters my argument about the limitations of liberal humanist criticism. He considers thinking and writing in depth about art, and using theory to elaborate ideas, as a way to intimidate others and 'flatter' oneself as a critic. This populist approach is in keeping with his argument in *Conversation Pieces*, in which Dada and Surrealism are criticized for adopting a disruptive stance that assumes superiority over an audience that needs to be 'educated'. His righteous aversion to authorship can only lead to the end of provocative art and thinking. I believe in the continued value of disruption, with all its philosophical anti-humanism, as a form of resistance to instrumental rationality and as a source of transformation. Without artistic gestures that recalibrate our perception, that allow multiple interpretations, that factor the problem of documentation/presentation into each project, and that have a life beyond an immediate social goal, we are left with pleasantly innocuous art. Not non-art, just bland art – and art that easily compensates for inadequate governmental policies.

A magazine is not the place to elaborate a theoretical position in depth, yet such discussion is crucial to avoid misunderstandings such as Kester's. The framework for my essay was Jacques Rancière's articulation of the relation between politics and aesthetics. In his schema, a political work of art disrupts the relationships among the visible, the sayable and the thinkable without having to use the terms of a message as a vehicle. It transmits meanings in the form of a rupture, rather than simply giving us an 'awareness' of the state of the world. As he writes in *The Politics of Aesthetics* (2000): 'Suitable political art would ensure, at one and the same time, the production of a double effect: the readability of a political signification and a sensible or perceptual shock caused, conversely, by the uncanny, by that which resists signification.' According to this perspective, we can no longer speak of old-fashioned autonomy versus radical engagement, since a dialectical pull between autonomy and heteronomy is itself constitutive of the aesthetic. Good art would therefore sustain this antinomy in the simultaneous impulse to preserve itself from instrumentality and to self-dissolve in social praxis. [...]

Claire Bishop, response to Grant Kester's letter in the previous issue, *Artforum*, vol. 44, no. 10 (June 2006) 24.

Lars Bang Larsen and Suely Rolnik
On Lygia Clark's *Structuring the Self* (1976–88)//2007

[...] Lygia Clark's *Estruturação do Self* (*Structuring the Self*, 1976–88) consisted of private sessions in which the artist would convey perceptual-sensorial experiences to clients, aiming at a treatment which would connect the aesthetic, the clinical and the political realms as an inseparable, existential force. In this way, far from being a variant of body art, *Estruturação do Self* opened up the resonating capacity of the body in the attempt to create a new, aesthetic subjectivity, in which the 'client' – as Clark called the participants of this proposition – would be open to become other, and other, in an endless process.

Going beyond questions of reconstruction and documentation, one of the central elements of Suely Rolnik's exhibition ['Lygia Clark: de l'oeuvre à l'événement' (Lygia Clark: From the Work to the Event), Musée des Beaux-Arts, Nantes/Pinacoteca do Estado de São Paulo, 2005–6] was thus the seventy-odd filmed interviews she conducted, producing a testimony of each phase of Clark's work within the ambient climate of the time. [...] *Lars Bang Larsen*

Suely Rolnik [...] In Lygia Clark I discovered an active quest for the politics of the sensible and thus of desire and subjectivity, deploying a sort of entirely singular zone that was cut through at once by the political, the aesthetic and the clinical, and which had real potential to open up possibilities in the existence of all those who approached it. And reciprocally, Lygia was interested in the universe that I brought with me, particularly Deleuze's philosophy (I was attending his seminar in Vincennes), and above all through his collaboration with Guattari (she was very interested in the *Anti-Oedipus* when it came out in 1972). She also took a great interest in the clinical practice that was going on around Guattari and the whole experience of La Borde [psychiatric clinic], in which I became involved, as well as the International Network of Alternatives to Psychiatry, which was shaking up the psychiatric field across Europe and changing how madness was seen. She thought that it might offer a possibility for understanding her own work and developing it theoretically. Retrospectively, I don't think she was wrong, and moreover what I found in that whole universe in response to my own questions – which helped increase their complexity – was very similar to what I had found in a different form in Lygia's work. At any rate, she asked me to do my thesis in clinical psychology at the University of Paris VII on *Structuring the Self* – a practice she had undertaken after her return to Brazil a year earlier. She was very much alone in this radicalization of her research, and was unable to find any interlocutors within the art world, and less still within the world of psychoanalysis. My doctoral dissertation was the first text that I wrote on Lygia. During the same period, I also collaborated with her on writing an article on *Structuring the Self* (the only one she ever wrote) for a little book on her work, which was published in Brazil at the time. [...]

I felt absolutely compelled to seek out strategies to communicate what was at play in these different practices. First of all, because her way of working dealt – in a subtle way, which proved effective in terms of affects – with this problematic field that had been so important to me since the 1960s in Brazil; and because I needed to carry out the project on the basis of what I had sketched out in my thesis – a kind of debt of gratitude with regard to Lygia and her work. But how is one to convey a work that is not visible, in as much as it is only produced in the sense-based experience of each individual viewer? It was at that point that I started envisaging the project of provoking a work of memory, and recording it cinematographically. What I was looking for in these interviews was not so much to conjure up the memory of the form of the different devices, actions and objects as they have been represented, as it was to provoke an immersion in the sensations lived in the experiences they enabled, but also to stimulate a work of elaboration through which these could become sayable, given that it was in the course of these experiences that the work itself actually 'happened'. These proposals implied a new mode of reception, whereby reception itself became not only a part of the work but its essential element: a fine and powerful intervention into the impoverished state of reception commonly known as the 'art system'.

In my opinion, this also explains why Lygia's persona was so present in her propositions. Indeed, her experience of teaching at the Sorbonne revealed that her presence was essential. Having borne witness from close up for the first time to the experiences of her propositions' receptors – as a teacher she was with her students during a whole school semester – she came to understand that to reactivate this quality of aesthetic experience could not be taken for granted; that is, that it was impossible to presuppose the capacity of being affected by the forces of the objects and the device in which they were presented and, through this experience, by the forces of the everyday environment. She had to accompany them one by one if it was to be possible. This is what subsequently led her to creating *Structuring the Self*, where her own presence in fact becomes an essential component of the device, without which the work, strictly speaking, which takes place in the receptor's sensibility, just cannot unfold in anything like its plenitude.

To raise the question of intervening in the dominant politics of subjectivation and relations with the other was very much part of the spirit of the times; parts of the cultural milieu were steeped in it in various ways. That implied not restricting the interviews to those who had been directly linked with Lygia, with her life and her work, but also to produce a memory of the context in which her practice originated and found its conditions of possibility. Not to restate the facts, and particularly not the allegedly heroic aura, which would make them into a model to be imitated. The point was instead to actualize the sensations of the affirmation of particularly bold poetic potential in its critical spirit – creative imagination and freedom of cultural and existential experimentation – which became possible in 1969–70 in Brazil because it was supported by a collective movement. I also wanted to make a certain reconstitution of the cultural movement of the same period in Paris, where the artist spent eight years beginning in 1968. In other words, I wanted to produce and transmit a body memory that this experience had affected and in which it was inscribed, in such a way that it might foster the reactivation of this potential in the present. [...]

Lars Bang Larsen and Suely Rolnik, extracts from 'On Lygia Clark's Structuring the Self', *Afterall* (Spring/Summer 2007) 1–6 [footnotes not included].

Harrell Fletcher
Some Thoughts on Art and Education//2009

Come Together

I was doing a week-long workshop at an art academy in Odensen, Denmark. All of the students there said that the town was not interesting so I asked them each to go out and find someone from the town who was willing to talk for ten minutes about something they knew and cared about. We then had all of those people come over to the academy and do their presentations one after another. It lasted about four hours. The students had to host and introduce the people they selected. The topics included healthcare, bus routes, skateboarding, scuba diving, furniture polishing, invisible social networks, playing music on the streets, etc. We were all blown away by the variety of knowledge that existed in one little town. Almost all of the presentations were truly interesting too. Since then I've used the same strategy for similar events in London; New York City; Austin, Texas, etc., and have done a separate series as part of the 'American War' travelling exhibition, which focused specifically on local people talking about war-related experiences. [...]

Aunt Grace

In my first year of grad school I made a Xerox book of a long transcribed interview that I'd done with my Great Aunt Grace when I visited her in a nursing home in a small town in Oklahoma just before she died at the age of ninety-eight. One of the people I gave a copy of the Aunt Grace book to told me that she took it home with her over winter break and showed it to her mother. She said her mother read it and loved it. That gave me pause. Did I want mothers to love my work? For a second that seemed somehow uncool. But then after thinking about it a little longer I realized that, yes, I did want mothers to love my work, I wanted all sorts of people to love my work and have all sorts of other emotions in regard to it also. [...]

Harrell Fletcher, extracts from 'Some thoughts on Art and Education', in *Educação para a arte, Arte para a educação*, ed. Gabriel Perez-Barreiro and Luis Camnitzer (Porto Alegre: Fundação Bienal de Artes Visuais do Mercosul, 2009) 310; 316.

Biographical Notes

Jorella Andrews is Head of the Department of Visual Culture, Goldsmiths, University of London.

Michael Archer is Reader in Art and Programme Director of Fine Art, Goldsmiths, University of London.

Hannah Arendt (1906–75) was a German-born political theorist based in the United States from 1941 onwards.

Roy Ascott is a British artist and theorist of cybernetics. He is Professor of Technoetic Arts at the University of Plymouth.

Elma Askham (now Thubron) is a British artist who taught at Leeds School of Art and at Goldsmiths College (pre-university status), London. She was married to the artist Harry Thubron (1915–85).

Dennis Atkinson is Professor of Art in Education at Goldsmiths, University of London.

Stuart Bailey is a graphic designer and co-editor, with David Reinfurt (under the joint workshop name Dexter Sinister) of *Dot Dot Dot*. He teaches at Parsons School of Design, New York.

Lars Bang Larsen is a critic and curator, and art historian at the University of Copenhagen.

Carol Becker is Professor of the Arts and Dean of the School of the Arts at Columbia University.

Caroline Benn (1926–2000) was an educationalist and writer who devoted her life to comprehensive education. American-born, she was the partner of the Labour politician Tony Benn from 1949.

Claire Bishop is Associate Professor of Art History at the Graduate Center, City University of New York.

Black Mountain College was an experimental college of liberal arts founded in 1933 at Black Mountain, North Carolina. It closed in 1957. The probable author of the prospectus reprinted here, the poet Charles Olson (1910–70), taught there from 1951 and was its final Rector.

Julie Brook is a British artist, based on the Isle of Skye, who develops land art projects internationally as well as regional art education projects.

Pierre Bourdieu (1930–2002) was a French sociologist, ethnographer and photographer.

Luis Camnitzer is a German-born Uraguayan artist, theorist and educator based in the United States. He is Professor Emeritus, State University of New York at Old Westbury, New York.

Paul Clements is a lecturer in arts and cultural policy in the Department of Drama at Goldsmiths, University of London.

Pen Dalton is a writer and artist based in London. She has taught in art colleges in the UK as well as internationally.

Alain Darbel (1932–75) was a French sociologist and statistician.

Paul Dash is a senior lecturer in Education, and Programme Leader for MA Artist Teachers at Goldsmiths, University of London.

John Dewey (1859–1952) was an American progressive philosopher, psychologist and educationalist.

Dinah Dossor is a therapist and counsellor who lectured on the creative and therapeutic applications of the visual arts at John Moores University Art School, Liverpool, from the 1970s to 2006.

Jimmie Durham is an American-born artist and writer based in Europe and a leading representative of Native American civil rights since the early 1970s.

Thierry de Duve is a Belgian art historian, critical theorist and curator, and Professor of Aesthetics and History of Art at the University of Lille III.

Elliot W. Eisner is Emeritus Professor of Education and Art at Stanford University.

David Elliott is a British-born curator who has worked in Sweden, Australia, Japan and Hong Kong. He was Director of the Museum of Modern Art, Oxford, from 1976 to 1996.

Alex Farquharson is a critic, curator and Director of the Centre for Contemporary Art, Nottingham.

Bruce Ferguson is Dean of the School of Humanities and Social Sciences, American University in Cairo (since 2010). He was formerly Dean of Columbia University School of the Arts (2000–2006).

Joanna Fiduccia is an art critic based in New York. With Chris Sharp, she co-curated the itinerant Zero Budget Biennial in Paris, Milan, London and Berlin (2009–2010).

Harrell Fletcher is an American artist based in Portland, Oregon, where he is Professor of Art at Portland State University.

Andrea Fraser is an American artist and Professor of New Genres at University of California at Los Angeles.

Paulo Freire (1921–97) was a Brazilian Christian socialist educator and theorist of critical pedagogy, who during the military regime worked outside Brazil from 1964 to 1979.

Johnny Gailey is an independent educationalist, formerly Children and Young People's Programme Manager at the Fruitmarket Gallery, Edinburgh.

Claire Gibb is an artist and tutor at Room 13 Lochyside, Scotland. Since 2002 she has worked with young people and artists to establish other studios in England, South Africa, India and Nepal.

Henry A. Giroux is Global Television Network Chair in Communication Studies at McMaster University, Hamilton, Ontario.

Dr Annette Gomperts is a fictional persona, in the artwork and book *Thin Air*, conceived by the British artist **Paul Rooney**, who has exhibited since 1999.

Janna Graham is a writer, organizer, educator and curator. She has collaborated with the collectives Ultra-Red and Micropolitics Research Group and co-initiated The Centre for Possible Studies.

Michael Hardt is a literary and political theorist and Professor of Literature and Italian Studies at Duke University.

Paula Harper is Associate Professor of modern art history and criticism at the University of Miami.

George E. Hein is Professor Emeritus, Lesley University Graduate School of Arts and Social Sciences, Cambridge, Massachusetts.

Pablo Helguera is a Mexican-born artist based in New York. Since 2007 he has been Director of Adult and Academic programs at The Museum of Modern Art, New York.

Patrick Heron (1920–99) was a British artist, critic and writer on art education.

Tom Holert is a Berlin-based art historian and cultural critic and former editor of *Texte zur Kunst* and *Spex*. He teaches art theory and cultural studies at the Akademie der bildenden Künste, Vienna.

Allan Kaprow (1927–2006) was an American artist, educator and writer whose work from the late 1950s onwards investigated the breaking down of boundaries between art and everyday life.

Vincent Katz is an American poet, translator, art critic, editor and curator. He is the editor of the poetry and arts journal *VANITAS* and of Libellum books.

Mary Kelly is an American-born artist who worked in London from 1968 to 1987. From 1996 she has been Professor of Art and Critical Theory at the University of California at Los Angeles.

Grant H. Kester is Chair of the Visual Arts Department at the University of California at San Diego.

Tamara Krikorian (1944–2009) was a British pioneer of video art and co-founder of London Video Arts. She also taught in art schools and was Director of the Welsh Sculpture Trust from 1984.

Suzanne Lacy is an American artist, writer, educator and organizer of collaborative projects. She is Chair of Fine Arts at Otis College of Art and Design, Los Angeles.

Darcy Lange (1946–2005) was a New Zealand-born artist who made work for some time in the United States and in Britain, such as *Work Studies in Schools* (Birmingham, 1976; Oxfordshire, 1977).

Les Levine is an Irish-born artist and critic based in New York who has been an innovator in working with technology in art since the 1960s.

Dieter Lesage is a Belgian philosopher and critic, and lecturer at the Department of Audiovisual and Performing Arts, RITS – Erasmushogeschool, Brussels.

Lawrence McDonald is a writer and curator based in Wellington, New Zealand. He is editor of the film and theatre journal *Illusions* and chair of the Emerging Artists Trust.

Carmen Mörsch is a German-born artist and Head of the Research Institute for Art Education at the Zürcher Hochschule der Künste, Zurich.

Antonio Negri is an Italian political philosopher. He founded the *Potere Operaio* (Workers' Power) group in 1969 and in the 1970s was a leader of the network movement *Autonomia Operaia*.

Emily Pethick is the director of The Showroom, London. From 2005 to 2008 she was the director of Casco – Office for Art, Design and Theory, Utrecht.

Andrea Phillips is a London-based critical writer on contemporary art, architecture and socio-political thought, and Reader in Fine Art at Goldsmiths, University of London.

Griselda Pollock is Professor of the Social and Critical Histories of Art at the University of Leeds.

Ernesto Pujol is a Cuban-born site-specific performance artist and social choreographer, based in the USA since 1979. He has taught in numerous American art schools and institutions.

Radical Philosophy Collective is the British editorial collective of ten academics who publish the journal *Radical Philosophy*, operating on a voluntary basis with no external support.

Jacques Rancière is a French philosopher and Emeritus Professor of Philosophy at the University of Paris VIII (Vincennes à Saint-Denis).

Herbert Read (1893–1968) was an art critic, educationalist and poet, associated with both formalism and surrealism. In 1947 he co-founded the Institute of Contemporary Arts, London.

Adrienne Rich is an American poet and writer based in California whose work has been published internationally since the early 1970s.

Bridget Riley is a London-based British painter who has exhibited since the early 1960s.

Irit Rogoff is Professor of Visual Culture at Goldsmiths, University of London.

Suely Rolnik is a psychoanalyst, cultural critic and curator based in Sao Paulo, Brazil. She was a close collaborator of Félix Guattari during her exile in Paris from the military dictatorship in Brazil.

Monica Ross is a British artist whose work is time-based and includes performance, installation, video, cd-rom and text works.

Ziauddin Sardar is a Pakistan-born British writer, broadcaster and cultural critic. He writes about religion, arts, politics and science and between 1999 and 2006, co-edited *Third Text*.

Eve Kosofsky Sedgwick (1950–2009) was an American critical theorist and scholar in the fields of literature, cultural and gender studies, and a pioneer of queer theory.

Allan Sekula is an American photographic artist, writer and theorist based at the California Institute of the Arts, Valencia, California.

Miriam Shapiro is a Canadian-born artist; a New York abstract expressionist in the 1950s and 1960s, she moved to California in the early 1970s, establishing the Feminist Art Program at the California Institute of the Arts with Judy Chicago.

Rebecca Sinker is a British artist and educator. With a background of research into digital arts education, she works with Tate's Learning department to produce online programmes with and for young people.

Frances Stark is an American artist and Assistant Professor of Painting and Drawing at San Francisco State University.

Harry Thubron (1915–85) was a British artist and from the 1950s onwards an influential art teacher, notably at Sunderland College of Art (1950–55) and Leeds College of Art (1955–65).

Lisa Tickner is Emeritus Professor of Art History at Middlesex University and Visiting Professor of Art History at the Courtauld Institute of Art, London.

Caroline Tisdall is Professor of the Department of Rural Future at Oxford Brookes University. As an art historian and critic she worked closely with Joseph Beuys and continues to explore his legacy in the Social Sculpture Research Unit at the university.

Jan Verwoert is an art critic based in Berlin. He is a contributing editor of *frieze* and has contributed essays for numerous catalogues and monographs and to the journals *Afterall* and *Metropolis M.*

Henry Ward is an artist and Head of the Faculty of Media and Visual Arts at Welling Specialist Art School, a British comprehensive school.

WEB (West–East Bag) was a collective network created in April 1971 to inform US women artists' groups from coast to coast of each others' political actions, techniques and methodologies.

Virginia Woolf (1882–1941) was a British modernist author, critical essayist, publisher and feminist.

Carey Young is a British artist based in London. Her projects and performances date from 1996.

Bibliography

This section comprises selected further reading and does not repeat the bibliographic references for writings included in the anthology. For these please see the citations at the end of each text.

Addison, Nicholas; Burgess, Lesley, eds, *Issues in Art and Design Teaching* (Routledge Falmer, 2003)

Adorno, Theodor. W., *Can One Live after Auschwitz?: A Philosophical Reader*, ed. Rolf Tiedemann (Stanford University Press, 2003)

Allen, Felicity, 'Situating Gallery Education', *Tate Encounters: Britishness and Visual Culture*, (e)dition 2 (February 2008) (http://www.tate.org.uk/research/tateresearch/majorprojects/tate-encounters/edition-2/papers.shtm)

Atkinson, Dennis, *Art, Equality and Learning: Pedagogies against the State* (Sense Publishers, 2011)

Ault, Julie, ed., *Show and Tell: A Chronicle of Group Material* (Four Corners Books, 2010)

Becker, Carol, 'The Education of Young Artists and the Issue of Audience', *Cultural Studies*, no. 7 (1993) 46–57

Belzer, Heike; Birnbaum, Daniel eds, *Teaching Art/Kunst Lehren* (Walther König, 2007)

Berry, Ian, ed, *Tim Rollins and K.O.S.: A History* (The MIT Press, 2009)

Bourriaud, Nicolas, ed., *Altermodern: Tate Triennial 2009* (Tate Publishing, 2009)

Braden, Su, *Artists and People* (Routledge & Kegan Paul, 1978)

Buber, Martin, *Between Man and Man* (1947) (Routledge, 2002)

Buchler, Pavel, *The Answer to the Question* (Information as Material, 2004)

Buckley, Brad; Conomos, John, eds, *Rethinking the Contemporary Art School: The Artist, the Ph.D and the Academy* (The Press of Nova Scotia College of Art and Design, 2009)

Buren, Daniel; Fauchereau, Serge; Hulten, Pontus; Sarkis, *Quand les artistes font école/Vingt-quatre journées de l'Institut des hautes études en arts plastiques 1988–1990* (Centre Pompidou, 2004)

Butler, David; Reiss, Vivienne, eds., *The Art of Negotiation* (Arts Council England/Cornerhouse, 2007)

Butler, Judith, *The Psychic Life of Power: Theories in Subjection* (Stanford University Press, 1997)

Carson, John; Stewart, Susanne, eds., *Out of the Bubble: Approaches to Contextual Practice within Fine Art Education* (London Institute, 1999)

Crickmay, Chris, *'Art and Social Context': Its Background, Inception and Development* (www.demandingconversations.org.uk/.../Art-and-Social-Context-by-Chris-Crickmay.pdf)

Desai, Dipti, 'Imagining Justice in Times of Perpetual War: Notes for the Classroom', *Journal of Curriculum and Pedagogy*, vol. 6, no. 2 (2009) 6–26

Dewdney, Andrew; Dibosa, David; Walsh, Victoria, eds., *Post Critical Museology: Theory and Practice in the Art Museum* (scheduled for publication by Routledge in 2012)

Dickson, Malcolm, ed., *Art with People* (AN [Artists' Newsletter] Publications, 1995)

Deleuze, Gilles; Guattari, Félix, *A Thousand Plateaux: Capitalism and Schizophrenia* (1980) (University of Minnesota Press, 1987)

ElDahab, Mai Abu; Vidokle, Anton; Waldvogel, Florian, eds, *Notes for an Art School* (Manifesta 6 School Books, 2006)

Elkins, James, *Why Art Cannot be Taught* (University of Illinois, 2001)

Encyclopaedia of informal education (http://www.infed.org/)

Filiou, Robert, *Teaching and Learning as Performing Arts* (Walther König, 1970)

Foucault, Michel, *Discipline and Punish* (1975) (Vintage, 1995)

Ganahl, Rainer, *Educational Complex* (1997) (http://www.ganahl.info/e.complex.html)

Garoian, Charles R; Gaudelius, Yvonne, *Spectacle Pedagogy: Art, Politics and Visual Culture* (SUNY, 2008)

Gaztambide-Fernández, Rubén, 'The Artist in Society: Understandings, Expectations, and Curriculum Implications', *Curriculum Enquiry*, vol. 3, no. 38 (2008)

Gorschlüter, Peter, ed., *The Fifth Floor: Ideas Taking Space* (Tate / Liverpool University Press, 2009)

Hak, Belinda, ed., with Faye Holdert, Joris de Jong, Judith Leijdekkers, Jammie Oostrum, Estra Yalçiner (junior eds) *JET: It's Not a Plane, It's Not a Girl's Name, It's a Book About Art* (Witte de With, 2010)

Hall, Stuart, 'Race, Culture and Communications', *Rethinking Marxism*, vol. 5, no. 1 (Spring 1992)

Harding, Anna, ed., *Magic Moments: Collaborations between Artists and Young People* (Black Dog, 2005)

Hartnett, Stephen John, ed., *Challenging the Prison Industrial Complex: Activism, Arts and Educational Alternatives* (University of Illinois Press, 2011)

Herne, Steve; Cox, Sue; Watts, Roberts, eds., *Readings in Primary Art Education* (Intellect, 2009)

Hickman, Richard, ed., *Art Education 11–18: Meaning, Purpose and Direction* (Continuum, 2004)

Holmes, Brian, *Games, Corporations, Distant Constellations* (http://brianholmes.wordpress.com/2009/06/16/games-corporations-distant-constellations)

hooks, bell, *Teaching to Transgress* (Routledge, 1994)

Hooper-Greenhill, Eilean, *Museums and Education: Purpose, Pedagogy, Performance* (Routledge, 2007)

Horkheimer, Max; Adorno, Theodor W., *Dialectic of Enlightenment* (1947) (Stanford, 2002)

Horlock, Naomi, ed., *Testing the Water: Young People in Art Galleries* (Tate Liverpool/Liverpool University Press, 2000)

Illich, Ivan, *Deschooling Society* (Marion Boyars, 2000)

Irigaray, Luce with Green, Mary, eds, *Luce Irigaray: Teaching* (Continuum, 2008)

Jacob, Mary Jane; Baas, Jacquelynn, eds, *Learning Mind: Experience into Art* (University of California Press, 2010)

Kaprow, Allan 'The Education of the Un-Artist' (3 parts) *ARTnews* (February 1971; May 1972); *Art in America* (January/February 1974)

– *Essays on the Blurring of Art and Life*, ed. Kelley, Jeff (University of California Press, 1993)

Kester, Grant H., *Conversation Pieces* (University of California Press, 2004)

Kwon, Miwon, *One Place After Another: Site-Specific Art and Locational Identity* (The MIT Press, 2002)

Lacy, Suzanne, *Leaving Art: Writings on Performance, Politics and Publics 1974–2007* (Duke, 2010)

Lazzarato, Maurizio, 'Immaterial Labour', in Virno, Paolo; Hardt, Michael, eds, *Radical Thought in Italy: A Potential Politics* (University of Minnesota Press, 1996)

Lee Podesva, Kristina 'A Pedagogical Turn: Brief Notes on Education as Art', *Fillip*, no. 6 (Summer 2007) http://fillip.ca/content/a-pedagogical-turn http://fillip.ca/content/a-pedagogical-turn

Lu Jie 'The Long March Project', *Fillip*, no. 2 (Winter 2006) http://fillip.ca/content/the-long-march-project

Maharaj, Sarat; Stanley, Nick, 'A Discussion', *Journal of Art & Design Education*, vol. 18, no 1 (1999) 63–7

Malik Okon, Rohini, *Participation of Black and Minority Ethnic Students in Higher Education Art and Design: Literature Review* (Arts Council England, September 2005)
McLaren, P; Sandlin, J.A., eds, *Critical Pedagogies of Consumption* (Routledge, 2010)
Madoff, Steven Henry, ed., *Art School (Propositions for the 21st Century)* (The MIT Press, 2009)
Meta Bauer, Ute, ed., *Education, Information, Entertainment* (Edition Selene, 2001)
Moreira, Maria, 'Rigor/Resonance + Art as Confrontation/ Repersonalização, Enfrentamento e Reversibilidade', *Item*, no. 5 (February 2002) 74–84 (http://www.acertainbrazilianness.net/htmlpages/rigor.html)
Mörsch, Carmen, 'Alliances for Unlearning: On the Possibility of Future Collaborations between Gallery Education and Institutions of Critique', *Afterall*, no. 26 (Spring 2011)
Mullin, David; Reardon, John, eds, *Ch-ch-ch-changes: Artists Talk about Teaching* (Ridinghouse, 2009)
Nollert, Angelika; Rogoff, Irit, eds, *A.C.A.D.E.M.Y* (Revolver, 2006)
Omar Tarar, Nadeem, 'Aesthetic Modernism in the Post-Colony: The Making of a National College of Art in Pakistan (1950–1960s)', *IJADE*, vol. 27, no. 3 (2008)
O'Neill, Paul, ed., *Curating Subjects* (Open Editions, 2007)
– ; Wilson, Mick, eds, *Curating and the Educational Turn* (Open Editions/de Appel, 2010)
Paik, Nam June, 'Expanded Education for the Paperless Society', *Interfunktionen* (1971)
Pollock, Griselda; Zemans, Joyce, *Museums after Modernism: Strategies of Engagement* (Blackwell, 2007)
Purves, Ted, *What We Want is Free: Generosity and Exchange in Recent Art* (SUNY, 2004)
Rancière, Jacques, *The Emancipated Spectator* (2008) (Verso, 2009)
Rogers, Carl R. and Freiberg, H.J., *Freedom to Learn* (1969) 3rd edition (Charles E. Merrill, 1993)
Rosler, Martha, *If You Lived Here: The City in Art, Theory, and Social Activism* (Bay Press, 1991)
Schön, Donald A., *Educating the Reflective Practitioner* (Jossey-Bass, 1987)
Sefton-Green, Julian; Thomson, Pat; Bresler, Liora; Jones, Ken, eds, *International Handbook of Creative Learning* (Routledge, 2011)
Sennett, Richard, *The Craftsman* (Allen Lane, 2008)
Singerman, Howard, *Art Subjects: Making Artists in the American University* (California, 1999)
Sladen, Mark, et al., eds., *Nought to Sixty* (Institute of Contemporary Arts London, 2009)
Spivak, Gayatri C., *Outside in the Teaching Machine* (Routledge, 1993)
– 'Can the Subaltern Speak?' in *Marxism and the Interpretation of Culture*, ed. Nelson, Cary; Grossberg, Larry (University of Illinois Press, 1988)
Stark, Frances, ed., *Primer (On the Future of Art School)* (Dexter Sinister, 2009)
Tallant, Sally; Coysh, Louise, eds, *Dis-Assembly* (Serpentine Gallery, 2006)
Tennant, M., *Psychology and Adult Learning* (Routledge, 1988; 1997)
Thompson, Nato; Sholette, Gregory, eds, *The Interventionists: User's Manual for the Creative Disruption of Everyday Life* (The MIT Press, 2004)
Verwoert, Jan, 'Lessons in Modesty', *Metropolis M: Expanding Academy*, no. 4 (2006) 46–53
Vishmidt, Marina, 'Creation Myth', *Mute*, no. 28 (July 2010) (http://www.metamute.org/en/content/creation_myth)
Vygotsky, Lev, *Mind and Society* (Harvard University Press, 1978)

Wallis, Brian, ed., *Democracy: A Project of Group Material* (Bay Press, 1990)

Ward, Colin; Fyson, Anthony, *Streetwork: The Exploding School* (Town and Country Planning Association, UK, 1973)

Wenger, Etienne, *Communities of Practice: Learning, Meaning and Identity* (Cambridge University Press, 1998)

Wood, Paul, 'Between God and the Saucepan: Some Aspects of Art Education in England from the Mid-Nineteenth Century until Today', in Stephens, Chris, ed., *The History of British Art: 1870 to Now* (Tate Publishing, 2008)

Art magazines with regular features or special issues on education

Art in America (May 2007) Raphael Rubinstein et al., 'Art Schools: A Group Crit.'

Art Journal, vol. 58, no. 1 (Spring 1999) 'Rethinking Studio Art Education'

Art Monthly, no. 320 (October 2008) Special Issue: 'The Future of Art Education', including Liam Gillick, 'The Fourth Way'

Afterall, no. 26 (Spring 2011) 'Education'

Artforum (February 2006), Claire Bishop, 'The Social Turn: Collaboration and its Discontents', 178–83; (Summer 2007), including Daniel Birnbaum, 'The Art of Education', 474–7; (May 2008), Tom Holert, 'Learning Curve: Radical Art and Education in Germany', 334–9; 406.

Cabinet, no. 39 (Fall 2010) 'Learning'

Control, no. 18 (April 2009) including Annette Krauss 'Hidden Curriculum', Steve Rushton 'Self-performance in the Social Studio'

e-flux journal, especially nos 1, 2, 3, 4, 11, 14 (http://www.e-flux.com/journal)

Engage, the international journal of visual art and gallery education, e.g. issue 22: 'Young People and Agency' (Summer 2008)

frieze, no. 101 (September 2006)

Journal of Educational Controversy, vol. 5, no. 1 (Winter 2010) 'Art, Social Imagination and Democratic Education', a special issue dedicated to Maxine Greene.

Metronome, no. 10 (2006) 'Future Academy: Shared, Mobile, Improvised, Underground, Hidden, Floating' (http://www.metronomepress.com/documenta12.html); no. 11 (2007) 'What is to be done?' ed. Clementine Deliss, special edition for Documenta 12 magazines.

n.paradoxa, vol. 26 (2010) 'Feminist Pedagogies'

Radical Philosophy, no. 141 (January/February 2007)

Tate Papers, no. 11 (http://www.tate.org.uk/research/tateresearch/tatepapers/09spring/)

Variant (http://www.variant.org.uk/) e.g. no. 39/40: John Beagles, 'In a Class All of Their Own: The Incomprehensiveness of Art Education'

Zehar, no. 60/61 (2007), 'The Open School'

Websites: school/art convergences

Alan Kane, Life Class: Today's Nude (http://www.artangel.org.uk//projects/2009/life_class/about_the_project/alan_kane_life_class_today_s_nude)

Art School Palestine (http://www.artschoolpalestine.com/index.php?option=com_frontpage&Itemid=1&lang=en)

Arte de Conducta (http://www.taniabruguera.com/arteconductaintro.html)

The Barefoot College (http://www.barefootcollege.org/)

Brown Mountain College (http://www.brownmountain.org.uk/about.html)

Center for Urban Pedagogy (http://www.anothercupdevelopment.org/)

Copenhagen Free University (http://www.copenhagenfreeuniversity.dk)

Colour School (http://www.colourschool.org/)

Community Arts Network (archived) (http://wayback.archive-it.org/2077/20100906195027/http://www.communityarts.net/archivefiles/visual_art/index.php)

Edufactory, Conflicts and Transformation of the University (http://www.edu-factory.org/wp/2011/04/)

Free International University World Art Collection (http://www.fiuwac.com/html/fiuwac_statement_-_www_fiuwac_.html)

La Lleca (The Street) (http://www.lalleca.net/english.html)

Manoa Free University (http://www.manoafreeuniversity.org/host_for/)

Micropolitics Research Group (http://micropolitics.wordpress.com/)

The Mountain School of Arts (http://www.themountainschoolofarts.org)

Open Source Embroidery: Curatorial Facilitation of Material Networks (http://issuu.com/icicccb/docs/material_network_final_text_ec_eng)

Our Literal Speed (http://www.ourliteralspeed.com/content/ols002a.html)

The Public School New York (http://nyc.thepublicschool.org/about)

Radical Education Collective (http://radical.temp.si/)

Reverse Pedagogy (http://www.modelart.ie/reversepedagogy.html)

School of Everything (http://schoolofeverything.com/)

School of Missing Studies (http://www.schoolofmissingstudies.net/)

Toronto School of Creativity and Inquiry (http://www.tsci.ca/)

Ultra-Red (http://www.ultrared.org/directory.html)

United Nations Plaza (http://www.unitednationsplaza.org/)

The University of Trash (http://www.sculpture-center.org/exhibitionsExhibition.htm?id=11909)

Index

ACKNOWLEDGEMENTS

Editor's acknowledgements

As well as the writers who have so generously allowed me to edit their work for this book, I should like to thank the series editor Ian Farr for the terrific – and educative – collaboration. My warm thanks also go to Iwona Blazwick for the invitation to develop this book and her continued interest since. I should like to thank Whitechapel colleagues, especially Sarah Auld and Hannah Holloway. Goldsmiths Library's Althea Greenan has modelled the generosity freelancers depend on: I am extremely grateful. Many others have contributed in different ways: I especially want to thank Rebecca Fortnum, David Garcia, Sally Tallant, Rebecca Sinker, Michael Archer, Henry Ward, Rob Fairley, Andrea Phillips, Dennis Atkinson, Claire Doherty, Veronica Sekules, Emily Pethick, Mary Kelly, Lisa Tickner, Griselda Pollock, Adrian Rifkin, Suzanne Lacy, Michele Jaquis, Toby Tannenbaum, Bob Sain, Kim Kanatani, Pablo Helguera, Marie Rouhète, Dominic Willsdon, Wendy Woon, Stephen Deuchar, Susan Ferleger Brades, Richard Wentworth, Eileen Daly, Jeremy Akerman, Carmen Mörsch, Victoria Walsh, Andrew Dewdney, David Dibosa, Nigel Llewellyn, Lindsey Fryer and many more former colleagues from Tate and beyond, Simon Smith, Stanley Allen and Dorothy Pickard.

Publisher's acknowledgements

Whitechapel Gallery is grateful to all those who gave their generous permission to reproduce the listed material. Every effort has been made to secure all permissions and we apologize for any inadvertent errors or omissions. If notified, we will endeavour to correct these at the earliest opportunity. We would like to express our thanks to all who contributed to the making of this volume, especially: Jorella Andrews, Michael Archer, Roy Ascott, Dennis Atkinson, Stuart Bailey, Carol Becker, Claire Bishop, Julie Brook, Luis Camnitzer, Paul Clements, Penelope Creeley, Pen Dalton, Paul Dash, Thierry de Duve, Dinah Dossor, Jimmie Durham, Elliot W. Eisner, David Elliott, Alex Farquharson, Bruce Ferguson, Joanna Fiduccia, Harrell Fletcher, Andrea Fraser, Vincent Katz, Johnny Gailey, Claire Gibb, Henry A. Giroux, Janna Graham, Peter Hallward, Michael Hardt, Paula Harper, George E. Hein, Pablo Helguera, Tom Holert, Estate of Allan Kaprow, Mary Kelly, Grant H. Kester, Suzanne Lacy, Lars Bang Larsen, Dieter Lesage, Les Levine, Lawrence McDonald, Janet McKenzie Spens, Chris Mooney, Carmen Mörsch, Jennifer Mundy, Antonio Negri, Emily Pethick, Andrea Phillips, Griselda Pollock, Ernesto Pujol, Jacques Rancière, Adrienne Rich, Bridget Riley, Irit Rogoff, Suely Rolnik,

Paul Rooney, Monica Ross, Fiona Russell, Ziauddin Sardar, Miriam Schapiro, Karsten Schubert, Hal Sedgwick, Allan Sekula, Rebecca Sinker, Frances Stark, Lisa Tickner, Caroline Tisdall, Jan Verwoert, Mercedes Vincente, Henry Ward. We also gratefully acknowledge the cooperation of: Afterall, Art Journal, Artforum, Bay Press, Blackwell Publishing, Book Works, University of California Press, Chicago University Press, Continuum Books, Dordrecht-Kluwer Academic Publishers, Duke University Press, e-flux journal, Engage, Faber & Faber, Librairie Artheme Fayard, The Fruitmarket Gallery, Hauser & Wirth, Estate of Patrick Heron, Houghton Mifflin Harcourt, IJADE, IKON, Kettles Yard, University of Cambridge, Estate of Darcy Lange, Lawrence & Wishart Books, The MIT Press, Modern Painters, Palgrave Macmillan, Penguin Group, Phaidon Press, The Radical Philosophy Collective, Galerie Michel Rein, Room 13 HQ, Routledge, The Serpentine Gallery, Simon and Schuster, The Society of Authors, Sprovieri Gallery, Stanford University Press Special Collections, Studio International, Tate Papers, The Wylie Agency, Verso, Virago Press, W.W. Norton and Company.

Whitechapel Gallery

www.whitechapelgallery.com

Whitechapel Gallery is supported by
Arts Council England

ARTS COUNCIL ENGLAND